Walsall Po

and the

Hotbed

of

Anarchy

An Avalanche of Anarchists,
Follow the Socialist Storm!

Paul Reeves

First Published in the United Kingdom in 2023

All rights reserved. No part of this publication may be reproduced, stored in a retrieval system, or transmitted in any form or by any means, without the prior permission in writing of the publisher, nor be otherwise circulated in any form of binding or cover other than that in which it is published and without a similar condition including this condition being imposed on the subsequent purchaser.

ISBN: 9798389093188
Imprint: Independently published.

Text copyright © Paul Reeves 2023

The right of Paul Reeves to be identified as the author of this work has been asserted by him in accordance with the Copyright, Designs and Patents Act 1988. VI

Although the author has made every effort to ensure that the information in this book was correct, the author does not assume and hereby disclaims any liability to any party for any loss, damage, or disruption caused by errors or omissions, whether such errors or omissions result from negligence, accident, or any other cause.

Every reasonable effort has been made to trace copyright-holders of material reproduced in this book, but if any have been inadvertently overlooked the publisher would be glad to hear from them.

Paul Reeves
Burntwood
Staffordshire

A TwoP Publication ©
2023

twop8540@gmail.com

Contents

Prologue	Page 1
Introduction	Page 2

Part One - Haydn Sanders

The Rise of the Socialists	Page 8
The Socialist Storm	Page 20
Councillor Haydn Sanders	Page 36

Part Two - The Walsall Bomb Plot

The Build Up	Page 59
The Cast of Characters	Page 64
The Lead Up To The Arrests	Page 71
The Arrests	Page 83
Magistrates Court - Committal Proceedings	Page 100
Stafford Assizes	Page 145
Just Rewards?	Page 166
The Mowbray and Nicoll Trial	Page 168

Part Three - What Happened, Next?

Haydn Sanders	Page 172
The Walsall Anarchist Case	Page 184
The Anarchist Literature Used at Trial	Page 205
About the Author - Paul Reeves	Page 212
Acknowledgements	Page 213
Further Reading	Page 214
Signposts to the Past - Source Records	Page 215

Prologue

Two dramatic historical events bind this book together, both happening within a few years of each other. It was a rich time for local history, our first story reaches its climax in 1888, when Haydn Sanders won his seat on Walsall Council, becoming the first Socialist councillor anywhere in England. Although his time in office was relatively short, it was nonetheless exceedingly colourful and eventful. Our second furore broke at the beginning of 1892, four years after the first. Walsall unimaginably was labelled, 'a Hotbed of Anarchy' a town tainted with a reputation for rebellion and revolution. The events of 1892, indelibly etched a mark on the history of Walsall for evermore. These times may have faded from living memory, but in 1892 every British broadsheet told the story of the Walsall Anarchists and their 'Bomb Plot.' This heinous crime was up there with the 'Jack the Ripper' case, as one of the Victorian crimes of the century.

To discover how Haydn Sanders came to power and how the Walsall Anarchists plot developed, we have to go deep back in time. Sanders may have been the first Socialist councillor in England, but he wasn't the first Socialist. Socialism rose steadily in popularity in the 1880s, and Sanders was at the forefront of the Walsall movement. We have to look at Socialism in general to have an idea how Sanders won his local acclaim. Whatever your own personal background, whether rich or poor, this is history, it can't be changed and it's wrong to judge what happened yesterday by applying the rules of today.

Introduction

After fifty years of service, Queen Victoria celebrated her Golden Jubilee in the June of 1887. Walsall rapidly expanded throughout her reign, changing from a Georgian semi-rural market town, into a significant hub of Black Country manufacturing. Walsall was originally missed off a list of towns to be included under the Reform Act of 1832, but it battled hard for reinstatement and retained its right to return a Member of Parliament to Westminster. One of the main considerations that influenced the change of mind, was the large growth in the towns population. After the Industrial Revolution, Walsall steadily grew, every street and courtyard being filled with dozens of thriving trades and businesses. By the 1880s, Walsall was already widely recognised for its excellent leather goods and equine wares, but it had a whole host of associated metal trades supporting the success. Saddlers, tanners, curriers, stirrup makers, harness makers, bit makers, spur makers, hame makers, to name but a few were everywhere. The skill and hard work of Walsall people certainly played its part in putting the 'Great' into Britain. The town had a high degree of manufacturing self sufficiency from its ingenuity and skills ability.

The new frenzy of industrial activity, brought the need for more people to continually feed the ever increasing workforce of manual labourers. Scores of local natives filled the factories, foundries and workshops, but they were not enough alone to meet the demand for labour. Hundreds of outsiders were sucked in, taking up the slack in the booming labour market. Men, women and children in their droves drifted into Walsall from the surrounding farms and countryside searching for higher paid work. These people were well accustomed to hard manual work, but industrial town life was something very different to experience. Few must have realised that fresh air and decent houses were the exception and not the rule in industrial towns. Working all day in dirty factories, doing backbreaking and tedious manual labour was no walk in the fields, but it was essential to keep the wheels of industry turning. As industrial growth continued, economic migrants from all over Britain, Europe and further afield competed with the rest to secure the best jobs available.

From the late 1840s, a large Irish Catholic community began arriving in Walsall, initially to escape starvation during the Irish potato famine. The contingent of 'Emerald Islanders' grew and grew over the next few decades, creating distinct Irish areas within in the town, such as Town End. Like so many new immigrant communities, they were expected to do the hardest and foulest jobs that nobody else wanted.

During the mid-1800s, a small group of Jewish settlers came to Walsall with their families. A very broad church of religious views existed, all praying for their own gods under the same town sky.

French, Italian, German, Belgian, Dutch and many more nationalities mingled together in close proximity, coexisting and integrating with the indigenous people. The basic foundations of a multicultural and cosmopolitan society were laid, with all seeking a better life for their families during these monumental times!

As numerous new inhabitants descended on the town its infrastructure inevitably began to creak and crack under the pressure. Poverty stricken people, squashed their families into an ancient and shoddy housing stock, once inhabited by their Georgian grandparents.

Firmly set in the Victorian period of invention and architecture, the late 1880s early 1890s, were times our Dickensian ancestors saw things changing fast. They lived through an extravaganza of local history created in days of unpredictability. Our stories focus largely on social history and politics of the day, so we need to look closely at how people lived during those times. Some may read this history and wonder, 'What's changed?'

Try to imagine, if you can, a world inhabited by two very different breeds of people, for ease I have called them, 'the Haves' and 'the Have Nots.' They both co-existed in parallel time together, but for all intents and purposes, they had very little in common with each other.

The 'Haves' possessed the greatest wealth, but were the minority by far. Although the smallest group, they lived in the biggest, most spacious and finely equipped mansions. Not only did they possess the lions share of the wealth and possessions, they also commanded all the power and authority. These people were Walsall's rich middle class residents, professionals, industrialists and entrepreneurs, not to mention some landed gentry. You couldn't mistake the 'Haves' with the 'Have Nots', as they looked very different. The 'Haves' men wore tailored suits, with top hats or bowlers and their ladies adorned fine long dresses, with bonnets or hats. They not only looked so different, they lived very differently too. The 'Haves' didn't trouble or bother themselves with menial tasks, they used their 'Have Not' servants to do all that. The minions did everything at their masters beck and call, responding to the sound of little bells. The 'Have Nots' stocked up raging coal fires, to warm the 'Haves' backsides and prepared their food from well stocked pantries.

By contrast, the 'Have Nots' were the vast majority, trudging monotonously day to day, through a life of comparative or sometimes severe poverty. Some 'Haves' called the 'Have Nots' the 'great unwashed,' as they lived in small smelly rooms within communal dosshouses. The vile, squalid overcrowded slums had no decent sanitation and hence their nickname. This under belly of society, lived in a world of adversity, with poor diets, no healthcare and minimal education. Many faced the annual winter dilemma of feed or freeze, when working every hour that God sent, was no guarantee of sustaining a decent lifestyle. Wilfully underpaid and grossly undervalued, the 'Have Nots' were the industrial 'beasts of burden.' The reality was, that the lowest in society found it near impossible to ward off illness, disease or a visit from the grim reaper. The 'Have Nots' were sadly the expendable human commodity who generated the money for the 'Haves.' An almost unassailable abyss, divided the 'Haves' from the 'Have Nots.' This chasmic divide was called 'social injustice,' and highlighted the very stark contrast between the two groups. Green eyes of 'Have Not' envy, gazed on as the rich paraded all the trappings of wealth before them. Top hatted 'Haves' with long dark coats travelled around in horse drawn carriages and first class trains. The dirty and scruffy looking 'Have Nots,' scurried about, doffing their flat caps, as the 'Haves' went by. While the rich carried walking canes as fashion accessories, the poor gripped crutches as disabled necessities. As the 'Haves' carriage wheels ground down the cobbles, the 'Have Nots' tip toed through boulders of oss muck left in their wake.

For those born into privilege and wealth, this was truly a 'Golden Age,' but for so many more it was a gruelling uphill struggle of hardship. Clanking hammers and rasping files rang a melody of misery in the ears of the poor, while the rich listened to chinking glasses and jangling jewellery. The brutal reality was, that your position at birth determined not only your life, but the life of future generations.

This was slavery in all but name, the 'Have Nots' were chained by circumstance to their masters treadmill of toil, men and women enslaved, bound and shackled to the hand that fed them. No work, meant no food, no home a simple reality. When times got too hard, many poor decent people considered death a better alternative to the workhouses or prisons. The chance of escaping poverty was remote, few avenues avoided the rat trap, with the majority of sons following their fathers onto the wheel of life. Generations of downtrodden Walsall folk, lived, loved and died in the town they called home. Our forefathers might have been poor, but they were tough and resourceful, determined to survive the hardships of an industrial town. Each strand of their DNA must have been coated in humanised kevlar, giving them superhuman powers of survival. Resilient blood pumped through every vein, driving the industrial output of every workshop, factory and yard.

It's not difficult to understand how working people became disgruntled with the extreme hardship. The poor of Walsall imagined better things for themselves and by the 1880s change had started, though at a slow tortoise like pace. Wanting things to happen faster, mouthpiece activists stirred up tensions by vocally calling out the unfairness in society. The constant strain on human endurance fuelled the social pressure cooker, creating an interesting recipe for change. Socialists led the charge of change, but they were divided. Influential people with humanitarian beliefs needed to be recruited to unite views and encourage people to make changes. To make any difference the

Socialists needed to change the very core of the establishment, which was easier said than done when the impervious fabric of Victorian society was finely woven and built upon a granite foundation. Monarchy, Government, the judiciary and the councils held all the power to maintain the status quo. The most powerful military and police in the world could keep any insurrection at bay, British society was not going to collapse in a hurry, after all said and done, it was not France! The law protected property and wealth, ensuring that the rich stayed rich and the poor stayed poor.

Walsall was ruled at this time by its Council from their Chamber at the Guildhall on the High Street. This Victorian edifice and centre of local government, occupied a prominent position near the top of the hill, where the Mayor presided as the most powerful man in town. The Mayor effectively controlled all the symbols of power and authority, the Council, the police, the magistrates court and the gaol. Only God's house of St. Matthew's perched on the hilltop held a more elevated position for the divine and spiritual support of the people.

In the late 1880s our Victorian ancestors were set to witness some of the most sensational and exciting episodes in Walsall's history. Things were about to get colourful in Walsall, as it started to attract tales of the unexpected like a magnet. Events which would be brightly illuminated under the spotlight of the national press, making the place notorious, even infamous in the columns of every broadsheet. Every detail they printed, painted a spectacular and scandalous picture of the town, for all to see under the public microscope. As the metaphoric grey clouds passed over Bill's mothers, a dark shadow of suspicion was cast over the town.

Victorian families would be amazed and astounded by the rich colourful drama to be acted out by every character in vivid detail. As Walsall folk bimbled around town, they unexpectedly bumbled into these sensational times. Every nerve of their senses, must have tingled in the tangled web of Victorian scandal. We can only guess what ran through the minds of our Victorian grandparents and great grandparents, when these stories broke. These times may have disappeared from living memory, but our forebears trekked up and down the same old High Street hill as we walk today. Carrying heavy loads, they walked to and fro through the crowded market, slowly eroding the cobbles of yesteryear. Precious clues of their existence remain on the worn stone doorsteps, while their now silent phantoms invisibly roam the air of Walsall. When the wind whistles through the crevasses and cracks in the old dark wooden Georgian pews of St. Matthew's Church gallery, you may even hear them singing to the vibes of that awesome church organ. The short walk along the historic route between The Bridge and St. Matthew's steps, has more stories trapped in the mist of time, than most people can possibly imagine. The High Street could easily challenge the spookiest of 'ghost walks,' anywhere in England, with every crack in the pavement oozing the very essence of a lost truth about times gone by. Many who walk that way today, are blissfully unaware they follow in the tracks and footsteps of mystery and magic.

Our Walsall forefathers certainly lived through some politically stormy times, wonderfully rich in valuable historic drama.

Glancing back in time gives a real opportunity to learn lessons from all those years ago and hopefully make things better for the future. Through the power of imagination, I hope this book will conjure up images, echoes and shadows to bring these times back to life, if only for a moment or two.

Part One - Haydn Sanders

The Rise of the Socialists

With social conditions like the ones I have described, it's no wonder the working man wanted his lot to change. Waiting for their proverbial 'Ship to come in,' never seemed to happen, most times it didn't even sail. The circle of poverty had to be broken if people wanted a better future for their children. Poor men and women could be clever and talented too, but they rarely got a fair chance or opportunity to prosper. The problem was the 'Have Nots' required sponsorship, good fortune or sheer good luck to apply their talent and those things were in short supply. More often than not, if such ability was recognised, their employers exploited them for their own personal gain. Both our stories have a Socialism theme running through them, so it would be useful to get a flavour of what was going on in the world, on the run up to our Haydn Sanders victory.

My political views are unimportant to this story, my father was a staunch Labour supporter and my mother a hardened Conservative so I consider myself fairly unbiased. My parents were both born in Walsall and grew up in working class families in the 1930s, so it just goes to show that Walsall has always been a place with diverse political views. I am by no means a self professed expert on the subject of Socialism, nor have I explored it in any great depth, but this pen picture hopefully shows how it started in Britain and more importantly in Walsall. My attempt to explain the basics, will help to show how all the main personalities are associated together. For those mainly interested in Walsall's history, it will set the scene and become clearer later.

The idea of Socialism was not exactly a new concept when it came to town in the 1880s. The Reform Bill of 1832, saw the emergence of the Chartists Movement, an organisation set up to fight for better conditions for working people. Incidentally, Walsall Borough Police was created on the 6th of July, 1832, so becoming the first regular force in the region and one of the first in the country. It was established partly to combat potential outbreaks of violence in the forthcoming Parliamentary elections, scheduled to take place at the end of 1832. Initially the police force consisted of one superintendent and three constables, so it's hardly surprising the numbers proved insufficient when violence did break out at the election and the military were called into restore order.

In 1843, Karl Heinrich Marx, who is generally seen as the father of Socialism was expelled from Prussia and took up residence in Paris, where he continued to spread his ideology with likeminded comrade Friedrich Engles. In 1845, the French asked Marx to leave because of the concerns about the Communist propaganda he was spreading. Marx settled in Brussels, promising the Belgians he would curb his controversial journalism.

In July 1845, Marx made his first visit to England to meet with Chartist leaders. Engles who lived in Manchester between 1842-1844, acted as his guide on this fact finding mission to gauge the strength of Socialist opinion in Great Britain.

Marx remained in contact with the French Socialists, from his base in Brussels, as political tensions gradually increased. Dark clouds of rebellion were being whipped up over France, as the continental bourgeois where subjected to verbal and written attacks. Violent protests spread like a plague over mainland Europe, with bloody riots breaking out in several major European cities. This cascading torrent of inflammatory Socialist propaganda, eventually culminated in the French Revolution of 1848, where the monarchy was overthrown. Political shockwaves ricocheted through many other European countries, including Great Britain, sending warning signals of potential social disaster. The concept of revolution, brought fear to the heart of every government and especially to the 'Haves,' in society. The notion that the 'Have Nots' could bring down society by standing together and overthrow their rulers, made everyone sit up and take notice. After the events in France, Marx's Belgian hosts were nervous enough to throw him out of the country. He moved back to Paris, where he thought the new regime would afford him a warmer reception for his support for the revolution.

Meanwhile back in England the Chartists were encouraged by the French Revolution and began to gather strength. The British Government, feared the worst and introduced new sedition laws to deter any treasonable threats made against the Queen or country. These new offences robustly tightened up the law, punishing would be offenders with lengthy terms of imprisonment or transportation to Australia. All around the country, police forces swore in hundreds of special constables to bolster their numbers in readiness for trouble. Several Chartists leaders were rounded up and made an example of in the courts, crushing their resolve. A few areas of the Black Country remained comparatively sympathetic for a while, but by the middle 1850s support had all but fizzled out. Many politicians saw how close things had come to a flashpoint and realised that real change was needed to placate the working classes. The threat to the establishment had subsided for the time being, but there was a genuine realisation that a new wave would come again if change didn't happen. The Government started to talk about making reforms and the wave of revolution eventually levelled off.

Marx continued his work from Paris publishing his 'Communist Manifesto' in 1848. His expectation of a better time in France was short lived however, because in May, 1849 after several run ins with the authorities he was ordered to leave. Running out of options, he moved to London in June, 1849, where he had a journalistic career writing for the New York Daily Tribune and continued his own literary works.

The wave of Socialism settled down in Britain, but like all fads and fashions, the works of Marx were set to make a come back, as soon as the economic and social climate was right. The establishment viewed the Socialists with suspicion, most likely because of the link to violence in order to achieve their aims. The truth was, Socialists had a very broad church of views, not all were militant extremists, but there was an element within it. In simple terms, Socialists wanted a redistribution of wealth in order to close the social gap. Amongst other things they sought fairer pay, better working conditions, affordable housing, education for their children and greater rights for the working man.

Opinions differed vastly between two extremes on how to achieve their aims, from political representation on the one side to violent revolution on the other. The majority of the working class had a great deal to gain from Socialist ideals, but a lot was at stake.

Our first story really starts in the late 1880s, so we now look at the run up to 1888 when the Haydn Sanders story began. On the 7th of June, 1881, Henry Mayers Hyndman, the son of a wealthy London business man started the Social Democratic Federation. He was a middle class graduate of Trinity College, Cambridge and a member of the Marylebone Cricket Club MCC. Hyndman was heavily influenced by the works of Karl Marx and was the first to translate and release his works in the English language. By early 1882, the Social Democratic Federation had become the leading Socialist organisation in Great Britain and was quickly recruiting and gathering the support of likeminded members. On the 13th of January, 1883, William Morris, better known as an artist and designer in the Art and Crafts Movement, joined the Social Democratic Federation. Like Hyndman, he was also a middle class graduate of Exeter College, Oxford, who had inherited wealth from his father. Eleanor Marx, Karl's daughter and her common-law husband Dr. Edward Aveling, were other prominent members of the Social Democratic Federation. Aveling was already married, but long separated from his legal wife. This nucleus of prominent personalities added credibility and money to the organisation and it steadily began to grow. Soon after William Morris joined the organisation, a decision was made to start holding open air meetings as a means of promoting Socialist doctrine to the general public. They recognised that the vast majority of people were illiterate, so word of mouth could reach many more than the written word alone, but they did start printing a new publication called 'Justice.'

On the 14th of March, 1884, William Morris led a large procession up the Tottenham Court Road to Highgate Cemetery, marking the first anniversary of Marx's death the previous year. The police refused the crowds admission to the cemetery, but Dr. Aveling as a virtual relative of Marx delivered a Socialist sermon anyway. This was really the beginning of things to come, the Socialists had started to rise in number and confrontation with the authorities was inevitable.

Hyndman lost a vote on the 27th of December, 1884 in a challenge to his leadership, but he refused to stand down as leader of the Social Democratic Federation. This resulted in a split in 1885, when William Morris, Eleanor Marx and Dr. Aveling left to form their own group called the Socialist League. They started their own Socialist newspaper called the 'Commonweal'. The Social Democratic Federation and Socialist League carried on as separate entities.

Charles Wilfred Mowbray, who became known as the 'Anarchist Tailor' because of his far left views, joined the Socialist League in the East End of London. Mowbray was born at Bishop Auckland in 1856, the son of a tailer, the trade he himself followed for most of his life. As a young man he served in the army being stationed at the barracks in Newcastle-upon-Tyne in 1871. Mowbray lived in Coronation Street, Bishopwearmouth in 1881, but within the next couple of years moved with his family to the East End of London, to be amongst other known Socialists. Mowbray plays a large part in our second story later. [1] [2] [3]

On the morning of Sunday the 20th of September, 1885, Mowbray led a large open air protest at Dod Street, Mile End of about a thousand people, who were claiming the right to free speech. The police had previously broken up their open air meetings and this time was no different, they moved into arrest the main speakers including Charles Mowbray. Mowbray appeared at Thames Court charged with resisting the police in the execution of their duties and was fined forty shillings or one month's imprisonment. [4]

Inadvertently the Socialists had stumbled upon something very dear to the heart of ordinary British people, 'freedom of speech.' Regardless of political persuasion, this topic got the sympathy of thousands of free thinking men and women, even if they weren't Socialists. To some extent this brought the general public and Socialists together consolidating opinion against the heavy handedness of the authorities.

Mowbray arranged an even bigger event on Sunday the 27th September, 1885, in protest of his treatment. On the day about fifty

Socialist leaders met at the Radical Club, Stepney Green to discuss tactics. The Police Commissioner, Sir Edmund Henderson told them they could not assemble in Dod Street, but in an act of total defiance, they ignored his order and a huge crowd made its way there. About forty to fifty thousand people gathered and the numbers took the police by complete surprise. Powerless to act, Dr. Aveling addressed the crowd in triumph and with the police on the ropes, they marched through the streets passing the police station. There they shouted loudly and waved red flags, but luckily for the police nothing more serious happened. At West India Dock gates, Mr. Hyndman declared the meeting a great victory for the freedom of speech. Both factions of the Socialists movement, the Social Democratic Federation and the Socialist League were united under one common cause, 'freedom of speech.' Over the coming months, the word of defiance was spreading and the idea of change was getting into the provinces. [5]

On the 8th of February, 1886, Hyndman and other prominent members of the Social Democratic Federation held a large Socialist rally in central London. Starting in Trafalgar Square they moved into Hyde Park, where several people gave politically charged speeches whipping the crowd into a frenzy. Like a swarm of bees, they made their way buzzing with violence from Hyde Park to Audley Street, where a riot started and shops were damaged and looted. This was the straw that broke the camels back, the police and authorities could not tolerate this kind of behaviour, it was just not British. Firm action was needed before things got too far out of hand. Hyndman and the others were summoned to appear at Bow Street Magistrates on the 17th of February, 1886, to answer charges of inciting insurrections, riot, tumult and breaches of the peace.

At a court appearance on the 3rd of March, 1886, Charles Mowbray gave evidence in defence of his former Social Democratic Federation friends. Despite this the magistrates committed the case for trial at the Central Criminal Court at the Old Bailey. William Morris stood bail for two Social Democratic Federation members, indicating the strong arm tactics of the authorities only served to consolidate the Socialists, which was the opposite of the desired effect.

The accused men appeared at the Old Bailey on the 6th of April, 1886 charged with uttering seditious words. The case took several days to be heard, one of the defence witnesses being Joseph Chamberlain MP for Birmingham, who had resigned from Gladstone's government only three days earlier. On the 9th of April, 1886, the jury found all the defendants not guilty. The Socialists claimed a great victory for their movement and the freedom of speech. [6][7][8][9][10][11]

A few weeks later in the United States, things turned drastically ugly at a Socialist demonstration, highlighting what could go wrong. On the 3rd May, 1886, in Haymarket Square, Chicago, a large group of picketers assembled and began heckling strikebreakers going into work. The police attempted to stop the intimidation, but violence broke out and one person ended up being killed in the fracas. The next day an even larger protest assembled and the police were compelled to move in to break up the violence again. This time, things got even worse when someone threw a bomb and shots were exchanged between the two sides. Extreme violence erupted, seven police officers were killed and a further sixty injured. At least eight civilians were killed and many more hurt in the fighting. After the event when the dust settled, eight men were arrested and later convicted of conspiracy to murder and five of those condemned to hang. The Socialists claimed foul play, as none of the men were identified as throwing the bomb and some could even prove they were not present at the time. There was a worldwide Socialist outcry over the severity of the Chicago sentences. Articles were published in all the Socialist newspapers about the unjust methods and extreme tyranny by the authorities in putting them down.

Back in Britain the Social Democratic Federation and Socialist League fell out once again, the split being even wider and more hostile. Hyndman accused the Socialist League of being all middle class men, while William Morris retaliated by accusing Hyndman of being a Tory agent.

On the 29th of May, 1886, Charles Mowbray and David Nicoll, were two of the eleven Socialists arrested during a large gathering at the the rear of Stratford Church. The accused appeared before West Ham Court charged with obstructing the Broadway a highway in Stratford. The case against Nicoll was dismissed, but Mowbray was fined ten shillings and costs. All the fines given to those convicted totalled five pounds seventeen shillings and all were paid by Dr. Aveling. [12]

The authorities change of tactic, meant they could no longer be accused of acting with any political bias over open air meetings. People were not being arrested for what they said, but for where they said it. It was simply a case that 'freedom of speech' could not take precedence over the 'freedom of movement.'

At about eight-thirty on the 12th of June, 1886, Mowbray was arrested again, this time for obstructing the Grove in Stratford, while addressing a crowd of between three and four hundred people. He refused a request from Police Constable 37 George Young to leave and a struggle occurred resulting in the officers coat being ripped. The magistrates made a point of telling Mowbray that his fine of twenty shillings was for blocking the road and had nothing to do with his political views. [13]

Mowbray's card was marked, he was the most vocal member of the Socialist League and the police watched his every move. In an attempt to escape police attention, Mowbray moved to Norwich. There he teamed up with fellow Socialist Fred Charles, who set up a Socialist League branch at his premises called Gordon café at 5, Duke Street in 1886. The cafe was a regular haunt of prominent Socialists, including William Morris and James Frederick Henderson, known as Fred. Regular outdoor meetings of a thousand plus were held at Norwich and Fred Charles, Charles Mowbray and David Nicoll represented the far left Anarchist views. Fred Charles infamous link to Walsall in 1892 will become blatantly apparent later.

At eleven o'clock on Friday the 14th of January, 1887, a large crowd of about five hundred assembled in the Haymarket, Norwich. Mowbray spoke about the Queen's immense wealth, while poor people starved to death. Fred Henderson followed with another inflammatory speech, exciting the people into rage against the authorities. Mowbray marched at the head of a crowd to the Guildhall, where he insisted on speaking to the Mayor. Aware of Mowbray's reputation, the Mayor tried to pacify him by agreeing to hold a public meeting at some point in the near future. Mowbray returned to delegation outside, condemning what the Mayor had offered as an insult. He said, "What were the men to do in the meantime who wanted food?" The speeches were the catalyst for violence and the crowd poured into the market place, intent on venting their rage. A riot broke out with the windows of Lacon's bank and several other premises being smashed. Police reinforcements were called in and with truncheon's drawn, they forced their way through the crowd to arrest the ringleaders, Mowbray, Henderson and two others. Several people were injured in the skirmish, later called the "Battle of the Ham Run," in reference to a butchers shop being looted and the offenders running off with the meat. [14]

On the 17th of January, 1887 at Norwich Magistrates Court, Charles Mowbray and Fred Henderson were committed to the assizes for, "riot and with force injuring buildings and assault". To avoid further violence, the prisoners were taken under the cloak of darkness to Norwich Castle gaol with a strong police escort. At Norwich Assizes on the 21st of January, 1887, Mowbray was sentenced to nine months imprisonment and Henderson to four months both with hard labour. Part of the punishment was to walk the treadmill at Norwich Castle prison. [15] [16]

In February, 1887, William Morris made a visit to the Midlands and met with the striking chain makers at Walsall. In the industrial heartlands of the Black Country and Birmingham, the Socialists were gaining huge support.

During the first part of 1887, two distinct factions appeared in the Socialist League causing a rift. One supported democratic representation in Parliament, while the other believed in anti-Parliamentary methods to achieve their aims. William Morris strongly believed in the latter view and he was prepared to stake his leadership on winning the issue. At the annual Socialist League conference on the 28th of May, 1887, there was a showdown over the issue. Morris and his anti-parliamentary group won by seventeen votes to eleven, but he did it with the support of the extremists, Charles Mowbray, Fred Charles and David Nicoll. Dr. Aveling in the opposing camp of the organisation held a secret meeting to discuss tactics against Morris.

In June, 1887, Queen Victoria celebrated her Golden Jubilee and for a time there was a resurgence in royalist feeling throughout the country.

On Sunday the 16th of October, 1887, Mowbray was released from prison. His train was due at Victoria station, Norwich at one o'clock and Fred Henderson had arranged a public reception to welcome him back. Flying a red flag, Henderson preached Socialism to the assembled crowd as they awaited the arrival. When Mowbray arrived, he lifted his young daughter Grace in the air and kissed her as a gesture of freedom. The procession was attended by many leading Socialists from all around the country, who made a resolution of sympathy towards the Chicago Socialists on Death Row. Afterwards some of the crowd surrounded the Guildhall, throwing sticks, oyster shells and rotten fish at the police. They shouted abuse at the Chief Constable as he cleared a space in front of the police station, but despite defiance by 'hangers on' the rest of the crowd dispersed with no arrests. [17]

On the 11th of November, 1887, four of the Chicago men were hanged for conspiracy to murder, while the fifth man managed to blow himself up with dynamite smuggled into his prison cell. Socialists and Anarchists on both sides of the Atlantic, believed the Chicago men were Martyrs. Henry George, the leader of the Knights of Labour, a prominent American Socialist organisation, publicly sided against the Chicago men and William Morris openly branded him a traitor. [18]

Feelings ran very high throughout the month of October, 1887, with almost daily large scale disturbances in Trafalgar Square and Hyde Park.

In early November, Sir Charles Warren the Metropolitan Police Commissioner decided to put his foot down. A Socialist meeting planned for Sunday the 13th of November, was declared illegal and

Warren prohibited anyone from attending. Sir Charles threw the gauntlet down to the Socialists and everyone anxiously awaited their response. On the day of the ban, about thirty thousand protesters turned up and gathered in Trafalgar Square, with another ten thousand in the surrounding streets. The protesters had several issues, freedom of speech, unemployment, police brutality and Irish home rule to name but a few. The stage was set for an all out showdown, but who was going to blink first, the police or the protesters? There were four thousand police officers on duty and four hundred of them were mounted. They were reinforced by infantry and cavalry soldiers standing by, including a detachment of three hundred Coldstream Guards. It was a recipe for inevitable disaster, it only took one wrong move and all hell would break out. Whatever the mood or determination of the crowd, they were never going to be a match for the disciplined power of the police and military.

The police identified two ringleaders, Robert Cunningham-Graham a suspended MP and the Socialist John Burns. As the police moved into arrest them, the crowd resisted and a signal was given for the mounted police to charge. The police brutally smashed into their ranks, resulting in a pitched battle resembling something from the Napoleonic wars in the middle of Trafalgar Square. In the midst of the violence, a surreal moment happened, when Marsham a London magistrate rode horse back into the Square to read out the riot act. Surrounding him was a bodyguard of two hundred First Life Guards, mounted on huge jet black horses and wearing their distinctive white helmets. Then red coated Foot Guards from St. George's Barracks, with fixed gleaming bayonets marched into the Square, ready for action. A procession of ten thousand Socialists, armed with sticks and waving red banners sang the 'Marseillaise' as they moved into Shaftesbury Avenue, meeting the police head on. Another eight thousand protesters entered Parliament Square. The authorities were determined to show the Socialists who owned the streets and the reality was that ordinary members of the public did not have 'a cat in hells chance' against professional soldiers, no matter what the numbers. The greater resistance shown, resulted in the more force being applied. There were scenes of open warfare, but ultimately there could only be one winner. Nearly all the leading Socialists, Hyndman, Morris and many more saw first hand what happens if the authorities were provoked too far. The defiance was a foolhardy failure and a futile attempt to unsettle the establishment. Over one hundred people attended hospitals with wounds, one civilian had a bayonet wound to the back and one police officer was stabbed by a rioter. About seventy-five people charged with riot related offences appeared at Bow Street Magistrates Court. This became known as 'Bloody Sunday.'

The following week there was another demonstration, the Commissioner did not ban it outright, but did order and specifically forbid them from entering Trafalgar Square. Initially the crowd of about forty thousand were peaceful in nature, a full warning had been issued by the police and perpetrators knew, they broke the rules at their own peril. The police stood by in the wings, poised and fully prepared to enforce their chief's orders. Despite the warnings a foolish contingent ventured towards and broke through into Trafalgar Square. Mounted police officers charged them down and battered the protestors unmercifully. In a commotion on the corner of Northumberland Avenue, one man named Alfred Linnell had his thigh crushed by a police horse. He was taken to Charring Cross Hospital seriously injured and died there on the 2nd of December, 1887. At the coroners inquest, no evidence was given about how his injuries were sustained, despite the official verdict being that he died from blood poisoning caused by the broken thigh. The matter was then closed. [19]

The Socialists were keen to make Alfred Linnell a martyr and at his funeral on the 18th of December, 1887, about one hundred and twenty thousand people formed a procession stretching one and a half miles. A virtual 'who's who' of Socialists attended to offer condolences and support the family. When the mournful cortege crawled to a halt at the gates of Bow Street cemetery, the police barred entry to anyone other than bona fide mourners. William Morris spoke at the grave side, while a melancholy choir sang a rendition of his own 'Death Song'. [20]

The Socialist Storm

Hopefully my introduction to the Socialist movement has given you a flavour of events on the lead up to 1887. My intention was not to deviate too far from Walsall, but by giving some of the major facts the reader is undoubtably better placed to understand how things happened and what went on.

The Borough of Walsall had a well respected and established Council in 1887. Historically, wealthy local men stood for election, without necessarily being aligned to any particular political idealism. The kind of men who generally stood for election, tended to be the 'Haves' of the town, businessmen or professionals. To carry out the duties of a councillor, men needed time on their hands and this meant they needed money independently of their day job. Councillors held a certain status and the position almost certainly rewarded them with a pecuniary advantage in their own private enterprises. Many councillors went onto become Justices of the Peace sitting on the Walsall Bench of Magistrates. The council and judiciary where bound together and both functioned under the same roof within the Guildhall. The Council formed its own Committees to oversee its various functions. One of these was the Watch Committee, consisting of council members who oversaw the management of the police. The Mayor was effectively the most powerful person in the town, ruling over the council, court and police.

Socialists believed that a minority of people, held the majority of power and this system of government helped proved their point to some extent. Socialists claimed that the system was corrupt, because local businessmen won their seats on the council by safeguarding jobs in return for their workers votes. It was things like this, that helped the Socialist movement gain support from the ordinary man in the street, as they could see for themselves the injustice. Changes were gradually introduced to make it easier for men to stand for election. The Municipal Corporations Act of 1882, removed the necessity of a resident ratepayer to satisfy a set of financial eligibility criteria. A small step in the right direction perhaps, but it hardly paved the way for a working man to be elected to the council. They had just as much chance of 'flying to the moon' or 'seeing pigs fly.'

Social injustice was very visible to most people in 1887, who could see with their own eyes what was wrong with society. Radical views in Walsall were gaining support, but nobody suspected that a working man, let alone a Socialist would ever be elected to the council. Sometimes however, when all the planets align, even the strangest of things with the longest of odds can inexplicably happen.

Haydn Sanders, took Walsall by storm in 1888, against all the odds. Some may have heard the name before, but few will know his story. Haydn Sanders was a local man born in Bloxwich in 1860, the son of William Henry Sanders and his wife Priscilla. The Sanders family were well established in the Bloxwich area throughout the Victorian period, owning both local property and businesses. Haydn's grandfather, Thomas Sanders was a lock maker by trade with his own business in Bloxwich. William Henry Sanders, Haydn's father and Thomas Sanders his uncle, both had their own businesses making locks in the borough. [21]

In 1861, Haydn was a baby living with his parents, an older sister Priscilla, and two older brothers John and Handel in Church Street, Bloxwich. His parents obviously had a musical influence by when naming their children, indicating a marginally higher level of education than the average working class family. [22]

By 1871, the Sanders family had moved to 35, Sandwell Street and his father employed two men and a boy at his lock making business. Haydn was an eleven year old scholar and his older sister Priscilla, was employed as a trainee music teacher. It is reasonable to assume the family were steadily moving up the social ladder as all the children were getting a good standard of education, empowering them to aspire to a better position in adult life. The Sanders family were respectable and well placed in the community, but not exactly part of the wealthy elite. [23]

Ten years on in 1881, the family had moved the short distance to 26, Bath Street and his father now employed three men at his business manufacturing trunk locks. Haydn was a twenty-one year old lock maker, having followed his fathers trade. Bath Street was within the heart of the industrial town, not the best, but not at the very bottom of the social scale. [24]

In 1882, Haydn Sanders married Louisa Arnold a twenty year old press worker in Birmingham. She was originally from Dudley, but lived in the Ladywood area of Birmingham after her fathers death. [25]

By the mid-1880s, Haydn Sanders was an intelligent and educated man in his mid-twenties, eager to prove himself amongst his peers. It's fair to say that Sanders was an opinionated character with strong Socialist views. He had become well versed in Socialism, having read many articles written by his fellow comrades, Hyndman, Morris, Mowbray, Charles and Nicoll. He obviously liked what he read and aspired to be the champion of the working man with a mission to break the circle of poverty and wrongdoing. In this crusade, he was ably assisted by the likeminded Joseph Thomas Deakin, his right hand man. Deakin, also an educated man, was a railway clerk who lived at 238, Stafford Street. Together the two men of similar age, set up and became the leaders of the Walsall Socialist movement. By November 1885, Sanders was the secretary of the Walsall branch of the Social Democratic Federation, registered with an address at 20, Victoria Street, Bloxwich. [26]

In February 1887, the Walsall Socialists switched allegiance from the Social Democratic Federation to the Socialist League. This coincided with a visit by William Morris to the chain makers of Walsall. Deakin was appointed secretary of the new, Walsall branch of the Socialist League and Sanders was the chief promoter and mouthpiece of the organisation. Deakin and Sanders held their first open air meeting of the Socialist League on Saturday the 30th April, 1887 on The Bridge. You have to imagine the scene, Sanders and Deakin made their way to a position just outside the George Hotel near to Sister Dora's statue, with a chair in one hand and a fistful of leaflets in the other. The chair was positioned in the most advantageous position to attract foot traffic, allowing anyone who wanted to listen to gather around. Sanders climbed onto his makeshift soap box as the front man of the outfit, to preach his Socialist sermon. There is little doubt that Sanders was a skilful orator and wordsmith, who commanded his audience through the power of his speech. With a persuasive, forceful and thought evoking style, he pulled people in to listen like a hypnotist. Like most politicians, he said what he thought people wanted to hear, something to their benefit. Sanders appealed to those who wanted a change from the day after day, back breaking work for little or no reward. He said the rich unfairly exploited their position and reaped all the profits from the workers hard labour. He resented the great wealth accumulated by the industrialists at the expense of the poor, who were in extreme poverty and struggling to eat. His message, it is no longer time to 'Shut up or put up,' they had been enslaved for far too long. He offered them a dream, a hope of better things for the working classes. Despite this most Walsall people were not stupid enough to believe he could actually deliver anything. [27] [28]

By the late 1880s, The Bridge, midway between St. Matthew's and the railway station, had become the obvious venue for public meetings in the town. The place got its name from a bridge crossing the brook that runs through the town towards the River Tame. The arches of the old bridge were visible until 1851, when they were covered over and hidden underground. The Bridge then became the main thoroughfare, where people passed numerous times on a daily basis. As the focal point of the town it accommodated the largest hotel, 'The George' and other major businesses, not forgetting the prestigious statue honouring Sister Dora and the 'Four Faced Liar.'

The power of speech was the number one means of communication at the end of the 1880s, as the majority of people were still unable to read or write. Several groups competed for positions on The Bridge, with the Salvationists and Socialists being the two main organisations who vied with each other to get the best pitches and to capture as many ears as possible. Sometimes this had raucous results with group members pushing and shoving each other in a rough rivalry to be top dogs. Views about the meetings differed, some Walsall people were happy to listen as a form of Victorian education and entertainment, while others despised them due to the nuisance they caused. The Bridge was after all a busy place, where people going about their business were disrupted and inconvenienced as they tried to get past. The Socialists and Salvationists were not to everyones taste, some saw them as troublemakers and a threat to the status quo.

One of the leading voices to air his complaints was William Henry Duignan, a local solicitor and historian. He had been Mayor of Walsall in 1869 and was generally considered to be a well respected elder statesman of the town. He lived at Rushall Hall at one time, but later moved to Gorway House. In April 1887, Mr. Duignan wrote to Walsall's Town Clerk describing the Salvation Army as a scandalous public nuisance to all the decent inhabitants in the locality. He said the 'blasphemous brutes' shamed the town making it an utterly unfit place for well bred people to live. Duignan claimed that Birmingham was a well governed town and would never permit this kind of nuisance in New Street (Birmingham did not become a city until 1889). Duignan often voiced his opinion, but generally speaking he was a man to be listened to. The Town Clerk, J. R. Cooper wrote back to him, saying he would refer the matter to the Chief Constable, but pointed out that several corporations had recently attempted to prevent similar types of nuisance only to be overruled for stopping 'free speech.'

When the council did meet to discuss the matter, several members expressed their objections calling the meetings, 'two rival armies on The Bridge' and 'a most disgraceful exhibition.' Councillors also expressed their annoyance at singing beggars who roamed the street late at night asking for money. They decided to ask the Chief Constable to take action against the Salvation Army or any body else who caused an obstruction on The Bridge. [29]

George Tewsley, was the Chief Constable of Walsall Borough Police at the time, but it appears he took no positive action to resolve the matter and things continued pretty much the same. In September 1887,

Christopher Taylor succeeded Tewsley as the head of Walsall Borough Police. It's worth pointing out that the police were only responsible for enforcing the law and maintaining the peace. The Chief Constable took his instructions from the Watch Committee and was guided in matters of law by the Town Clerk (the towns legal adviser). The Watch Committee of the Borough Council, governed, appointed and dismissed the officers of Walsall Police, so they were not an independent body.

The sport of challenging the authorities had arrived and confidence was growing. Haydn Sanders and Joseph Deakin were two young men, both eager and ready to engage the authorities at the first available opportunity. Amid a backdrop of social unrest in the country, Sanders was well versed and well positioned to be the Socialist champion for the cause in Walsall. The Sanders and Deakin's roadshow was already touring local towns, including Wednesbury, Cradley, Pelsall, Dudley, West Bromwich, Smethwick and Oldbury to name but a few. Sanders was a rising star in the Socialist movement, having the ability to inspire and draw in likeminded men and women and slowly his word was getting around. Sanders speeches were drawing in larger and larger audiences and it wasn't long before his inspiration resulted in another branch of the Socialist League being set up at Wednesbury.

It was a pivotal year in 1887 for the Socialists, Mowbray was released from prison, the Chicago hangings took place, there were riots in Trafalgar Square and finally came Alfred Linnell's funeral. Socialist stories spread like the proverbial plague all over the newspapers, with gossip and passions running high. William Morris was slowly losing control of the Socialist League as the Anarchists Charles Mowbray, David Nicoll and Fred Charles slowly prized it away from his grip.

Every Monday, Sanders and Deakin held regular group meetings at the Temperance Hall in Freer Street and membership of the Walsall Socialists grew stronger. In December 1887, the famous Russian Anarchist, Peter Kropotkin visited the Walsall Socialists. He was a major player in the Anarchist movement and delivered a speech, on the effects of prisons on prisoners. [30]

In February, 1888, Edmond Guillemard gave a speech to the Walsall branch of Socialists. He makes several appearances later in this book, when we move on to our second story. At the same meeting Sanders spoke about, 'Revolution, what the Socialists mean by it and why they believe it inevitable.' [31] [32]

By April 1888, Sanders and Deakin were drawing in large regular crowds at their Saturday meetings on The Bridge and reporting good sales of the 'Commonweal.' The Socialist meetings were usually closely monitored by the constable who had the The Bridge assigned as part of his beat. Before long, large groups began to stop and listen to the rants from the podium, which inevitably caused a disruption to the free flow of pedestrian and vehicular traffic.

In May, 1888, the Chief Constable Christopher Taylor warned the Watch Committee, that Salvation Army leaders were failing to keep their promises in respect to meetings on The Bridge. He asked for their instructions on how to handle the situation. Christopher Taylor was very aware that several members of the Watch Committee were also borough magistrates, who would hear any cases he took to court. The Town Clerk, said the Salvation Army had recently changed leadership and the new one may not be aware of the situation. The Town Clerk advised, that if the Chief Constable took action against the Salvation Army, he was duty bound in the interests of fairness, to act against the Socialists and anyone else who broke the rules.

Mayor Lindop thought that The Bridge should be kept clear of nuisance at all times. Councillor Beddows said while he had no sympathy with the Socialists, interference would only strengthen their cause. They instructed the Chief Constable to speak to the new captain of the Salvation Army to hopefully prevent further problems on The Bridge. [33]

When the Watch Committee met in July 1888, they had received numerous complaints from Walsall residents about the Salvation Army and others groups causing nuisances on The Bridge. The Chief Constable said he had spoken to the culprits as requested, but that was all he was instructed to do at the last meeting. Councillor Beddows thought it wrong to interfere with any group unless there was violence and totally inappropriate to get involved in matters of religion, such as with the Salvationists. Alderman Williams said he had heard no complaints about the Salvationists, but some very bad things about the Socialists that should never be allowed. [34]

At this point Walsall Council hesitated to take any positive action and there was obviously some reluctance amongst the members to act.

Haydn Sanders profile in the Midlands continued to rise, which in turn helped him make a name for himself in national Socialist circles. On Sunday the 6th of August, 1888, he gave an outside Socialist speech at Council House Square in Birmingham with John Burns. That same evening he gave another speech near the statue of Joseph Sturge at Five Ways. [35]

When the Watch Committee met again in October 1888, Alderman Brewer reported a disturbance connected to the gatherings on The Bridge with stone throwing. He understood the incident was virtually a riot and expressed his grave concerns about possible damage to the Sister Dora statue and surrounding property. The Town Clerk, advised that anyone who caused an obstruction on The Bridge, could be summoned to court for assembling there. He reminded councillors, that before they made a decision they should know they, "could not make flesh of one and fish of another." If they got rid of one group, they were bound by fairness to get rid of them all. Alderman Brewer proposed a resolution 'to direct the Chief Constable to require people causing an obstruction to move on.' This was seconded by the Mayor and unanimously carried. Councillor Beddows thought it was a great shame to reduce anyones liberty, as he personally wanted to leave the place for meetings, he conceded however that stone throwing could not be tolerated. The Mayor regretted being forced to take action, but ultimately the railings around Sister Dora's statue already looked tired from the gatherings and were only a few months old. [36]

The Chief Constable personally visited Haydn Sanders on the 9th of October, 1888 to inform him of the new rules. He was told the Borough Council had decided that in future meetings on The Bridge, would render him liable to prosecution. The following day, Mr. Taylor wrote to Sanders to confirm the instructions in writing, no doubt he anticipated further problems.

On the 11th of October, 1888, Sanders wrote to the editor of the Walsall Observer, confirming that the Chief Constable had served him with a notice of prohibition, but denied any of his meetings on The Bridge had any disturbances or stone throwing. Sanders said the police always attended his meetings so knew this to be true and appealed to the council to immediately withdraw their orders to the police, on the grounds that they had never caused a problem. Sanders said he told the Chief Constable, that he fully intended to continue to meet on The Bridge to defend his right to 'free speech.' It was an absolute right, that he was not prepared to let the Chief Constable or anyone else take from him. He warned the council that confrontation was on the cards, as they could only govern with the consent of the people and the vast majority believed in 'free speech.' Sanders letter of defiance was published sending a direct challenge to the police that a showdown was on the horizon. An uneasy feeling of trouble brewed and gossip circulated, who was going to make the first move? The inhabitants of Walsall did not have to wait too long to find out.

Walsall people, whatever their other views strongly believed in the basic right to speak their own mind and these new rules grated on their sense of fairness. Haydn Sanders seized the opportunity to present himself as the ordinary people's champion fighting for their rights. His ultimatum to the police, finally gave him the chance to take on the authorities. The general feeling around the town was that the council had overreacted, even some councillors had misgivings about the ban and only supported it because it was the 'lesser of two evils.'

Coincidentally, Sanders showdown with the authorities coincided with an extraordinary councillor vacancy arising in the St. George's Ward of Walsall. Councillor Amos Parsons, the owner of several grocery shops in Walsall was declared bankrupt, effectively disqualifying him from being a councillor. His removal from office, brought on a by-election where two candidates James Allen, a known

Liberal Unionist with no political affiliation and John Venables from the Liberal Association expressed an early interest. This election was only a few weeks ahead of the annual November elections, where several more seats would come up for re-election. [37]

Haydn Sanders sensed the time was right to chance his hand at the politics game and declared his intention to contest the St. George's election. His uncle Thomas Sanders was already an established councillor in the Foreign Ward of Bloxwich. Haydn Sanders caused something of a revelation in the local press, who described him as 'a Socialist agitator, extremely idealistic and without realistic prospects.' [38]

By standing for election, Sanders went against the anti-parliamentary policy of the Socialist League and although they remained members, the Walsall Socialists started to drift apart from the movement.

Sanders planned his 'ban on The Bridge' protest meeting for five o'clock on the evening of Saturday the 13th of October, 1888 and had some handbills printed and circulated around town to advertise it. Mr. Taylor's 'eyes and ears' soon let him know what Sanders was planning and he sent out his own warnings to deter people from attending. Everyone knew from the events in London the previous year, what could happen when things went wrong. Despite the hype, as five o'clock approached the initial turnout was lower than Sanders was expecting. The first few who turned up seemed unsympathetic to the Socialist cause, but at the allotted time Haydn Sanders and Joseph Deakin marched onto The Bridge and placed their chair next to Sister Dora's statue. A ring of about thirty strangers, all hardcore Birmingham Socialists came to support him and protected his position. Another one hundred and fifty men and boys soon gathered to form a crowd. Sanders climbed on to his make shift podium and declared the Town Council unjust and unreasonable, for imposing unnecessary restrictions upon them. He questioned the Council's right in law to authorise the police to take such action. The Chief Constable made his way through the crowd in full uniform and gave Sanders a polite though forceful warning to stand the meeting down. Sanders could not back down and still retain any credibility in the presence of his supporters, so continued to speak totally ignoring Mr. Taylor. Sanders suggested setting up a 'free speech' committee to legally challenge the council, Joseph Deakin instantaneously seconded the idea and it was carried. Mr. Taylor was concerned that the crowd grew larger and larger by the minute, so anxious to maintain the peace, he issued further requests for Sanders to stop. Spectators were attending in pure anticipation of seeing a showdown with the law. The Chief Constable was in a difficult position as he did not want to be branded the aggressor, especially as there had been no violence or disturbance up to that point. On the other hand he had his duty to do and had received his orders. The atmosphere became very tense as Sanders and Taylor closely watched each others every move, neither wanting to blink first. It was a Mexican standoff, both sides held their nerve waiting for their adversary to show their hand. As the police patience was running out, a horse drawn cart full of passengers left the yard of the George Hotel. Turning sharply onto The Bridge, the large crowd forced the driver to deviate the wrong way around Sister Dora statue. Manoeuvring around the obstruction was suddenly interrupted by a loud drastic crack, as the axle on the cart snapped. Screaming terrified passengers were unceremoniously thrown into the roadway. Amid the wails and commotion, a human stampede began as horrified people scrambled to get out of danger. In the blink of an eye, Sanders spotted the police moving in and realised his arrest was imminent. Fearing reprisals from the public, Sanders and his band of adherents made a hasty retreat and ran off up Bradford Street. [39]

 The moment had passed without any physical conflict between the Socialists and the police, but it had come very close and it was unlikely the Chief Constable would hesitate to enforce the restrictions next time Sanders broke the rules. One thing was for sure, the Chief Constable and the Council needed no further proof about the dangers from obstructions, their course of action had been vindicated by the catastrophe.

 On Tuesday the 16th of October, 1888, Haydn Sanders held his pre-election meeting in Bath Street Board School hall. He said everyone had a right to peace, prosperity and happiness and he would fight anyone with a fearless spirit to get them all a better life. Sanders pledged that everyman should be rewarded with the fruits of their own labour and promised to use a seat on the council for everyone's benefit. Sanders saw the forthcoming election as a chance to test his own popularity, after all the hard work and study he had done. He was now both ready and willing and although the opposition branded him an extremist, his new ideas were based on common sense, necessity and the duty of one man towards another. He advocated an eight hour day, artisan dwellings and a fair price of gas. The council's ban on meetings on The Bridge, was he said, their attempt 'to filch, rob and curtail the peoples rights and liberties.' He was never going to give up the right to meet and speak, it was their birthright and he would not standby while a few councillors sold them out. He said the Chief Constable, 'might wear a gold rim around his hat, but it did not belong to him,' meaning that he was a public servant employed to serve them. Sanders said he was a working man from Walsall too, who struggled to keep body and soul together and promised that his voice, would be their voice on the council. Cheers of approval came from the audience for their candidate and then John Haddon, a Birmingham Socialist spoke in his support. [40]

At around eight o'clock on the evening of Saturday the 20th of October, 1888, Haydn Sanders returned to The Bridge intent on testing the Chief Constable's patience again. Under the watchful eye of the police, he continually kept walking around the Sister Dora statue, possibly under the impression that if he kept moving he could never be accused of causing an obstruction. The police heard him asking people to donate money to pay the magistrates if he was fined and he goaded the officers shouting over on numerous occasions, "Move on, or you will get fined ten shillings and costs." This time Mr. Taylor was in no mood for nonsense and determined to make a stand, so he ordered one of his officers to issue Sanders with a formal and final warning to leave. A crowd of nearly a thousand people had built up on The Bridge, completely blocking the area outside the George Hotel. Most were attending specifically to see the spectacle of Sanders taking on Mr. Taylor. Sanders continued shouting, exciting the crowd to become more and more rowdy as every second passed. Eventually the Chief Constable's patience was exhausted, it was obvious Sanders was unprepared to listen to reason, so instructed several of his officers to arrest Sanders to prevent a breach of the peace. Uniformed police officers surrounded Sanders, took hold of him and marched him up the High Street towards the police station. One officer was kicked by someone in the crowd, but the police presence deterred anything more serious occurring. An entourage of Sanders supporters followed the police up the High Street and assembled outside the gaol. Inside the Chief Constable told Sanders, he was prepared to release him with two sureties standing for bail. Mr. Taylor hoped the prospect of freedom, would help to disperse the hostile crowd outside. Sanders was searched before being placed into the cells and later Joseph Deakin provided one of the two sureties to secure his release. [41]

At eight o'clock on the morning of Monday the 22nd of October, 1888, polling opened for the St. George's ward election. There were three candidates standing, Dr. J. Scott Wilson, Independent, John Venables, Liberal Association and Haydn Sanders, Socialist Labour. Tensions ran high throughout the day with a great deal of speculation about the pending results. Voting closed at eight o'clock that evening and then the ballot papers were counted inside the Guildhall. With great trepidation, Alderman Brewer came onto the steps outside, to a larger than usual crowd of people to read out the results. Wilson 1,002, Venables 646 and Sanders 445. Sanders had come last, but with over twenty percent of the vote he had done far better than most expected.

Undeterred by the setback, two days after losing the election, Sanders added his name to the list of candidates for the annual council elections being held on Thursday the 1st of November, 1888. [42]

In the meantime Sanders had to face two charges of obstructing The Bridge on the 13th and the 20th of October, 1888. He appeared at Walsall Magistrates Court on Friday the 26th of October, 1888, pleading not guilty. The prosecuting solicitor was none other than Mr. Duignan, the same man who made the initial complaint about the nuisances on the The Bridge. He opened the prosecution by quoting the Highway Act passed during the reign of William IV and made reference to recent local cases at Sedgley and Birmingham's Bull Ring, where obstructions had been upheld by the magistrates.

The Chief Constable told the court that The Bridge was the main route through the town where highways converged and that meetings did cause obstructions to the thoroughfare, forcing people heading for Digbeth to go out of their way.

The Town Clerk confirmed that according to his legal understanding, the whole of The Bridge should be considered a highway for the purposes of the law.

Sanders conducting his own defence did not contest that the meetings took place, nor did he blame the Chief Constable for carrying out his orders as he was only doing his job as servant of the town. The reason he refused to obey Mr. Taylor, was simply because he believed the council ban was unlawful. Sanders disputed asking anyone for money to pay his fines, claiming it was to start a fund to defend 'free speech.' Sanders told the magistrates that every citizen had a right to hold a meeting on The Bridge, it was a privilege handed down from generation to generation from time immemorial and was upheld by common law. He quoted the Bill of Rights, allowing people to meet and discuss their grievances.

The Magistrates Clerk said Sanders argument was invalid, because highways had an even greater right, the right to 'freedom of passage' which trumped 'freedom of speech.'

Sanders quoted the principal of majority rule 'the greatest happiness for the greatest number,' and appealed for the Bench to give way on the issue. He said, the Council only wanted The Bridge to be considered a highway when it suited them, as they closed the road themselves to make money, selling the rights to hold markets and fairs. Sanders was reminded that markets and fairs came under the ancient Borough Market provisions. He then wanted to know if by paying the appropriate market fee, he could obstruct the road, but was told his suggestion was ridiculous and in any case he was not a stall holder.

Sanders called his fellow Socialist, Edmond Guillemard to give evidence in his defence, but this input did little to help support his case.

   Mr. Duignan attempted to settle the matter amicably, asking the magistrates to adjourn any judgement for three months, providing Haydn Sanders promised to stay off The Bridge in the meantime. Sanders outright refused the offer and told the Bench they would have to accept responsibility for the consequences of any ruling against him. The Magistrates Clerk, considered Sanders remark a veiled threat and warned him, stating that the justices had a duty to make decisions. The magistrates retired for a ten minute recess to deliberate their decision. During the break, Sanders cheekily distributed election leaflets from the dock for the forthcoming election. The Bench found the case proved and fined Sanders ten shillings, but only for one of the two offences charged. Sanders said he was unable to pay the fine, they gave him seven days to settle, or he would spend a week in gaol.

   Albert Mayers from the Salvation Army also appeared at court that day. He point blank refused to stop holding meetings and was fined ten shillings. He refused to pay the fine on principle and elected to go straight to gaol for seven days. [43]

   Both of Haydn Sanders opponents for the St. Georges ward election, were serving councillors up for re-election. The first was, Edmund Septimus Hildick, a saddlers ironmonger and merchant with a premises at 13½ Park Street and the second, John Nicholls Lester, an iron merchant, of 9½ Stafford Street.

   John Lester held a pre-election meeting and spoke of Haydn Sanders in derogatory terms, saying "to have a class of men like him would be akin to Communism in Paris."   Edmund Hildick branded most of Sanders principles as absurd, with the rest being impossible to execute without costing the ratepayers a fortune. Hildick did however agree with Sanders on one thing, if he won he would rescind the council order to ban meetings on The Bridge.

   The voting booths opened on the morning, of Thursday the 1st of November, 1888, with Sanders still considered the underdog against the more established candidates. At the close of business there was a general expectation that the result might be closer this time around. The ballot papers went off to be counted and people assembled outside on the steps of the Guildhall waiting anxiously for the final result to be read out. As the council official emerged, everyone listening intensely as the outcome was declared, Sanders 1,055, Hildick 986 and Lester 901. Sanders had done it, he had won the first Socialist seat on a council anywhere in England. Jubilant supporters raised Sanders onto their shoulders and carried him off towards The Bridge, cheering all the way down the High Street. He attempted to make a speech, but the police prevented him from doing so. [44] [45] [46]

Councillor Haydn Sanders

Haydn Sanders won his seat on Walsall Council by storm to the surprise and astonishment of many people in the town. He had promised his supporters a better world and now had his chance to improve working conditions. Expectations were high, it just remained to be seen if he could make the dreams he spoke about actually appear.

On the 7th of November, 1888, Sanders wrote to a local newspaper, publicly requesting the Council to call off the Chief Constable and back down on The Bridge issue. The letter written from Sanders marital home of 27, Brace Street intimated he was prepared to go to gaol, if they did not meet the publics demands. [47]

The first council meeting Sanders attended was on Friday the 9th of November, 1888. The main business was Mr. Lindop standing down as Mayor at the end of his term of office. Mr. Russell succeeded him and he received a warm welcome to his new appointment by all the councillors.

The next business after the formalities was to appoint councillors to the various committees for the forthcoming year. Councillor Beardsley raised an objection to the number of unelected Aldermen sitting on the Watch Committee, suggesting at least half should be elected councillors. He proposed Aldermen Brewer, Evans and Williams should be substituted by Councillors Brownhill, Powell and Wheway. Councillor Sanders suggested that he should be given a place on the Watch Committee, which controlled the police. Everyone in the room must have been suspicious about his motivation, knowing only too well Haydn Sanders views about the police. Councillor Powell was opposed to Sanders idea on the grounds that only tried and trusted members should be on the Watch Committee. There was a vote resulting in no changes being made to the existing structure of the committee. (Aldermen were abolished under the Local Government Act of 1972) [48]

Haydn Sanders supporters met at the Temperance Hall, in Freer Street to celebrate his victory on the 20th of November, 1888. Joseph

Deakin presided and among the Socialists attending were Edmond Guillemard from Walsall and Haddon, Tanner and John Burns prominent members of the Birmingham Socialist Democratic Federation. Deakin said, finally they had a workman, one of their own class elected to office and he felt sure their loyalty and trust would be repaid. Overwhelming applause filled the smokey room as Sanders got up to speak. Jubilantly, Sanders proclaimed himself as the first Socialist Councillor elected anywhere in England. His victory was so much sweeter, without having to rely on his own employees votes, like the industrial men he stood against. He said his opponents used dirty tactics, spreading terrible lies against him in both the press and from the pulpits. Sanders thought every man and woman had a right to earn a respectable living and he would fight all the way to defend 'free speech' on The Bridge. He accused the Police with 'helmets and staves' of doing their masters bidding, just because he had the audacity to represent the, 'great unwashed.'

Sanders said the greatest sadness of the whole campaign, was being betrayed by the man he trusted the most. He had followed the influence and ideals of this man, who taught him the principal that governments could not operate without the consent of the people. Without that mandate they were nothing but despots, who should be met if necessary by free and brave people in the bloodiest resistance. His pain was made all the worse, because his trusted tutor and friend, turned out to be the first person to raise a hand to prosecute him. That man was none other than Mr. William Henry Duignan.

Sanders announced that he declined his invitation to attend the Mayor's banquet as a conscientious objector. He couldn't bare the idea of free food while people were starving. He said the Mayor had understood his reasons for not attending and had been a perfect gentleman about the matter. [49]

At the Council meeting in December, 1888, the Chief Constable's salary was discussed. Christopher Taylor had recently taken over control of the Borough Fire Brigade and Councillor Franks tabled a motion to increase his pay by forty pounds a year as compensation for the extra work and responsibility. The Mayor seconded the proposal, but Councillor Sanders instantly piped up, moving that no increase should be given. He said the Council could not morally raise his pay, when they had men in their employment working for a starvation wage of sixteen shillings a week. Alderman Evans responded by saying it was hardly worth replying to the nonsense and other members expressed the opinion that educated men were worth more money. His idea that everyone should earn the same wage was branded ridiculous. Councillors argued that if a good man was not paid his true worth, they would find employment elsewhere and they would ultimately lose out. Only Haydn Sanders voted against Mr. Taylor's increase in salary, so his pay rise was approved. [50]

After only two meetings, there was evidently a 'cat amongst the pigeons' in Walsall's Council Chamber. The boat was certainly rocking, but would they throw Sanders overboard or let the ship go down?

On Thursday the 27th of December, 1888, William Henry Sanders, Haydn's father, chaired a meeting at Palfrey Infant School to discuss 'free speech' on The Bridge. About thirty or so enthusiastic Socialists turned up to hear that the Mayor had totally blocked any discussion on the subject, even if Sanders managed to get ten thousand signatures in support. Haydn Sanders called Mr. Duignan a hypocrite over his conviction, but expressed a hope that he would soon return to practice what he once preached. He claimed the other councillors were being unjustly hostile towards him, especially over his challenge to the unnecessary increase in the Chief Constable's pay. His objective for the next monthly council meeting was to challenge the price of gas, as he was disgusted the richest people got the best discounts at the expense of the poor. John Westley requested that councillors be canvassed for their opinions about the Chief Constable interfering with meetings on The Bridge, if they remained peaceful. This suggestion gained unanimous support. John Westley plays a leading role in our next story. [51]

The next monthly council meeting was on the 14th of January, 1889 when Haydn Sanders started with his trademark opener of making a complaint. Sanders alleged that no prior reports for the meeting had been received. The Mayor immediately summoned the council messenger into the chamber to explain. In front of the whole assembly the messenger produced his delivered book for inspection, clearly showing that all reports were personally handed to Mrs. Sanders the previous Saturday morning. The very unimpressed Mayor asked Sanders if he wanted to say anymore on the matter, but he declined to do so.

The next topic was the price of gas produced by the corporation owned gasworks. Sanders entered the debate on the attack, by accusing certain council members of winning their seats by promising to reduce gas prices, but failing to do so. His words were undoubtably offensive to some in the room and downright insulting to others. Sanders demanded to know why those getting the best gas prices, also benefited from the lions share of the profits. It was fair and proper, he said to air the peoples grievances at the meetings. He insisted on knowing why officials at the gasworks point blank refused to answer his questions about the specifics of gas pricing and constantly closed him down on the subject. The Mayor, was also the chair of the Gas Committee and he defensively told Sanders it was quite reasonable for bigger consumers to get more favourable rates, as that's how business worked. He passionately defended the fairness of Walsall gas prices, as some of the keenest prices in the country. He then told everyone that the gasworks were protected from outside applications for information in order to safeguard their operations. Any requests would not be answered without the strict permission of the Gas Committee. Looking at Sanders, the Mayor said the principal reason why he personally had not been answered, was because of the rude and threatening way he chose to word his request. Everyone present agreed to the question of gas prices being referred for consideration to the General Purpose Committee with the exception of Haydn Sanders. [52]

Intentionally or not, Sanders was upsetting just about every person on the council, including those who may have probably given him a fair chance and the benefit of the doubt. After just a few appearances in the chamber, Sanders made himself as popular as an unwanted guest at a wedding. Some elder statesmen on the council had years of experience in public matters and had earned great respect for their knowledge. Sanders lack of wisdom and bombastic attitude was disliked by his counterparts, who saw him as a disrespectful novice. He appeared to have underestimated the real power of such men, believing his prowess as a speaker could make people listen. His social skills failed miserably to connect him with his fellow councillors. He knew so little about the internal workings of the corporation, that his arguments were filled full of schoolboy errors and some of the elder statesmen saw him as a fool. Any good ideas he did have, needed their support to succeed and he was never going to get that so long as he continued to rub them all up the wrong way.

At the February monthly meeting, Councillor Sanders was quick out of the traps to ask two quick fire questions. Firstly, who paid the presiding officer and election officials and secondly, would the Chief Constable be taking action against the police band for playing on The Bridge on the 28th of December, 1888.

The Mayor confirmed that elections had nothing at all to do with the council and the Chief Constable would not take any action against the police band.

Unsatisfied, Sanders asked if there was going to be a public inquiry about the police interfering with the meetings on The Bridge. A frustrated Mayor said Sanders knew the position perfectly well, because he had already received a written reply on the subject. Sanders said he did not like the Town Clerks tone in the letter he received. The Mayor called Sanders insinuation, impudent and disgraceful and the chamber resounded with a loud round of applause in agreement. The Town Clerk was perhaps the most respected person within the council and very few people thought to criticise him. Sanders looked around the room at the clapping councillors and called them unfair. The Mayor repudiated his remark saying there was nothing unfair, which received another round of applause. Several words of animosity and disagreement, between Sanders and the Town Clerk took place. In the space of just a few short minutes, Sanders had totally offended the Mayor and the Town Clerk the two most influential members of the council.

Sanders insisted that firms who did not pay their men Trade Union wages should not get council contracts awarded to them. At this point in the proceedings any respect he did have was gone, one member wanted to know if he was entitled to ask questions, without giving proper formal notice. Sanders accused them all of ganging up and being prejudiced against him, but the Mayor said he had given him more time to speak than anyone else, which received another a rapturous applause signalling agreement of the other councillors. [53]

There was a proposal at the March monthly council meeting, to turn Caldmore Green into a public park. Sanders jumped in to suggest they erect a platform and use the area for public meetings. The other councillors ignored his idea and with nobody to second it, the matter was was closed. In response to being rebuffed, Sanders continued to bombard them with further questions not on the agenda, making the meeting almost impossible to manage or direct. The topics he introduced were random and unpredictable, he even advocated the nationalisation of the railways, accusing the bond holders of making too much profit. Senior councillors knew of course this subject was nothing to do with the council and the Mayor, verbalised his disbelief by saying, it was so strange that Mr. Sanders seemed to know everything, while everybody else knew nothing. Councillor Brownhill, informed Sanders he had more chance of abolishing the Ten Commandments, than sorting out the railways, which was nothing to do with the council anyway.

The unstoppable Sanders, did not seem to care how deep he dug the hole for himself and pressed on saying he wanted fair wages for all contractors engaged in doing council work. The Mayor told him his idea was totally impractical, as council contracts were awarded to tenders with the keenest price and in any case they had no power to dictate wages to private contractors. The Mayor allowed Sanders to put the motion to a vote and it lost by eighteen to his one. Very little normal business was being achieved as the Mayor struggled to stem the flow of Sanders constant questions. The Council Chamber started to become restless, infuriating the Mayor who tried to regain order. Unrelenting, Sanders asked what law prevented him from putting questions about the gas prices. The Mayor told him that no individual member of the council had a right to demand information from officials, it wasn't statute law, but the law of common sense. By this he intimated that Sanders had no common sense at all. The Mayor told Sanders, that most of what he was so rudely asking for was printed every year by the council and was readily available to anyone. [54]

A scathing article in the Walsall Advertiser on the 19th of March, 1889, described someones views about Haydn Sanders. It said, "for hour after hour this shallow ignorant fellow hindered public business by his verbose and conceited twaddle." The article also claimed he was, "the personification of vulgarity and obstruction, he disgusts not only those who opposed his return, but also those who were prepared to welcome him." Allegedly Councillor Lindop said he, "felt humiliated to go there, time after time to listen for hours to the rubbish Mr. Sanders uttered." [55]

At the April meeting, Sanders quickly demanded a full breakdown of all council employees, age, service, role, hours and wages. The Mayor asked him how long he thought it would take to prepare such a document and Councillor Baker wanted to know if Sanders would be paying himself for the extra work he wanted doing. Antagonising the others members, Sanders requested to be supplied with copies of the Acts of Parliament and rule books governing council business.

Councillor Powell got to his feet, waving a copy of the Birmingham Daily Post in his hand and forcefully challenged Sanders about an article in it. The report about the Birmingham Trades Council on the 6th of April, 1889, quoted Sanders as saying that Walsall Council consisted of, "bald headed, pot bellied old town councillors fonder of guzzling than justice." Sanders responded saying the report was not completely true and denied using the language mentioned. The whole council declared their disgust, forcing the Mayor to motion a resolution to request the newspaper to share their reporters notes to ascertain the truth. Sanders told the Mayor that he should abide by his own rules and stop moving unscheduled resolutions.

Councillor Wheway said, if the language quoted in the press was true, it was a disgrace to the working men Sanders professed to represent. He asked Sanders outright, if he had used the words quoted and he admitted using the word "guzzling", but said that the report misrepresented what he actually said.

After the main meeting concluded the General Purposes Committee sat. The general public left, but the press remained to listen. Sanders got up to leave, but looked over to the reporters and said the press deliberately misreported what he said. The Town Clerk was tasked with making urgent enquiries at the newspaper concerned to fully investigate whether the allegations were true. The Mayor said if found to be true, Sanders attack on the council was disgraceful. He personally considered Sanders to be a young man without, "birth, age, talent, experience or money to back up his boasts of a reformation."

After only half a dozen council meetings, the state of play was that Haydn Sanders had managed to insult, infuriate or offend everyone who sat as a councillor. When he didn't get the answers he wanted, his passion to speak completely overwhelmed his ability to listen, effectively alienating himself from everyone else at the Guildhall. Councillor Sanders, in a very short space of time had brought the council meetings to a virtual standstill. Instead of achieving any of his aims or objectives, no business was moving forward at all. Everyone was getting very frustrated and angry and tempers and tensions were strained to breaking point. Nobody seemed to know what to expect next, how bad could things actually get in the Council Chamber at Walsall and how long could it all go on for?

While the 'slagging off' investigation in the paper was still ongoing, another story broke about Sanders conduct. Apparently, after making the "guzzling," speech, he caught the train home from Birmingham to Walsall. The press reported him being so drunk on the return journey that he made things very unpleasant for his fellow passengers. [56] [57] [58]

When the General Purpose Committee met on Monday the 6th May, 1889, to discuss the allegations in the newspaper, Haydn Sanders got up to leave. He told them that he would never get justice so long as the press were present. Everyone else was very keen to hear the results of the Town Clerk's investigation, but perhaps there was something Sanders preferred not to hear himself. The Town Clerk read out the letter he had received from the editor of the Birmingham Daily Post. It simply said the report printed in the paper accurately reflected his reporters notes of the meeting.

Councillor Baker thought enough time had been wasted on the matter already and they should leave it. He said nobody in Walsall believed a single thing Mr. Sanders had to say anyway. Councillor Marshall thought that Haydn Sanders was chasing notoriety and would do anything to get it, he believed the most dignified course of action would be to treat Sanders with the contempt he deserved.

After a great deal of discussion, a resolution was passed 'condemning Mr. Sanders for using disgusting and vulgar language, calculated to bring ridicule and contempt on members of the council.' At the vote there were eleven votes to five, one of those voting against him was his uncle Thomas Sanders. [59]

At the June Finance Committee meeting, Haydn Sanders continually interrupted and disrupted the proceedings by bringing up business without prior notice. Every time the chairman, Councillor Baker attempted to intercede, Sanders ignored him and continued to speak. Eventually the Mayor intervened asking him to obey the chairman and the Town Clerk told him that rules dictated he must give notice of any business he wanted to raise. Several members asked him to sit down, but he said, "I shall certainly decline to let the business go on." Eventually councillors got up to leave the fiasco, with Sanders calling them, 'Mean and cowardly' as they walked out. The Mayor called Sanders 'cowardly' and the Town Clerk declared him, 'Out of Order.' Members slowly returned in support of the Mayor, as they did not want Sanders antics to succeed. Many members called upon the Mayor to use his special powers to settle the matter, but Sanders maintained his right to speak. The ex-mayor, Mr. Lindop, out of sheer frustration offered to personally throw Sanders out by force if asked, but Sanders continued to shout over the proceedings. After a twenty minute adjournment, Sanders returned and continued to shout over every other member and point blank refused to be quiet. The meeting ended up being abandoned with councillors leaving while he was still on his feet shouting. In his quest to get things done, he had single handedly brought the town council to a grinding halt. [60]

The adjourned meeting recommenced on Monday the 17th of June, 1889, with Haydn Sanders immediately demanding to know why his business was not listened to at the last meeting. The Town Clerk spelt out the rules for everyone present and declared Mr. Sanders had been told the them already. Sanders was informed that not all matters raised resulted in a vote being taken and that was normal.

Councillor Sanders moved that the Watch Committee withdraw their order to the Chief Constable about prosecuting meetings on The Bridge. A serious discussion took place with several members giving their views. There were two votes for and eight against Sanders motion. [61]

In June, 1889, the bit forgers and filers of Walsall went out on strike, in demand for more money. The strike committee was awarded ten pounds by the Knights of Labour organisation. [62]

At the council meeting on Monday the 8th of July, 1889, Councillor Sanders made a long speech about the state of Walsall's slums. He said they were unfit for human habitation and thought the council should exercise its powers to provide affordable housing. On this subject he was right and possibly could have started to get some members on his side, but he followed up by making slurs on the character of certain members of the Health Committee and several people took exception to his remarks. Sanders then brought everyones attention to two newspaper reports, both on the 15th of June, one in the Evening Express and Star and the other in the Walsall Free Press. He said certain members of the council had made threats of violence towards others and described Councillor Baker's behaviour at the end of the Health Committee meeting on the 29th of June as disgusting. The Mayor called

Sanders 'out of order,' saying it saddened him that he felt the need to bring the matter up at all. The Mayor refused to have either issue discussed, but told Councillor Sanders, that if and when he had something good to say about the town, he would be only too happy to listen. Sanders tried to speak, but the Mayor declared the meeting over and everyone got up and walked out. [63]

On the 24th of July, 1889, a large group of bit forgers and filers met at the Railway Inn run by Mr. Towe at Broadstone, to discuss their strike action. Several guest speakers attended to promote the merits of forming a local branch of the Knights of Labour. Many of those attending indicated a positive response and a willingness to join the organisation. [64]

At the next meeting of the council on the 12th of August, 1889, Councillor Sanders started by attacking the Mayor by declaring him out of order. He demanded to know why he refused to listen to him at the previous meeting, but the Mayor told Sanders there was nothing further to say on the matter.

Sanders then verbally attacked Councillor Baker, calling him a disgrace. Councillor Baker said in retaliation, that a man like Sanders born without any sense, could not acquire it later in life, he was a simpleton and it was rich for Sanders to talk of disgrace, when he had never done a graceful act in his life. Baker said he was more than happy to repeat in public what he said about Sanders in private, if anyone wanted him to hear it.

The council then discussed a failed legal action they had taken against Mr. Boys. Again, Sanders was heavily criticised for the words he used in a debate, which ended with him being a lone voice with his views on the subject.

Not content, Sanders argued against everyone else about the market tolls. The Mayor said he thought Sanders must be the only man in the borough who didn't know the facts, as they were published in the press week after week for everyone to see.

Sanders then aired his concerns about increasing police numbers, especially as they had appointed a shorthand writer recently. He wanted assurances from the Mayor, that this officer had not been instructed to take notes at outdoor meetings. The Mayor simply replied by saying that Mr. Sanders should not be afraid of the police. [65]

It was around this time that Sanders formed an allegiance between the Walsall Socialists and the Knights of Labour. This organisation began in Pennsylvania, United States in 1869 and between 1884 and 1894, they set up over thirty branches all across Britain to promote workers rights and improved employment conditions. This was a distinct move away from the Socialist League, who had branded the Knights of Labour 'traitors' over the events in Chicago. Knights of Labour branches had similar aims to trade unions, but were a secret society organised into lodges similar to freemasonry. Haydn Sanders, was the 'Master Workman' of Walsall branch (LA454) and he later refers to taking the pledge of Secrecy, Obedience and Mutual Assistance (SOMA). [66]

Haydn Sanders was the president of the Walsall branch of the Knights of Labour, which held their first meeting at the Temperance Hall on Monday the 26th of August, 1889. Sanders said the Knights of Labour had subscribed fifty pounds to the Walsall bit forgers and filers to help settle their strike, despite many of them not even being members of the organisation. Sanders said many had wrongly called the Knights of Labour a strike machine or employer crusher. Mr. Archibald from New York, was introduced as a brother from the Far West and Commissioner to Europe. Archibald said the organisation was neither political or religious in belief, but only worked for the interest of the labour movement. [67]

The following night, Haydn Sanders chaired a meeting to promote the Knights of Labour at the Turk's Head Inn, in Digbeth and to raise money for the dock labourers strike. The meeting was well attended and they resolved to do a penny collection around local factories and workshops. The stewards appointed were, David Young (plays a part in our second story later), Howells, P. Russell and F. Eglington. [68]

At the September council meeting, Councillor Sanders made very few remarks, other than to say he thought the council should acquire land to build workmen's houses. Mr. Brownhill said his prophesy was starting to come true that, 'Mr. Sanders was becoming a true Conservative,'. [69]

Haydn Sanders held a Knights of Labour meeting on Thursday the 19th of October, 1889. This was to select candidates for the local Walsall elections in November. They decided two men would fight the election under the Knights of Labour banner and the Socialist's would not have separate candidates. Those selected were, William Henry Sanders, Haydn's father, for the St. George's ward and Mr. F. Eglington, for the Foreign ward. [70]

On Tuesday the 22nd of October, 1889, an election campaign meeting was chaired by Haydn Sanders for his father at Palfrey Board School. The two men standing against him were Lester and Franks, who Sanders said were both enemies of the working man, because they voted against him on many matters, including the Chief Constable's pay. He told them, 'if working men wanted better wages, then they must send men to the council pledged for labour and not for capital.'

The following night Sanders held another meeting in support of the other Knights of Labour candidate, Mr. F. Eglington. During the meeting someone told Sanders that the other candidates, Beddows and Baker, had the support of the Pelsall Miners Association. This was in fact untrue and Sanders claimed they were the victims of a smear tactic by their enemies. [71]

Only about a quarter of the electorate turned out to vote at the elections held on Friday the 1st of November, 1889. St. George's ward results were, Lester 1,401, Franks 1,055 and W. H. Sanders 758. The Foreign Ward ended, Baker 711, Beddows 767 and Eglington 706. As the first two in each ward were elected, neither of the Knights of Labour candidates were successful. The prospect of getting the support of another Socialist on the council was over for another year. Sanders was very much alone at Walsall Council, in more ways than one. Was it possible for Haydn Sanders to make things anymore difficult for himself? [72]

When the Gas Committee met on the 12th of November, 1889, Councillor Sanders who was not a member, took a seat with his notebook. He told the Mayor, that he had a perfect right to be present and would not be leaving. Both the Mayor and Town Clerk asked him to go, but their attempts to persuade him were in vain, he was having none of it. Eventually he agreed to step out, while his attendance was discussed, but promised he would be back. Sanders impatience got the better of him and a short time later the sound of scuffling came from directly outside the room, followed by the door bursting wide open. Sanders made a dramatic entrance to the chamber, dragging a bedraggled doorkeeper behind him, who was miserably failing to restrain the demon from coming in. Several members in total disbelief of what they witnessed, pleaded with him to leave peacefully. Sanders refused to listen to a word they said and retook his seat, forcefully proclaiming his intention to fight for the rights of the working man.

The Mayor tried and exhausted all attempts to reason with him, to no avail. Eventually, he told Sanders that if he refused to leave he would have him forcibly ejected. This of course was a challenge Sanders revelled in, so in typical fashion he point blank refused the request. The Mayor sent out for assistance and shortly after Police Sergeant Wiltshire and Police Constable Mason marched in from the station next door. As the officers entered, Sanders showered them with a torrent of threats, including taking them to court if they dared to touch him. They tried to reason with him, but eventually the Mayor signalled his order for them to throw him out. The officers lifted Sanders chair with him still in it and carried him towards the door. Sanders made one last ditched attempt to throw himself backwards, but the officers predicted his defiant move and he failed to stop them throwing him out.

Two days later on the 14th of November, Haydn Sanders wrote to the Walsall Observer to give his side of the story. Despite the fact he had previously accused the press of printing wildly exaggerated accounts, they published his letter.

His version of events said he politely asked the Mayor's permission to be present and although refused, the Town Clerk could provide no legal reason for him to go. He therefore stayed, believing all council meetings should be open to scrutiny. He strongly denied struggling or resisting, but described the police as, 'the two well paid hirelings in blue, who cheerfully did the dirty work.' He claimed a right to be present as he was the treasurer of the Corporation Gas Workers Union and they were discussing gas prices. [73]

The reality was Sanders actions and interruptions had turned the Council into a circus, almost to the point of being comical. What he failed to understand was that the Mayor was the ringmaster and he was looking like a clown. Haydn Sanders just didn't seem to know when to give up on a lost cause.

On the 22nd of November, 1889, Haydn Sanders went to Walsall Magistrates Court to ask them to issue summonses against the two police officers who he claimed assaulted him. He said the police had no right to interfere with council proceedings and his removal was both unfair and illegal. The magistrates deliberated for forty-five minutes, but they failed to agree with him and threw out his application. [74]

In December, 1889, the Walsall Socialists moved to their new club premises at 18, Goodall Street. It was open to members every night for meetings and the club plays a major role in our second story. If only those old walls could tell now! [75]

There was a lively council discussion on Monday the 9th of December, 1889, regarding a claim from the gas workers for a pay rise. Sanders was the treasurer of the union and to his surprise the Mayor supported the recommendation for an increase from the Gas Committee. Sanders jubilation backfired, when the Mayor announced the pay rise would be financed from either an increase in the rates or in gas prices. Councillor Sanders exchanged some adversary words with Councillor Baker, over the true value of men. Councillor Wheway told Sanders, "You would make people believe you are a very God send from heaven." Wheway told Sanders, that many council members were far better friends to the working man than him and he hoped they would soon turn their backs on him.

Councillors Beardsley and Sanders then argued over the appointment of a member to the Free Library Committee. The squabble became heated and Councillor Baker accused Sanders of being a liar. Sanders told Baker his comments were rich coming from a lawyer.

Councillor Sanders had submitted a series of questions to the Mayor, regarding his ejection from the meeting. When it was time for the them to be dealt with, Sanders got up to speak. The Town Clerk stopped him in his tracks and said, members putting questions could not make speeches, as it was contrary to standing orders.

Sanders first question was, "Can councillors attend committee meetings when not a member?" The Town Clerk answered by saying, people could not attend committee meetings, without the committees permission. His second question was, "What law allows the Gas Committee to call in the police?" The answer given by the Clerk was, that common law protected all meetings and assemblies from obstruction or disturbance. Anyone attending a committee meeting uninvited was liable to be ejected. The Clerk said that was his professional opinion and it was supported by the law officers at the Municipal Corporations Association. The last question was, "What law allows the police to interfere with meetings?" The Town Clerk explained that the police had been called in after Mr. Sanders assaulted the doorman by forcing his way in. As a breach of the peace had occurred and all reasonable methods of removal failed, the police or anyone else had the right in law to use reasonable force to eject him, if acting on the orders of the chairman.

Councillor Sanders told the Town Clerk that he was contradicting himself, because he previously decided that common law did not apply to meetings on The Bridge and then went further accusing him of interpreting the law to suit himself. The other councillors were horrified by Sanders outrageous level of rudeness and called his behaviour ungentlemanly and totally 'out of order.'

The Mayor asked everyone if they were happy with the answers given by the Town Clerk, to which he received a resounding, 'Yes!'

Councillor Baker told Sanders that he should pay for his own lawyer in future, if he needed answers to legal questions.

The Town Clerk, lost his patience and told Sanders that if he was not happy with his advice, he was welcome to sue him. Sanders claimed poverty prevented him from doing so. The Mayor declared the meeting over, but before they could leave, Haydn Sanders told them he would disrupt the next meeting until he felt the matter had been settled to his satisfaction. The Mayor said he and everyone else were ashamed of the way he behaved, Sanders replied this is, "Might against right." [76]

The bridges were blazing brightly behind him, when he left the Council Chamber that cold December night. He was certainly in the cold and could expect to be 'sent to Coventry' from that point forward. Councillor Baker who was a lawyer, called him a liar and Sanders insinuated that all lawyers told lies as it was synonymous with their trade. He accused the Clerk of making up his own laws and threatened everyone that his disruption tactics would continue. Councillor Beddows said it was a great pity that Haydn Sanders felt it necessary to add a 'sting in the tail' to everything he had to say.

On the 27th of December, 1889, the awl blade makers met at the Stag Inn, Bloxwich to discuss an increase in wages. Mr. Roebuck who presided said most workers in the district had a decent Christmas, but the awl blade makers pay had lagged behind the other trades for many years. Haydn Sanders who was there to promote the Knights of Labour organisation, said it was good to see men taking practical steps to better themselves. He advised them against strike action, saying it was better to settle their differences in a conciliatory way. Mr. Harper pointed out that when the trade societies broke down employers took advantage of them, but he hoped many would join the Knights of Labour with him. [77]

On Wednesday the 1st of January, 1890, the saddle tree makers of Walsall went out on strike, having failed to reach an agreement with their employers. Councillor Sanders chaired a meeting at the Temperance Hall that evening, saying it was very unfortunate they could not reach agreement, because the longer it went on the worse it would be for everybody. He called for the bosses and workmen to share the company profits more fairly. He said the Knights of Labour had helped defeat many employers and the Walsall lock makers had just won their dispute. He said it was in the employers own interest to settle the dispute, because for one hundred pounds they could set up a cooperative cutting them out altogether and the Knights of Labour might make that money available. Sanders insisted that he had no intentions to set 'master against servant,' but did want to get better wages for all the working people. [78]

At the council meeting on Monday the 13th of January, 1890, Councillor Sanders asked for a debate about how the Gas Committee illegally and unjustly ejected him from the meeting. Dumfounded members began to leave the room rather than to listen to another word from him on the subject. Sanders motion was deliberately seconded by Councillor Wheway who wanted him to get the answer he deserved. Wheway expressed the view that Sanders should have gone when requested, rather than force himself onto everyone present. The council overwhelmingly voted to uphold the Gas Committee's action in ejecting him from the meeting. Sanders went on to bring several other resolutions at the same meeting, all of which were voted down. [79]

Any opportunity Haydn Sanders may have had by winning his seat on the council was rapidly slipping away. So far his 'sledge hammer' approach was miserably failing to make any positive changes to impact on the lives of the people he was supposed to be representing. Walsall Socialists must have been very sad that nothing constructive came from all their efforts, all their hopes and aspirations were dwindling away. On top of everything else the Council had won their point on the subject of 'free speech,' by closing the debate.

Haydn Sanders must have seen the writing on the wall, his days were numbered and he began to lose interest in the affairs of Walsall Council. On the 14th of April, 1890, a local newspaper reported that Haydn Sanders had addressed a meeting of striking stove and grate makers from Sheffield and Rotherham, with a speech allegedly bordered on being revolutionary. He told them he was happy to take up their cause as he was fed up with "everyman looking out for himself and the Devil take hindmost." His original mission at Rotherham was to promote the Knights of Labour organisation. [80]

At the end of May, 1890, after nine weeks of strike the stove and grate makers in Rotherham achieved a ten percent pay rise for six months and fixed uniform prices afterwards. Haydn Sanders who helped them achieve their victory was hailed as a hero. The workers decided to set up a Stove and Grate Workers Union and asked Sanders to become their temporary General Secretary. It was estimated that the men on strike lost between eleven and twelve thousand pounds, so they were very thankful to get back to work with a result in their favour.

A meeting at the Cooperative Hall in Rotherham, heard Sanders say he hoped the new Stove Grates Workers Union would be structured on a national level. The new union was to be entirely separate from the Knights of Labour organisation, although workers would be free to be members of both. [81]

After Sanders success in Rotherham it was clearly apparent that he lost any interest in his position at Walsall. His brand of politics had a new opportunity and he was instrumental in setting up a second branch of the Knights of Labour (LA1266) at Rotherham. Not long after this, Haydn Sanders announced that he intended to accept the permanent position as General Secretary of the Stove and Grate Workers Union and moved his family from Walsall to a new home in Rotherham. Technically, he was still a councillor in Walsall, but his political career in the town was coming to a self determined end as a result of his absence. [82]

He did turn up at the Walsall Council meeting on Monday the 9th of June, 1990, but his attitude was very subdued compared to his usual presence. He spoke about the closure of the Wolverhampton Street gas works, but it was fairly clear he had a new mission at the union and his energy at the council had been diverted to that cause. [83]

There is no record of him attending any more monthly meetings of Walsall Council after that, but if he did there was no more conflict. At the December meeting, the Town Clerk announced Sanders had been a none resident of the town for six months so the council could declare his seat vacant. Peace had finally been restored in the Guildhall Council Chamber and it was business as normal. [84]

Haydn Sanders firebrand of politics was still very much alive and kicking he hadn't settled for a quiet life just yet. Manningham Mill was a major employer in the Bradford textile industry, providing work for about five thousand workers, mainly women. The mill was one of the largest of its kind anywhere in the world at the end of 1890, when a strike broke out for more pay. Outdoor meetings were attended by between sixty to ninety thousand people and these huge numbers eventually led to the authorities banning them. The strike committee of the Bradford Trades Council was furious over the loss of free speech.

The scenario was the perfect cue for Sanders to re-enter the political stage. This was exactly his cup of tea and the kind of mission he liked to get involved in. Maybe he thought he would have more success than he did at Walsall.

The police refused the strikers permission to meet in the square outside Bradford Town Hall on Sunday the 12th of April, 1891. An alternative venue further away was offered, but the authorities knew they were unlikely to accept it. In preparation, one hundred and fifty policemen were precautionary billeted inside Bradford Town Hall, ready if strikers defied the ban. At three o'clock that afternoon, Haydn Sanders led a group of five hundred protestors into the square. The Bradford Chief Constable James Withers requested him to disperse immediately, but he refused to do so. He had been in exactly the same position before at Walsall, this was history repeating itself. Bradford Police were in no mood for games and officers marched out of the Town Hall, forcing their way through the crowds with truncheons drawn, to form a defensive square. In the scuffle, Haydn Sanders was allegedly hit in the stomach by a constable, which instantly convinced the shouting and hooting crowd to start a gradually dispersion.

That evening, the crowd outside the Town Hall began to swell again and at eight o'clock, Sanders went into the police station to request permission to address them. This police refused, but he went back outside without permission to speak anyway. The police watched him begin to speak, then two officers moved into arrest him, while others were deployed to scatter the crowd in every direction. Sanders was taken into the police station where the Mayor and Town Clerk greeted him. They told him he was free to go, as their only intention was to stop the meeting occurring. Sanders insisted on being taken before a magistrate to hear his case, but they refused to listen and set him free.

On Monday morning, Sanders aided by a barrister applied for a summons at Bradford Magistrates Court against the police for false arrest. He had tried this previously at Walsall without success, maybe he thought he could get a different result or maybe he had not learnt the lessons from the past. The court case took almost the whole day, with Sanders managing to bring up nearly every legal argument he could think of. Eventually the stipendiary magistrate had heard enough and told Haydn Sanders that by obstructing the police, he rendered himself liable to arrest and dismissed his case.

That afternoon another large crowd assembled in the square and inflammatory leaflets circulated entitled, "Communists Appeal to Criminals - signed, Your Brothers and Comrades in the Social Revolution, the Sheffield Group of Communists and Anarchists." Had Sanders become an Anarchist or had they tagged on to his campaign? Interestingly at this time one of the people involved with the Sheffield Anarchists was Fred Charles, who plays a major part in our next story. As the crowd increased in numbers, tensions grew stronger and stronger with every agitators rant.

The Chief Constable protected by a large body of officers emerged and took the names of the ring leaders. As the crowd grew bigger and bigger, the police sent for reinforcements and in the meantime formed a defensive cordon around the Town Hall building to hold control of the square. Violence erupted when the police were bombarded with stones, smashing windows and injuring officers. The mob made several rushes attempting to break though the police lines, until the mounted branch charged and forced the protestors back. The Chief Constable and his senior officers were pelted with stones as they desperately appealed for the crowd to go home. A large contingent of factory girls from the mill joined the rioters and things were getting completely out of control. The powerless Mayor came out to read the Riot Act, but this had no effect on the excited crowd and all possible peaceful ways to restore order were exhausted.

The Mayor had one last trump card to play and he signalled for the one hundred and eighty red coated troops of the Durham Light Infantry to enter the square. Each soldier was pre-issued with forty live rounds, but their very presence frightened the demonstrators enough for them to quickly start to disperse. This ended things abruptly, but not before several people were injured during the rioting.

On Tuesday morning, when some of those arrested were being taken to the railway station for transport to gaol, unsuccessful attempts were made to rescue them. On the evening crowds formed again to ridicule the police and soldiers. Men and woman turned out to protest, but many more just to spectate. At six o'clock, Major Woodland marched his troops into the town and through the crowds, this time with swords drawn as a show of strength. They entered the Town hall to reinforce the special constables who were protecting the building.

As nightfall began, the militants extinguished the gas lamps outside the Town Hall plunging it into darkness, then they threw stones smashing the windows. Both the Mayor and Town Clerk were hit by flying stones and patience was running out. The police and military were ultimately never going to back down, no matter how enormous the numbers grew outside. It had been shown previously in the capital, that it was foolish to take on well prepared authorities in a game of violence. When the order was finally given, the military marched out forcibly driving the protestors into the surrounding side streets and scattering them to the four winds. Later at court several of the rioters were imprisoned or fined for their parts in the disorder.

On the 27th of April, 1891, after nineteen weeks, the Bradford strike broke down and the defeated and bewildered workers reluctantly agreed to return to work. Many of them were destitute and ruined with the bailiffs at their doors. On this occasion the Socialists had totally failed to achieve the aspirations of the demoralised mill workers. [85]

On the 5th of April, 1891, when the census was taken, Haydn Sanders lived at 67, St. Ann's Road, Rotherham. He was thirty-one years old and the secretary of the Stove Grate Workers Union. His wife and four children all lived with him. [86]

In October 1891, Sanders seat on Walsall Council was up for election subject to the usual rotation. He had been absent for months and was ineligible for re-election due to his residency outside the borough. Haydn Sanders involvement in Walsall politics had finally come to an end. He had already demonstrated that he had no intention of returning to Walsall, when he was heavily defeated in the East ward of Sheffield election in 1891. Interestingly the Socialists did not enter any candidates in the 1891 Walsall elections. Before the end of 1891, his allegiance to the Knights of Labour organisation had also dissolved away, both at Walsall and Rotherham. [87]

Despite all the odds being against him, Haydn Sanders somehow managed to pull off becoming the first Socialist Councillor in England, by winning his seat on Walsall Council in November 1888. Whether Sanders was a success or failure is up to you to decide, I know what I think. Whatever your thoughts, Haydn Sanders left an indelible mark on Walsall Council, one which for many years was going to be very hard to erase. We will return to Haydn Sanders life after Walsall later, now it's time for, 'The Walsall Anarchists.'

Part Two - The Walsall Bomb Plot

The Build Up

The Walsall Bomb Plot has all the necessary ingredients for a gripping television or film production, plotting, intrigue, mystery, conspiracy, unanswered questions and so much more. The colourful characters alone make a rainbow look black and white. It's hard to imagine that in Victorian Walsall, a group of men walked almost invisibly amongst the people, clutching a dark secret plan to cause abominable human carnage. They had in their possession drawings of bombs and part made grenades, intended to maim and kill men and women indiscriminately. Their crazy notions and ideas involved blowing up theatres and music halls, to butcher their fellow man for committing the crime of being rich. Walsall people may have been down trodden, poor, even hungry, but this was something else. This was murderous terrorism of the most extreme kind, so abominable it was unimaginable to almost every sole in Walsall. This is the picture painted by the authorities about what the accused men were plotting. This sort of thing didn't happen in England and certainly didn't happen in Walsall, or did it? We have already seen that some strange things happen in Walsall against all the odds.

Three of the six men involved in the bombing conspiracy were from Walsall, all well known and respected in the town beforehand. The other three consisted of a well known Anarchist from Norwich and two extremist foreign fugitives. For months without the slightest suspicion, these people mixed amongst their fellow inhabitants of Walsall. Harbouring dastardly thoughts of making a bomb, they met and plotted in the Victorian streets and alleyways and from their headquarters at the Socialist Club in Goodall Street

Mr. Taylor, Walsall's Chief Constable commanded a force consisting of sixty-nine officers including himself. He was a thirty-six year old former soldier, who first joined Kent police in 1873 and worked his way through the ranks to be chief at Walsall. He is one of our leading characters, a visibly imposing man with a large handlebar moustache and walking cane. He wore a military style blue uniform similar to that of a Rifles officer and a gold braided peaked forage cap with a bear and ragged staff emblem at the front. He commanded a team of three experienced detectives, who although were well versed in hunting down local villains, bomb plotters were very different creatures. These bombers were not common felons, they had respectable jobs and they could move around unsuspected of their devious views.

The story about the Anarchists is shrouded in controversy, with conspiracy theories having been banded about since the original story broke in 1892. These theories relate to an alleged high level sanctioned plan designed to break up the Anarchist movement in the country. Some believe police informants were tasked as agent provocateurs to convict innocent men, just because of their Anarchist views. The idea of making them scapegoats by dragging them to court and severely punishing them is just one opinion. Several people have written about the Anarchists and the views of the authors have varied enormously. I have to say, some are wild and wacky, some politically distorted and others fundamentally incorrect, but few concentrate on the facts.

It's true that Walsall Borough Police and detectives from New Scotland Yard combined their efforts to investigate the case, but the enquiry was run and owned by Chief Constable Taylor. It is also true that the detective who came from New Scotland Yard to assist in the investigation, could have stepped straight out of a Conan Doyle book. While Sherlock Holmes was fiction, Detective Inspector William Melville was very real and had already earned himself a well respected reputation for his exploits against terrorists in London.

In 1892, the Walsall Anarchists story headlined as a major national crime of terrorism. This consortium of men had actually commenced the production of bombs, intent on striking at and destroying the heart of Victorian capitalist society in England. The Anarchists trial remains the most notorious court case in the whole history of Walsall. As for conspiracy theories, who did what, where, when and why, you can be the jury and I will present the evidence.

What are the questions that need to be answered? Was this the governments answer to getting rid of Anarchists, by infiltrating and breaking up their network? Were the police involved in intrigue and entrapment to remove a perceived dangerous element from society? Were the Walsall Anarchists innocent victims, set up by a man who told the police what they wanted to hear in return for money? Or were they a dangerous and deadly terrorist network of organised criminals with their sights set on bringing down society, by causing bloodshed and carnage?

In considering these questions it is important in the interests of fairness to remember that Victorian crime investigation was still fairly basic. There were rules about giving cautions to suspects, but the rules of evidence were not entirely standardised. These were pioneering police investigations, from which all the rights and entitlements known today were born! It's also important to realise that the police have always used informants, narks, grasses, snitches, or as they were called in Walsall sarbuts. These people invariably told the police a story in return for financial gain and the more serious the crime, the more money they could make. For a long time, the Home Office had offered large rewards for information in murder cases. Even if an informant was used, it did not necessarily mean that the offenders had been set up, the information may have been perfectly true. The reader must work out for themselves if they were guilty or not. Some of the people mentioned did not stand trial at all, so you will have to consider why that was. To make a reasoned and fair assessment, you will have to look closely at all the evidence and the character of the people involved.

The reason, Haydn Sanders formed the first part of this book was because he is intrinsically linked to the Walsall Socialist Club, which plays such a big part. The club is at the core of both our stories and Joseph Thomas Deakin is the man at the centre who links them both together. Even while Sanders was a councillor at Walsall, the Anarchist movement was developing and gathering pace. Sanders was a fine example of why the electoral route of Socialism was not working and why many decided to take an alternative and more violent route towards power. To look at where the Anarchist movement was we at the time, will need to return for a while to our Socialist characters from earlier.

In January 1889, Charles Mowbray left Norwich and returned to London. Fred Charles followed at about the same time, taking up residence in the East End, where he continued with other anti-parliamentary communists to preach mass propaganda. [88]

In February 1889, Mowbray began holding large open air meetings in Victoria Park with Fred Henderson, drawing crowds numbering around fifty thousand. [89]

In 1890, Mowbray wrote 'Reform and Revolution' an article which concluded by saying, "Revolution is now inevitable.' [90]

At the Socialist League conference on the 25th of May, 1890, William Morris lost control of the 'Commonweal,' when David Nicoll with William Mowbray replaced him as editor and publisher. The Anarchist element had now taken complete control of the Socialist League and the new leadership began to publish more revolutionary ideas. William Morris remained a member of the Hammersmith branch for a while, but on the 21st of November 1890, he severed all links with them.

On the 17th of March, 1891, the Socialist League celebrated the Commune in Paris at the Banner Street hall in London, where the guest speakers included prominent Anarchists, Charles Mowbray, David Nicoll, Fred Charles, Auguste Coulon and Louise Michel. [91]

In March 1891, seven French Anarchist's were tried following a violent demonstration in Paris. Only one man with a gun was convicted and the rest were sensationally acquitted. The French Anarchists shift towards violence, caused the French government to instruct their police to harass, frustrate and break up their network. The consequence of the French authorities action was to effectively drive the Anarchists out of the country, as they found their bomb making activities almost impossible to carry out without being caught. This mass exodus of Anarchist terrorists saw many of them coming to England, where they were comparatively free from interference. [92]

The Autonomie Club at 6 Windmill Street, London hosted an International Anarchist Conference on the 29th of March, 1891. This was a major meeting point for British Anarchists and a safe haven for foreign fugitives. This place plays a central part in the Walsall story and was most likely the location where the whole thing started.

On the 9th of May, 1891 the 'Commonweal' started referring to itself as, 'A Revolutionary Journal of Anarchist Communism.'

At this time Charles Mowbray started an intensive anti-militarist propaganda campaign, by distributing thousands of leaflets and copies of the Commonweal to army barracks at Rochester, Colchester and Chatham. The leaflets encouraged working class soldiers to disobey orders to fire on civilians. Mowbray's own son, Charles was imprisoned and discharged from the army for his anti-militarist views. The warning signals were all there to show that the Anarchists intended to start a war against the establishment.

Fred Charles, who was almost certainly the leader of the Walsall Anarchists disappeared from London and for a time met up with Dr. John Creaghe in Sheffield. They set up and published a new newspaper, 'The Sheffield Anarchist.' Not too long after this, Fred Charles inexplicably vanished from Sheffield and turned up in Walsall, meeting up with his old comrade Joseph Deakin.

Dr. Creaghe held a meeting in August, 1891 at the Monolith in Sheffield. The crowd turned ugly and Creaghe was booed and jeered when he mentioned the use of dynamite and bombs. The Anarchists retreated back towards their club in Westbar Green and the angry mob surrounded their premises. Foolishly the Anarchist's threw their literature out of the upper windows, inflaming the mob to pelt them with stones. It was ten o'clock, before the police eventually were able to clear the streets. John Creaghe, later became an active member of the Argentinean Anarchist movement. [93]

The Cast of Characters

When Haydn Sanders up-sticks and left for Rotherham in 1890, he left the Walsall Socialists like a headless power vacuum. Sanders was not only the mouthpiece, he held the whole Socialist caboodle together. He was almost certainly the driving force behind changing their allegiance from the Social Democratic Federation to the Socialist League and then to the Knights of Labour. It was whatever suited his own agenda. Sanders was the person who fought the law, got arrested, got elected and then disappeared leaving his old friends high and dry. The truth was, Walsall proved to be a nut too hard for Sanders to crack, so he left it all behind to try his hand in pastures new. His old friend Joseph Deakin was left in charge of the Socialist Club in Goodall Street without his political partners steer. Under Deakin the club moved slowly but surely towards the more militant views of Mowbray, Charles and Nicoll. The disillusioned Socialists were beginning to convince themselves, that there was no peaceful solution to achieve their aims. By 1891, there is little doubt that the men of Goodall Street club had turned the corner towards Anarchy and had started calling themselves Anarchists.

So who were the people involved in Walsall's most serious crime of the century. The term 'Walsall Anarchists' was given to the six men who faced trial at Stafford Assizes in 1892. Those men were, Joseph Thomas Deakin, Fred Charles, Victor Marie Cails, Jean Joseph Battolla, John Westley and William Ditchfield. We now need to take a closer look at who these men were and how three local men got wrapped up with, an Italian, a Frenchman and a revolutionary from Norwich. These six men were the ones who faced trial, but there were plenty more people involved in this affair, who never went before the court.

Joseph Thomas Deakin, was the son of a railway wheel turner, who was born at Wednesbury in 1858. The family lived at 12, Constable's Row, Wednesbury in 1871 and in 1881 at Station Road, Cannock. By 1891, the family lived at 238, Stafford Street, next door to the Prince Blucher public house. Deakin worked as a clerk for the London and

North Western Railway Company at the company's Albion Station in West Bromwich and he was also the secretary of the Walsall Socialist Club in Goodall Street. [94] [95] [96] [97]

John Westley was born at Walsall in 1861, the son of a stirrup maker. At the time of his birth his parents John and Emma and his two sisters lived at 4, St. Paul's Row. In 1871 the family resided at 51, Dudley Street. On the 29th of December, 1884, Westley, married a local girl Ellen Elizabeth Larkkom at St. John's Church, Walsall. Between 1885 and 1896 they had six children, five girls and one boy. His only son, Horace died aged two in 1889. In 1891 the Westley family lived at 17, Goodall Street, next door to the Walsall Socialist Club. As a socialist and neighbour, Westley acted as a casual caretaker and key holder for the club. Westley's views were well known around Walsall, he had been a member of the Socialist Club since the time of Haydn Sanders. He made no attempt to hide his beliefs, in fact he was a strong advocate and spoke out with considerable force and ability both in public and in the press. Westley was recognised in the town as a well respected and successful businessman, trading as a self employed brushmaker. [98] [99] [100] [101] [102] [103] [104]

William Ditchfield was born at Walsall on the 21st of June, 1848, the son of Thomas and Mary. On the 2nd of April, 1871 Ditchfield lodged at 72, Green Lane and worked as a bit filer. Six days later on the 8th of April, 1871, he married Ellen Edwards at St. John's Church, Walsall. The marriage produced nine children between 1872 and 1891, two sons and seven daughters. In 1881 Ditchfield lived with his wife and four children at House 4, Court 1, Blue Lane West. Ditchfield was also a member of Walsall Socialist Club and in 1891 he lived at 272, Green Lane with his wife and six children. [105] [106] [107] [108] [109] [110] [111]

The fourth man was Fred Charles, who was born in Norwich in 1864, his original birth name being Frederick Christopher Slaughter. His father was Christopher Slaughter, who died when he was just three years old. Fred Charles parents had a curious relationship, his mother Lucy was his fathers third wife and forty years his junior. Before they married she was employed as his housekeeper, but was also described as his niece. In 1871 at the age of six, Charles lived at Gildengate, Norwich with his widowed mother Lucy and his four year old sister. His mother ran a pork shop and they had a live in servant. Ten years later in 1881, he worked as a commercial clerk and lived with his mother and sister at Old Palace Road, Norwich. [112] [113] [114] [115] [116]

As early as 1886, Charles started using the name Fred Charles, when he became one of the leading Socialists in Norwich. He set up a branch of the Socialist League at his premises at 5, Duke Street, where he frequently met with William Morris and James Frederick Henderson, better known as just Fred. Fred Henderson later became his brother-in-law when he married Charles sister Lucy Bowman Slaughter in 1892.

Charles moved to London after the 'Ham Run' riot affair in 1887, to continue his Socialist campaign. Joseph Deakin and Fred Charles first became acquainted in July, 1889 in Paris. In April 1891, Fred Charles was working as a clerk and lodged at 26, Cawley Road, Hackney with the German born women's rights activist, Gertrude Guillaume-Schack. Soon after this and without any apparent reason, Charles turned up in Sheffield to assist Dr. John Creaghe with the 'Sheffield Anarchist' newspaper. Charles didn't stay there for very long, because by July 1891, he had moved under suspicious circumstances to Walsall. There he linked up with Deakin, Ditchfield and Westley and became a member of the Walsall Socialist Club, which united four of the men together. [117]

Victor Louis Marie Cails was a Frenchman born in Nantes on the 16th of February, 1858. As a teenager, he became a marine engineer and went to sea. In his early 20s, he became a militant following the teachings of the imprisoned Anarchist, Clément Duval. While at sea he travelled to Devil's Island and covertly exchanged letters with Duval who was imprisoned there. Cails was one of the instigators of the 1891, May Day riotous demonstration in Nantes. To evade being arrested Cails fled France, arriving first at Glasgow, where he got work as a stoker on a riverboat. Not too long after he made his way to the Autonomie Club in London, which had become a nest of Anarchists frequented by two other key people in our story, Jean Joseph Battolla an

Italian and Auguste Coulon. At the Court of Assizes in Nantes on the 2nd of July, 1891, Cails was sentenced to eighteen months imprisonment in his absence, for "distribution of writings, exciting crimes of murder, looting and burning."

The last of the Anarchists, was Jean Joseph Battolla who was born in Porto Venere, La Spezia, Italy on 8th of December, 1862. He married Josephine Eugenie Barthelemy in Marseilles on 8th of December 1883, but was already an Anarchist by then. To disguise his identity Battolla often used his mothers maiden name of Degiani as a 'nom de guerre.'
118

In February, 1891, Battolla fled from the French authorities after his revolutionary activities attracted their attention and they banned him from ever returning. He sought refuge in London, where he also met with Auguste Coulon at the Autonomie Club. By trade Battolla was a shoemaker, but he always dressed exceptionally well. He had a mass of dark curly hair and a dark moustache waxed at the ends. New Scotland Yard appear to have regarded him as a 'professor' in the dark and mysterious art of explosives and he was treated with suspicion from the time he arrived in the country. Battolla was probably placed under surveillance as soon as the authorities realised he was in London.

Anarchists like any other likeminded group of people networked with each other, either meeting at rallies or knowing each other by reputation from their written work. There is no doubt that some of these men had dangerous intentions, Battolla and Cails were Anarchist fugitives from France with reputations for militant and violent action. Fred Charles was a skilled linguist, but also a cunning activist who moved around the country to evade police attention. Charles was a prominent Anarchist, even before he arrived in Walsall and Deakin was well aware of that having met him in Paris two years earlier. Charles knew Deakin was the leader of the Walsall Socialist and that he was an Anarchist sympathiser.

That summarises the six men who appeared in court, but there were almost certainly others involved in this plot. Some of the prominent characters who did not appear at court, are mentioned below for completeness. How much they were involved is open to opinion, you decide.

Edmond Josephe Guillemard was born in France in 1857, but came to Walsall at a young age. He married a local girl Rhoda Elizabeth Acton at St. Michael's Church, Rushall on the 11th of March, 1878. In 1881, Guillemard lived with his family at 23, Hatherton Street and was employed as a malleable iron caster. In 1891, he was a thirty-four year old iron caster living at 244, Green Lane, with his wife and two children. [119] [120] [121] [122]

The one thing that can not be overlooked, is that when Haydn Sanders left Walsall, Edmond Guillemard was a rising star in the ranks of the Walsall Socialists and a key figure when they turned the corner towards Anarchism. It would be hard to believe that Deakin never asked for his linguistic help when he spoke with his foreign plotters. Some researchers have suggested that Edmond Guillemard assumed the leadership of the Walsall Socialists from Deakin after Sanders left, but there is no firm evidence of this. Guillemard would have certainly been in an ideal position to assist with planning a bomb project, as he was an iron caster and his brother Jules Guillemard was a metal pattern maker who lived just off Green Lane, at 6 Nelson Terrace. [123] [124]

Last but not least on the list of key people involved was Auguste Marcial Coulon, considered a Frenchman, but born in Mouscron, Belgium in 1844. Coulon was an accomplished linguist, fluent in French, German, Dutch, Italian, Spanish and English. At some point Coulon took up residence in Dublin, where in 1884 he married a German woman, Helena Ulmschneider. In 1885 Coulon was one of the original members of a new Dublin branch of the Socialist League. He described himself as a Professor of Modern Languages in 1889 and his family lived at 10, Leeson Street, Dublin. He also rented 50, Dawson Street, where he ran a language school with his wife and held the Socialist League meetings. [125] [126] [127] [128]

Coulon left Dublin in 1889 for Paris, from where he wrote several articles that appeared in the 'Commonweal.' By April 1890 he had become a well known Socialist and moved to London. There he joined the North London branch of the Socialist League and gave a lecture entitled, "The French Revolution" at the Clarendon Coffee Tavern. [129]

Coulon and his family lived at 37, London Street, Tottenham Court at the time of the 1891 census and described himself as a forty year old translator of language. [130]

The North London Socialist League held their meetings at the Autonomie Club in Windmill Street, where Coulon gave regular lectures. He also assisted Louise Michel open a Socialist and International School at the club premises, which later relocated to larger premises at 19, Fitzroy Street, London.

The final person we are going to talk about is Detective Inspector William Melville. He was born on the 25th of April, 1850 at Sneem, in County Kerry, the son of a baker and publican. As a young man he moved to London, where on the 16th of September, 1872, he joined the Metropolitan Police. [131]

At the beginning of 1879, Melville married Catherine Rielly at Lambeth and later that year on the 14th of June, he was promoted to Detective Sergeant on the Criminal Investigation Department. [132]

In 1881, Melville was a twenty-nine year old police officer, living with his wife and one year old daughter at 44, Liverpool Street, Lambeth. [133]

On the 17th of March, 1883, Chief Inspector Littlechild took command of the 'Special Irish Branch,' a new department at New Scotland Yard and Melville was one of the twelve original members. Most of the men were of Irish descent and their remit was to counter the Irish American Fenians, involved in the 'Dynamite War.' In 1884, Melville was posted to the port of Le Havre, in France. Two of his children were born there, James Benjamin in 1885 and Cecile Victorine in 1886. On the 3rd of February 1887, he was promoted to Detective Inspector and transferred to D Section of the CID called, 'Special Branch.' This unit consisted of only four officers, Chief Inspector Littlechild and Inspectors Melville, Quinn and Pope. The team was funded by HM Treasury and came under the direction of the Home Office. This small group of men were responsible for foiling the

'Jubilee Plot,' a conspiracy to bomb Westminster Abbey, during Queen Victoria's, 1887 jubilee service.

Unsubstantiated accounts claim that while at Le Havre, Melville was involved in the pursuit of Francis Tumblety, a suspect in the 'Jack the Ripper' case, who managed to escape to the United States. I have found no documentary evidence except speculation of his involvement in the case, but nothing can be ruled out in Melville's unbelievable career.

The Melville family returned to London sometime late in 1888 or early 1889. We know this for sure, because his wife died in Lambeth of pneumonia early in 1889, leaving him a single parent with four children all under the age of seven. [134]

At the time of the 1891 census, Melville was a forty year old Inspector of Police living with his four children at 51, Nursery Road, Lambeth. Visiting at the address was Amelia Foy, the widow of a former constable on his team. He married her later that year on the Isle of Wight, probably while he working on Royal protection duty at Osborne House. [135] [136]

The real story of William Melville's career is the envy of fictional crime writers, he really was a most formidable Victorian detective on whom a whole book could be written.

The Lead up to the Arrests

The French authorities implemented a major clampdown against the militants after the Paris affair in March, 1891. The vigorous police activity caused a mass exodus of Anarchists, with many of them arriving in London. Several of these people were convicted felons or wanted men in their own countries and now their dubious intentions were the problem of the British police. The British Government did not place an outright ban on the Anarchists coming, most likely because it was too difficult to implement with travel being far simpler back then. That said, many of the prominent Anarchists were known to the police and their names were on a watch list. Almost immediately after arrival, many of the known activists began to associate with known British Anarchists. This set alarm bells ringing at Whitehall and the authorities knew they needed to put measures in place, before they got too established. They knew perfectly well that Anarchist doctrine included destructive beliefs and potential bloodshed.

New Scotland Yard had a specialist department 'Special Branch,' tasked to monitor and make sure the Anarchists did not get free rein to do as they liked. These men were highly trained and experienced detectives with language skills. They also had expert knowledge of their targets and a proven track record of bringing down militants and sniffing out terrorists.

Detective Inspector Melville was one of the key Special Branch officers deployed on this anti-terrorist unit in the capital. Their mission was to infiltrate, gain information and break up Anarchist terror cells. Sometime during 1891, Melville managed to infiltrate the Autonomie Club where the Anarchists met. He found out about the plan to make bombs, which led him to the Socialist Club in Walsall. The bombers had unwittingly drifted into the crosshairs of perhaps the most iconic detective of the day. Melville was ruthless like a terrier with a rat, which he was going to shake to death. There can be little doubt that the information came from a well placed informant under Melville's control and all the fingers seemed to point at Auguste Coulon. Melville was locked on, he had smelt the blood of another conviction on the horizon and his extraordinary policing sense was to wait for the most favourable time to go in for the kill. While the Autonomie Club became the focus of Melville's investigation in London, the Socialist Club in Walsall was soon discovered as the epicentre in the Midlands.

The Socialist Club in Goodall Street, was literally just down the road from Walsall police station. Haydn Sanders left a lasting impression on the Chief Constable as the proverbial 'wasp in his ear.' Sanders battles with Mr. Taylor meant the Socialists were already treated with suspicion and under the watchful eye of the police. It's very likely that the Chief Constable wanted to know every move they made and his men were best placed to see any activity.

Fred Charles, was the first Anarchist from outside to arrive in Walsall at the beginning of July, 1891. His motives for turning up in Walsall have to be suspect, he was the man with the most influence, attitude and ability and has to be considered the leader of the group. He was a tall slim man with what some described as a refined look and he was a fluent speaker in French and other foreign languages. Having met Deakin at Paris previously in 1889, Charles turned up in Walsall seemingly destitute. John Westley gave him a job selling brushes to tide him over while he settled in with his fellow Socialists at the club. On the 15th of July, 1891, he secured a position as a clerk at Thomas Gameson and Son, iron founders in Lower Rushall Street. He apparently supplied Gameson's with excellent references from previous employments in Nottingham and Sheffield. His talents were attractive to his new employers, as being able to read and write in French they occasionally asked him to deal with French correspondence for them. It is very unlikely that Gameson's knew about his political activities in Norwich, London or Sheffield. Despite being a notorious Anarchist on the national scene, he came to Walsall keeping a very low profile. He never spoke about himself or Socialism at Gameson's, but worked steadily and accurately to gain an exemplary reputation as a thoroughly reliable clerk. Charles had gone from a high profile Anarchist to a man who wanted to disappear into the community! Westley found Charles lodgings at 57, Long Street, which was his mother-in-laws house. Unknown to Charles, his best attempts to evade detection and stay invisible and under the radar had failed. The Chief Constable was tipped off about his presence in the town from August, 1891, which was not long after his arrival. Something or someone had given him away but little escaped Mr. Taylor's attention.

In August 1891, there was a Socialist International Revolutionary Congress at Brussels, where all Anarchists delegates were expelled. On the way back from Brussels several Anarchists met at the Autonomie Club in London. According to David Nicoll, Auguste Coulon asked Joseph Deakin how Fred Charles was doing in Walsall. Deakin allegedly told Coulon he was working in a local foundry to which he replied, "that could be useful in making bombs for us." [137]

Coulon corresponded by letter with Charles from the Autonomie Club, asking if the Walsall Socialists could accommodate and find work for two Frenchmen who had fled the troubles in France. The subject was discussed at Walsall Socialist Club and they agreed to accommodate one man only at Charles's lodgings. Charles said he would confirm their offer for one man with Coulon by letter.

On the afternoon of Saturday the 8th of August, 1891, Victor Cails and another Frenchman George Laplace arrived in Walsall. Charles met them both at the railway station and took them to eat at Wright's Dining Rooms, in Park Street. Laplace ending up lodging with Charles in Long Street and Ditchfield found a temporary place for Cails at the club's expense. The day they arrived, Deakin nominated Fred Charles, Victor Cails and George Laplace for membership of the club, Westley seconded them and they joined.

George Laplace was an opera glass maker by trade and struggled to find suitable work in Walsall. He only could only manage to kept the wolf from the door by doing casual work for Ditchfield and after only a short time he decided to return to London.

Victor Cails looked and dressed like a typical working class Frenchmen, with blouse and peaked cap attire. He was short and stout in stature with a heavy brow. Underneath his deceptive simple looks an intelligent, ruthless and wanted fugitive was hiding. Initially, club members helped him find a job at Messrs. Glaze's, at Butts Mill, but this proved physically too hard. Then a fellow club member David Young, from 54, Green Lane, helped the destitute Frenchman out by taking him on as a trainee chainmaker.

On Sunday the 10th of September, 1891, Cails attended an open air meeting in Walsall, where Joseph Deakin spoke about the Anarchists being expelled from the Socialists Congress of Brussels. Cails was eager to speak himself, but felt his English was not quite good enough to make a positive contribution. Almost immediately after arriving in Walsall, unlike Charles, Cails did want to become actively involved in the Anarchists work.

In October, a woman Marie Josephine Piberne came from Nantes in France to live with Cails. David Young, thought Piberne was his wife, but they were not married, although they lodged together. Piberne was an 'English and Parisian dressmaker' by trade, but found it difficult to find work as she could not speak any English. She got small odd jobs, but unfortunately neither of them were capable of earning decent money. During their time lodging with David Young, Cails received several letters with foreign postmarks. He had a habit of getting up early each morning to check the post before anyone else got up. Charles, Cails and Piberne would read the letters together, but they only ever spoke in French so nobody else could understand what they were saying.

Cails wrote a letter on the 4th of October, 1891, which appeared in the 'Sheffield Anarchist' newspaper. The article said, nineteen twentieths of all people were poor and were maddened and irritated by the sight of wealth held by the few. He claimed modern day society took even the basic privileges of a savage away from the working class man. The enslaved poor were forced to do the most vile and distressing work, without even the promise of bread to eat. He said the law granted the poor imaginary rights, but in reality they were abandoned to chance, with no guarantee of food or education. Society only repressed, punished and chastised poor men, women and children who he advised should not submit to its law. [138]

Cails and Piberne relied heavily on Fred Charles to supply them with food to keep them alive.

In late October, 1891, Cails and Charles received a letter signed 'Degiani,' containing the sketch of a bomb and instructions in French on how to construct it. Battolla was the author, but anyone who could understand French was obviously aware of what was going on at this point. Battolla, Cails and Charles were certainly in the know.

In November 1891 the Walsall Socialists sent a greeting card to the national Anarchists commemoration for the Chicago Murders saying, 'Walsall anarchists join in remembering murdered Chicago comrades and look hopefully for the speedy success of Social Revolution and triumph of Anarchy!' This shows beyond much doubt that Walsall men were subscribing to the cause of Anarchy. [139]

Deakin, Cails, Charles and Westley discussed the bomb sketch at the clubhouse and decided they needed to make a pattern to cast it in iron. Edmond Guillemard supposedly had a pattern maker brother in Brussels and they decided to write to him for his advice. The brother did allegedly visit, but they had already decided to make it for themselves by then. The brother did end up clearing all Edmond's debts for him. This information came from Deakin himself, but Edmond Guillemard did have a brother named Jules who was a pattern maker living in Walsall. Charles kept the bomb sketch and not too long after this, with Deakin and Westley, a rough wooden pattern was made on a Sunday afternoon. Ditchfield advised them the walls were too thick, so Westley and Charles made them thinner by shaving the sides. Deakin, Charles, Westley and Ditchfield all collaborated in double checking the measurements with a pair of engineers callipers. They agreed to call it an, 'electric cell,' to avoid suspicion when they spoke about it. Charles agreed to pay the casting costs, but was against asking Gameson's foundry where he worked to do the work.

Early in November, 1891, William Ditchfield met an unemployed brass caster named Bernard Ross in Jessel Road. Ross was given the two halves of the wooden pear shaped pattern, together with a wooden model of a bolt. Ross who lived just down the road at 9, Birchills Street was asked to cast them and told it was for electrical lighting, designed by a student named Purchase at the Science and Art institute. Purchase supposedly worked at Matthews and Bliss's linen drapers on The Bridge and lived in Long Street. Bernard Ross agreed to make the castings in return for a sovereign. Ross made plaster casts from Ditchfield's patterns, then took them to his brother Thomas Ross, who could make them in metal, with the promise of half a sovereign. Thomas Ross lived at 17, Bulls Head Yard and he was assisted by a friend, Thomas Brown to make the moulds at Lambert Brothers, Alpha Tube Works in Ablewell Street. He made a lead model, a brass casting, core stocks and the bolt.

After Bernard Ross had finished with the plaster moulds, he decided to return them to Purchase in Long Street. He went to the house where he thought Purchase lived, but nobody by that name lived there. He enquired at Matthews and Bliss about Purchase, but they had never heard of him either.

Thomas Ross returned the castings to his brother when they were finished. Bernard sent the castings with his wife Edith to Ditchfield house to get his money. Ditchfield only gave her two shillings saying she would get the rest when he got paid himself. That night Ditchfield went to the club to get the money Charles promised, but he never arrived as expected. Ditchfield was furious at being let down and had to be given the contents of the club till to buy his family's Sunday meal. Ditchfield went away a very unhappy man and when Deakin found out the next day, he went round to his house and gave him a sovereign to cool him down. When Charles and Ditchfield did meet they exchanged a few strong words, but Ditchfield paid Edith Ross another fourteen shillings on the following Saturday.

Ditchfield later asked Bernard Ross to enlarge the model and put three holes in the bottom. Ross told him it was impossible to cast with three holes and they had to be drilled later. A new plaster cast and shortened bolt was made, which Edith Ross took back to Ditchfield with a request for five shillings. Ditchfield was only prepared to pay one shilling and sixpence, so she went away unhappy threatening that her husband would be coming to see him about the money. Thomas Ross expected to be paid half a sovereign for his work, but ended up receiving nothing from his brother.

With the patterns now complete, they were taken to the Socialist Club and put on a shelf. They they now just needed to work out how they could get them made in large numbers. Eventually they concocted a plan to move their evil bomb making experiment forward. Charles wrote a letter, purporting to be from George Laplace, from 54, Green Lane, where Cails lodged. It read, 'Kindly quote by bearer your very lowest cash price for three dozen castings, pattern sent, common iron, and is wanted for a customer and if satisfactory I can probably secure his orders for a considerable quantity. Let me know by bearer the very earliest date at which you could supply them. Yours faithfully, George Laplace.' The pattern and core stocks for the bomb were wrapped up in brown paper tied with string and taken to Westley's workshop, which was next to the Socialist Club, in Goodall Street.

On the morning of Monday the 23rd of November, 1891, Westley's twelve year old errand boy, William Nicholls from 109, Paddock Lane, arrived at the workshop for work. Nicholls was given the parcel and the letter written by Charles and instructed to take them to Bullows's foundry in Long Street. He was told to tell Mr. Bullows they were for Mr. Laplace. Nicholls innocently did as his master told him and made his way through the town, blissfully unaware of what was going on. The cogs in the bomb making machine had started to turn. When Nicholls arrived at the foundry, he handed the parcel containing the pattern, core-stocks and letter to the thirty-two year old warehouse woman named Sarah Higgins. She took them into the foundry and gave them to her boss Mr. Frank Bullows. The foundry frequently had bits of work like this coming in off the street, it was after all the age of invention so Mr. Bullows had no reason to suspect anything untoward. He looked at the job and thought it looked troublesome to make and really didn't want the bother of the business. To put the customer off, he decided to quote an exaggerated price and wrote '20s. per cwt,' (twenty shillings per hundredweight) on the letter. Sarah Higgins took the quote back to Nicholls who was waiting in the yard and he immediately scurried back to Westley's shop, where he handed the reply to his master. Westley looked at it and wrote on the same letter, 'Yes, price will do. Please say when sample three dozen will be done.' Westley directed Nicholls to take his reply straight back to Bullows foundry with the message, "tell them to get them done as soon as they could." Only a quarter of an hour after leaving, Sarah Higgins saw Nicholls come back into the foundry yard. Frank Bullows was surprised at the speedy return and the acceptance of the quote, but answered Westley's question, by saying "they would be done at the end of the following week."

The Walsall Bomb Plot had moved from planning to production, the Anarchists were about to become bomb makers with prototypes on the way. Everything was almost ready to go!

Believing that Bullows was going to do the work, Cails wrote to Auguste Coulon, at Fitzroy Street to tell him the exciting news. Cails received a letter back to say a man would collect some of the bombs on the after delivery Saturday.

Despite the Anarchists optimism there was a problem. The caster at Bullows foundry could not complete the job, because he found the core was too large for the mould and it was unworkable without some adaptations. He informed Mr. Bullows of the problem who personally examined the pattern and core stocks and concluded they were the work of an amateur. Mr. Bullows wrote a postcard to Mr. Laplace at 54, Green Lane, asking him to collect his pattern as they could not do the work. This was the home address of David Young, where Cails and Marie Piberne were lodging. Having read the postcard, the postman was told that Laplace did not live there. The postman returned the postcard to Bullows as 'a dead letter,' meaning that the person was not known at the address and he burnt it.

Cails wrote to Auguste Coulon at the Autonomie Club to tell him about the holdup at Bullows foundry. Maybe the letter arrived too late, or the information was not passed on, but whatever happened the wheels kept turning. Battolla was still going to Walsall to inspect the bombs and someone had informed Detective Inspector Melville at New Scotland Yard of what was going on.

Melville needed to get the evidence himself, so on the morning of Saturday the 5th of December, 1891, he travelled by train from London. When his train ground to a halt at Walsall railway station, it must have seemed like something from a different age compared to the capital, but Melville was at home where ever he was. He made his way down Park Street, across The Bridge and up the High Street to Goodall Street. At the Police Station, Melville spoke directly in the strictest of confidence with Christopher Taylor, spelling out the seriousness of the case. Melville informed Mr. Taylor that Battolla one of the bomb makers would be arriving in the town later that day. Melville had connections at the highest level and the Chief Constable was well aware that this was a case involving national security.

At just after three o'clock that afternoon, Inspector Melville and the Chief Constable went incognito to Walsall railway station, where they watched and waited for Battolla's to arrive. Melville had known Battolla through his investigations into the London Anarchists for about ten months and seemed to know the Anarchists every move. The two men waited in the shadows of the station platform, as the London train arrived. Melville instantly spotted Battolla the distinctive man from London, snappily dressed all in black, wearing a black silk top hat and Inverness cape. He looked like a stereotypical magician with his waxed moustache as he moved slowly but confidently out of the station concourse and into Park Street. He asked a young lad on the footpath for directions and was led to Goodall Street, where they parted company. Battolla walked up and down furtively on the footpath opposite the Socialist Club. The only plausible explanations for his suspicious behaviour was he was either being careful not to be seen entering the Socialist Club or he was waiting for someone to arrive. Eventually as nightfall descended on that cold December evening,

Battolla went inside, while Mr. Taylor and Melville kept watch on the club.

They waited for almost an hour before Battolla emerged in company with Cails and Marie Piberne. Together they walked through the town to 54, Green Lane, where Piberne went in alone. Battolla and Cails continued walking up Green Lane until they reached Ditchfield's house at number 272, where they went in. Inside Battolla examined the brass casting and said three holes in a triangular formation were needed in the bottom. Battolla and Cails stayed at Ditchfield's house for about thirty minutes before they returned to 54, Green Lane. Observations continued in Green Lane until about eight o'clock when Battolla and Cails came out of the front door and headed back towards the town. They walked directly to the Socialist Club in Goodall Street, where Deakin and Charles were both observed to enter and Westley, who lived next door, went in and out two or three times, while the others were there. When Mr. Taylor and Detective Inspector Melville left, Detective Sergeant Charles Cliffe continued the careful vigil. When Battolla finally left, he went to stay the night at Hodgkins, Midland Coffee House in Bradford Street.

Early on the morning of Sunday the 6th of December, 1891, the Chief Constable and Detective Inspector Melville continued their surveillance outside Hodgkins coffee house in Bradford Street. Deakin arrived to meet with Battolla and together they walked the short distance up to the Socialist Club. Battolla went inside, but Deakin almost immediately left him and was followed to Charles lodgings in Long Street. Deakin and Charles had a short conversation on the doorstep and then Deakin returned to the Socialist Club. At dinner time, Battolla left the club and went to Cails lodgings at 54, Green Lane, where he stayed until about three o'clock in the afternoon. When Battolla and Cails left the address together, the Chief Constable and Detective Inspector Melville covertly followed them returning to the club. Away from prying eyes, Battolla showed them how to make a casting using some sand and mortar. At five o'clock that afternoon under the cover of darkness, Battolla, Charles, Westley, Cails and David Young came out of the club. They walked up Park Street to the railway station, where they all waited for the ten to six train to London. On the platform, Cails told Battolla in French, "Give my compliments to all the London pals." Battolla stepped onto the steaming and hissing train and Detective Inspector Melville jumped into an adjoining carriage and watched him carefully during the return trip to London. At Euston, Melville was first to leave the train and Battolla followed him out. Outside the station, Melville stopped and put his bag down to put on his gloves and Battolla who was right behind passed him by and they went their separate ways.

The joint forces of Walsall Borough Police and the Metropolitan Police were convinced they had uncovered a serious threat to national security and things were put into place to bring them to justice. Walsall Police kept the Socialist Club under strict surveillance for another fortnight, with the intention of identifying targets and gathering evidence. During this time Ditchfield was formally identified as being one of the club members.

On the run up to Christmas 1891, Cails proved himself simply useless at chainmaking. He was lucky to earn a meagre 9s. 6d., a week, so ultimately David Young was forced to dispense with his services. Out of sympathy John Westley took him on as a trainee brushmaker, but despite this help Cails and Marie Piberne were totally destitute and struggling to keep the roof over their heads.

During that cold and dark Christmas, the ordinary people of Walsall had no idea a desperate and evil gang of terrorists walked in the shadows of their Victorian streets. They had no reason to even suspect that the people living amongst them were planning to commit heinous acts of bloodshed and carnage. Unknown to the syndicate of killers, they had been rumbled and the net was closing in on their planned acts of mass destruction. This small circle of extremists had been fools to carry out their activities right under the noses of Walsall Borough Police, who now with the help of Melville were onto them. This band of Anarchists from around the globe, with ideas of retribution and revolution, had underestimated the ability of the police. The Anarchists were united in Walsall planning to bring the capitalists down, while the police had combined resources to bring the curtain down on them.

By New Year 1892, Cails and Piberne could no longer pay David Young his rent, so on Monday the 4th of January, 1892, they were forced to move into an unoccupied upstairs room at the Socialist Club in Goodall Street.

With their business at Bullows foundry on hold, the Anarchists had to rethink their plans and calculate how to get their bomb making business back on track. Whatever they did, the clear intelligence coming from the London kept Melville one step ahead of them. The information must have originated from the Autonomie Club, making Auguste Coulon the obvious suspect as the nark.

At the beginning of January 1892, other members of the Autonomie Club were becoming suspicious of Coulon and he was losing their trust. His usefulness to the police was running out and would shortly come to a swift end. Although Coulon was almost certainly the informant in London, it's not beyond the realms of possibility that the resourceful Chief Constable of Walsall aided by his trusted Detective Sergeant Charles Cliffe cultivated their own informants. The main suspects for this hypothesis would be Edmond Guillemard, David Young and Bernard Ross. There is no doubt that Walsall police would have offered financial incentives for good information against these men.

With intelligence drying up and bomb making getting closer, it was time to make a move.

The Arrests

At about eight-thirty in the evening on Wednesday the 6th of January, 1892, Euston railway station was once again the venue for a stakeout by Detective Inspector Melville and his colleague Detective Inspector Patrick Quinn from New Scotland Yard. Concealing themselves with a view of the platform they waited for a man who they suspected would be arriving from Walsall. Believing this man would be met by a London connection, they set their lair early. Who knows whether this information came from Walsall or London but it was very accurate. As Melville discretely watched from a distance, he observed the darkly clothed figure of Battolla making his way towards platform number one, where he waited for the train to arrive. Battolla stood alone when the train came and he carefully watched all the passengers get off as if he was looking for someone in particular. The platform cleared, but whoever he went to meet did not arrive. Unknown to Battolla he had made a mistake, this was not the train from Walsall, that train had been delayed. He left before realising and walked out of the station on his own.

Melville held his nerve realising Battolla's mistake and his officers held their positions. He was right, just a short time later the anticipated train from Walsall arrived late at platform number two. As the steam cleared, Melville immediately recognised the unsuspecting Joseph Deakin getting off the train. Deakin was the leader of the Walsall Socialists, the head man from the Midlands. Deakin walked down the platform with a suspicious looking parcel tucked under his arm, looking around furtively as if expecting to meet someone, but Battolla had gone. He walked out of Euston station towards the Tottenham Court Road, closely tailed by Metropolitan Police's finest men. Keeping in near proximity, Deakin was heard to ask someone for directions to Windmill Street, where the Autonomie Club was located. Melville had to make a decision fast, he needed to find out what Deakin was carrying before he had chance to reach his destination. It was nine o'clock on that cold dark night as Deakin approached the police station on Tottenham Court

Road. The decision was made to strike, Detective Inspector Quinn, a large man of Irish descent approached Deakin taking him by surprise. Quinn introduced himself as a detective from New Scotland Yard and asked Deakin what he had in the parcel, to which he replied, "Nothing." He was taken through the front doors of Tottenham Court Road police station, where inside he confessed to having a bottle of chloroform in his parcel. The parcel was carefully unwrapped and found to contain a cigar box packed full of sawdust, concealing a small glass bottle, about three quarters full of a clear and colourless liquid, labelled 'chloroform.' Deakin appeared nervous and his behaviour was extremely suspicious giving evasive answers about the strange way the chloroform was concealed. He would not tell Inspector Quinn why he brought the chloroform to London, where it came from or where it was destined to go. He would only say it was for a friend who he refused to name, because he thought it was lawful for anyone to possess it. His failure to give a satisfactory account led to him being physically searched. He was carrying a copy of the 'Commonweal,' a season rail ticket between Walsall and Albion and a return train ticket from London to Walsall.

Melville knew Deakin was involved in the bigger job and needed him tucked away, while he thought about his next move. Deakin was confined to the cells on a charge of having in his possession suspected stolen property and remanded in custody for the next available court. With Deakin out of the way, the next part of the plan was to round up the rest before they got wind of what had happened. Detective Inspector Melville immediately returned to Euston station after Deakin's arrest and caught the last train back to Walsall.

Travelling through the night he arrived back in Walsall on the morning of Thursday the 7th of January, 1892. Melville's arrival at Walsall police station was unexpected, as he was informed the Chief Constable was at home ill in bed. He insisted that Mr. Taylor's personal attendance was of the utmost importance, so a messenger was sent to his home address of 129, Lichfield Street, alerting him of his arrival. The Chief Constable despite his incapacity, hastily returned to his office to find Melville waiting with the news about Deakin's arrest. Deakin was appearing at court later that day, so consequently they had to act quickly and decisively. Taking charge of the matter immediately, the Chief Constable summoned his three detectives, Detective Sergeant Charles Cliffe and Detective Constables John Smith and John Ingram to his office. Nobody knew about Deakin's arrest at that time and the plan was to keep it a secret until the rest were rounded up.

Later that morning, Deakin appeared at Marlborough Street Police Court, charged with the unlawful possession of a cigar box, containing a bottle of fluid, without being able to give a reasonable explanation for it. Deakin requested a solicitor to defend him and appealed for the magistrates to grant him bail, but it was refused and he was remanded in custody for a week. With Deakin safely secured in London it was time to make the first moves in Walsall.

At around midday the Chief Constable, Melville and all the Walsall detectives went to William Ditchfield's house at 272, Green Lane. They were convinced Ditchfield knew something about the bomb making and was possibly the weakest link, but they were unsure how involved he was in the overall conspiracy. They knew Cails and Battolla had visited Ditchfield in December, so chanced their arm to see if he would spill the beans with a little bit of friendly police persuasion. Ditchfield was in his workshop at the rear of his house working at his trade as a saddle bar filer. None of the officers were in uniform when they turned up and Ditchfield mistook them for bailiffs after money. Mr. Taylor asked, "Where's Swain work?" This was the name Ditchfield used until he was twenty-one years of age, as his father died when he was young and his mother remarried a man named Swain. As the officers moved around his workshop, the Chief Constable saw the plaster cast made by Bernard Ross in an open box. Realising what it was, Mr. Taylor picked it up and Melville said to Ditchfield, "you will have to give an account of it." Without much prompting, Ditchfield said, "That is for George Laplace. It's a French lubricator, a model for casting." Ditchfield was asked if he had seen Laplace, he replied, "No a Frenchman named Cails brought it to me." Ditchfield seemed only to happy in mentioning Cails, Deakin and Charles by name. He told them that on one Saturday in

December, Cails had brought a brass casting to him with an Italian who examined it. He could not understand what they were saying to each other in French, but they did ask him to drill three holes in the bottom of the 'electrical lubricator.' He bored three holes in a line at the bottom as requested, but they told him it was wrong, as they needed to be in a triangular pattern. They agreed to pay him threepence for each 'lubricator' he drilled three holes in the bottom of and for putting a threaded hole in the top. Cails and Charles also gave him a letter to take to Mr. Bullows foundry, but he had lost it. Ditchfield was not arrested at that point, as it appeared he was cooperating and had supplied some valuable information. Detective Smith took him to the police station as a witness, to help with their enquiries. The Chief Constable wanted Ditchfield somewhere safe were he could not alert the other suspects. He also wanted time to consider what Ditchfield's precise position was in the gang. After extracting what they could from Ditchfield, the officers regrouped.

At one o'clock the police secured all entrances and exits to the Socialist Club in Goodall Street before raiding the premises. Entering the place by surprise they gave no one an opportunity to escape. Fred Charles, Victor Cails and Maria Piberne were found all together and were quickly secured and arrested on suspicion of conspiracy to manufacture bombs for the Anarchists. The police suspected they could be dangerous and subjected each prisoner to a physical search. Fred Charles had a large bore loaded revolver in his pocket, with five bullets in the chambers and another eight loose ones in his trouser pocket. The metal on the weapon was worn shiny and bright, from regularly being carried. Cails and Piberne occupied an upstairs room as a bedroom. In that room was a portmanteau belonging to Cails, inside of which was a copy of a German Anarchist journal, 'Die Autonomie,' printed in London and a large number of other documents. There was also a reel of explosive fuse, similar to that used for blasting in mines. In the bar of the club the police found three books, marked 'The Minute Book,' the 'Nomination Book' and the 'Visitor Book.' The 'Minute Book', containing the club rules, stated that the club was opened in 1889.

Members had to be over sixteen years of age and show allegiance to the Social Democratic Federation. Membership applications needed to be supported by two members in writing and confirmation by the committee. All entries in the book were made and signed by J. T. Deakin, as secretary. One entry was a resolution for J. T. Deakin to attend the Anarchist Congress in Brussels and the International Congress. His presence accompanied by Ditchfield was confirmed at both. This entry must have shone more light of suspicion towards Ditchfield as an active member of the gang. The 'Nomination Book,' contained an entry dated the 8th of August, 1891, showing that 'F. Charles, V. Cails and G. Laplace,' were nominated for membership by Deakin and seconded by Westley. Two days after this their membership was confirmed by the committee and entered on to the roll of members as numbers 47, 48, and 49. The 'Visitor Book,' was examined for the 5th and 6th of December, 1891, but there was no reference to Battolla visiting the club. The prisoners Cails and Piberne were taken to the police station and allocated cells in the gaol.

The Chief Constable and Detective Inspector Melville took Fred Charles in a cab to his lodging house at 57, Long Street. The cab pulled up a few doors short, to prevent anybody being alerted as they walked up to the door. A careful watch was kept on Charles, who was given no chance to escape. Charles was invited to open the door with his key to confirm his residence. Inside, Charles explained to his landlady Mrs. Elizabeth Larkkom, that his companions were members of the police, who had come to search his room. He may well have told her they were the police, so that she would not say anything incriminating. Mrs. Larkkom was in fact, the widowed mother-in-law of John Westley. They went upstairs to the back bedroom occupied by Charles, where the officers found a black bag belonging to him, containing lots of documents, both handwritten and printed. Amongst the papers was the sketch of the bomb with some written instructions, "The substance cast-iron, The screw at this height and very strong, The dimension of the bomb like a big pear, not larger. It is understood that you don't trouble about caps. Make three holes at the places and the same size."

Sketch of bomb

A screw at this height and

The substance cast

The dimensions of the bomb, like a big pear, not

caps

It is understood you don't trouble about caps. Make three holes at the places and the same size.

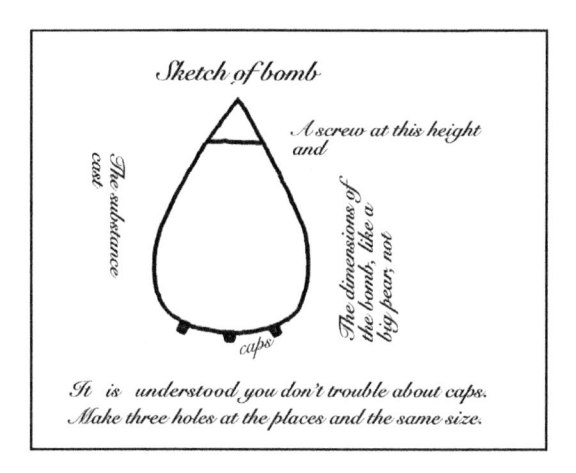

Charles black bag also contained two further documents which the police believed were proof of his intentions. The first was a handwritten manuscript by Cails called, 'The Means of Emancipation' dated and signed, 'V. Cails' at Walsall on the 1st of December, 1891. The second was a copy of Number 7, 'L' International,' with an article entitled, 'An Anarchist Feast at the Opera.' This article gave instructions on how to blow up public buildings using bombs. There were also several copies of a leaflet entitled, 'Fight or Starve' (see The Anarchist Literature in Contents). In a little address book there was an entry, 'Degiani, 50 Fitzroy Street,' this was Battolla's address in London.

Detective Inspector Melville found a lead model of a bolt, similar to the threaded bolt required to finish off the top of a bomb. Charles refused to say what the bolt was intended for, but he did say, "I regard the police as my enemies." After this Charles was returned to the gaol.

The Chief Constable then visited Alfred Bullows foundry in Long Street, where he spoke to Frank Bullows. He told him the story of how the boy had brought the pattern and core stocks to him. Luckily, he still had them in his possession, together with the letter signed by 'Laplace,' and he gave them to the Chief Constable. Mr. Bullows had no idea who the errand boy was who brought the things to his workshop, or any knowledge of the man Laplace. Mr. Taylor was very keen to know if there was any possibility that an actual casting could be made from the pattern. The Chief Constable asked Mr. Bullows to attempt a further experiment to make a casting, which he agreed to do under his own watchful eye. Later after Mr. Taylor had left, Mr. Bullows was able to produce a perfect casting by coating the moulds with charcoal blacking.

Later that day in Mr. Taylor's office, he and Melville interviewed Fred Charles. They asked him if he wanted to give any explanation for the incriminating items found at his lodgings, but he said, "I must refuse to do so." After being cautioned and charged with the offences, all he had to say was "Alright."

The next to be interviewed was Cails, who Detective Inspector Melville spoke to in fluent French. At the close of the conversation, Cails pointed to the articles produced and said in English, "I never see."

William Ditchfield had been at the police station nearly all day waiting for the Chief Constable to speak to him. Although he was supposedly helping the police with their enquires, he was left in the pen within the cell block, referred to as the dock. It was evidently freezing cold, because after an hour under police guard, he began to physically shiver and shake. Inspector Thomas Bailey spotted that Ditchfield was suffering and took him through to the report writing room with a fire, to warm up. It was not until six o'clock, that Detective Sergeant Cliffe arrived and led Ditchfield through to the Chief Constable's office. The Chief and Melville could see that Ditchfield looked unwell. Mr. Taylor handed him a glass of whisky and Melville gave him a cigar. After speaking for a while Ditchfield agreed to make a written statement. Ditchfield was left in the presence of the Chief Constable's clerk, Police Sergeant John Cullinan, who wrote the statement down for him. In essence the statement said that sometime in November he saw the bomb pattern at the Socialist Club. Deakin, Charles and some of the others were talking about it being too rough and he agreed to file it for them. When it was finished, he took it back to the club and put it on the shelf. Deakin, Charles and Cails visited his workshop with a casting, which they told him was for a French electric lubricator. He agreed to drill three holes for threepence and remembered them giving him a note for Bullows's foundry in the name of Laplace. He never went to Bullows's as he didn't like the idea and had since lost the note. On one Saturday before Christmas, Cails and an Italian in a top hat visited his workshop. They told him that the three holes needed to be made in a triangular shape in the thick end of the object. He agreed to punch the three holes and to thread the top aperture for threepence each item. They told him there would be a lot of them to do. His statement was read over to him and he made his mark. After making his statement, Ditchfield took the Chief Constable and Detective Inspector Melville back to his house, where from a drawer he produced a brass threaded bolt with a hole through the head. He told them it was the screw bolt for the top of the lubricator.

At six-thirty that evening, Chief Constable Taylor went back to make a thorough search of the Socialist Club in Goodall Street. In the cellar of the club premises, he found a parcel of mortar, sand and hair, which he believed was suitable for making a mould for casting.

Fred Charles, Victor Cails and Marie Piberne made their first appearance at Walsall Magistrates on the morning of Friday the 8th of January, 1892 before W. Bayliss and William. E. Blyth.

Marie Piberne looked a pitiful sight whimpering in the dock and to spare her any further misery the Chief Constable informed the Bench that he had already decided to offer no evidence against her. The Bench ordered her immediate release from the dock and Detective Inspector Melville translated and explained it to her.

Cails and Charles faced charges under Section 4 of the Explosive Substances Act of 1883. This offence states that, any person who makes or knowingly has in his possession or under his control any explosive substance, in circumstances that give rise to a reasonable suspicion it is not for a lawful object, shall unless they can show a lawful object be guilty of felony, and on conviction, shall be liable to penal servitude for a term not exceeding fourteen years, or to imprisonment for a term not exceeding two years with or without hard labour, and the explosive substance shall be forfeited.

The expression 'explosive substance' for the purpose of the Act, includes any materials for making explosive substances, but also any apparatus, machine, implement, or materials used, intended, or adapted, to aid or cause any explosion. It also includes any part of any such apparatus, machine, or implement.

Mr. Taylor opened by saying he had conclusive evidence to prove that over the last two months, Charles and Cails had in their possession materials for making bombs and he indicated to the magistrates that it was part of a serious and well organised national Anarchist plot.

This was certainly no ordinary run of the mill Friday morning offence for the Bench to deal with. The Chief Constable introduced Detective Inspector Melville from the Metropolitan Police Special Branch, who was ably assisting him with the investigation. Mr. Taylor informed the Walsall Bench that the prosecution was sanctioned by HM Treasury and the highest authorities in London. He said he would be making a further report to the men in London, asking for their instructions on how to proceed with the matter. This really was the proverbial 'Big London Job,' coming to town.

The Chief Constable theatrically handed the magistrates a specimen bomb to examine, which had been made by Mr. Bullows for the police from the pattern supplied. The bomb was shaped like a large pear, between three or four inches long, with a hole in the top. The hole was used to load the explosive and then closed and secured by a threaded bolt. At the bottom, there were three holes to fit detonators or percussion caps. Mr. Taylor told the court that when it was thrown, it would strike the ground and the weight would cause it to detonate and explode. He explained that the pattern had been recovered from Mr. Bullows foundry and a bolt suitable to secure the top was found at Charles lodgings. Mr. Taylor said that he did not propose to offer any further evidence, as there were several lines of enquiry still ongoing. He asked the court to remand both men in custody, so that he could continue the investigations and protect the public from any potential harm.

Charles raised no objections to being remanded in custody, but Cails protested energetically by waving and pointing towards Mr. Taylor. Through Detective Inspector Melville's interpretation, he disputed having anything in his possession and requested to be granted bail. The police made strong objections to his request and Mr. Taylor informed them that the London magistrates had already remanded Deakin. This was the first indication that Deakin would be brought into the enquiry at Walsall. Charles asked to be supplied with a pen and paper for writing, which Mr. Taylor agreed to. Charles also asked for better blankets and food, complaining that he only had been given dry bread to eat. Mr. Taylor, who was officially the Borough Gaoler told the court that prisoners were, "given enough food to keep them alive," but friends and relatives could bring in as much as they wanted. After considering their decision the magistrates remanded them both of them to Stafford gaol to await trial. The magistrates clerk Mr. Newman, told Charles and Cails to make any complaints to the Stafford Governor and they were both taken down.

Only the few regular people who normally attended initial court appearances were present. Up until then the police had managed to keep the lid on their secret investigation, but now the 'cat was out the bag' and it wasn't long before the news of this sensational crime spread like a wild fire all around town. Within the hour the locked up Anarchists were the talk of the town and everybody's main topic of conversation. Before the court sessions ended that day, a crowd of curious spectators started to assemble outside the Guildhall, hoping to catch a glimpse of Cails and Charles leaving for Stafford. Eventually the two men were led out by Inspector John Hamilton and Detective Constable John Smith and loaded into the horse drawn 'Black Mariah' police van. As they drove the vehicle through the streets, there was a weird disbelief of what was going on. Another crowd assembled at the railway station to see the two outsiders unloaded from the van. Men from Walsall Borough Police kept a watchful eye to prevent any escape attempt as both shackled men boarded the three-forty train to Stafford.

A buzz of excitement vibrated through the town and speculation increased even higher, when the police issued an urgent appeal. The police sought crucial information to help them identify the unknown errand boy who took the patterns and core stocks to Mr. Bullows foundry. People, young and old in every corner of the town waited with bated breath in anticipation of what would happen next. One question on everyones mind and causing a great deal concern was how many more bombers were still at large? [140]

The national press were quick off the mark to get all over the story. A reporter from the 'Sheffield Telegraph,' tracked down Haydn Sanders in Rotherham and asked him to comment about his relationship with Joseph Deakin. Sanders affectionately said Deakin, "bears a delicate expression, and his large eyes with a dreamy expression, bespeak a man filled with the best possible spirit." Sanders said that Deakin and the Socialist Club in Goodall Street had played a huge part in him becoming a councillor at Walsall. He believed Deakin was innocent and only guilty of extending his hand of friendship to the foreigners. Deakin, he said, was a single man who did not drink or smoke, but gave everything to look after his disabled mother and father. Sanders called, Deakin "the most sincere enthusiast I ever met in my life and I would make any sacrifice on his behalf."

A reporter from the 'Gazette' went in search of Marie Piberne at the Socialist Club. They arrived just in time to find her sitting alone, in her coat and hat ready to leave. Sobbing and looking miserable, she was staring into the last few embers of a flickering fire, with a despondent look on her face. Piberne was left stranded high and dry, all alone in a foreign country with people who could not understand a word she spoke. She informed the reporter, "I am going to London, to leave this pestiferous village, wished to God I had never set foot in it." She planned to find enough work dressmaking in the French quarter of London to earn her passage back to her home town of Nantes. She had a son and a fourteen old daughter in Nantes, but Cails was not their father, she had only known him for three years. She made it plainly obvious that her experience in England had been a bad one and she had an even poorer impression of 'pestiferous Walsall.' It's hardly surprising her time in Walsall had been no holiday and ended in disaster. [141]

After the police issued their appeal to find the errand boy, John Westley knew his days were numbered. He knew William Nicholls would come forward to tell the police the truth and reveal his involvement in the case. On the morning of Saturday the 9th of January, 1892, Westley made his move by going to Walsall railway station and catching the train to London. Westley knew from his mother-in-law, Elizabeth Larkkom that the police had found the sketch of the bomb after Charles was arrested. Whether Westley wanted to visit Deakin or warn the men in London is open to speculation, but he left town just in time to evade arrest. That day, William Nicholls came forward to tell Mr. Taylor, that he was the boy who took the order to Mr. Bullows's foundry in Long Street. He spilt the beans on Westley being the person who sent him to the foundry and also that Westley employed both Cails and Charles at different times in his workshop. When the police went for Westley they discovered he had flown the nest and gone to London, but his wife did expect him to be back later that day.

Mr. Taylor immediately obtained a warrant for Westley's arrest from Walsall Magistrates. The Chief Constable deployed his detective's to lie in wait, monitoring every train arriving at Walsall station. Members of the public soon became aware of the increased police presence around the town and a general air of excitement wafted about as people wondered what would happen next. That night to Mr. Taylor's disappointed Westley failed to show up as expected.

Police surveillance continued throughout Sunday the 10th of January, 1892, but again there was no word from Westley and he failed to turn up. It's almost certain that Westley took the time to visit the Autonomie Club in London and let them know what was happening. The Autonomie Club held an impromptu meeting, where members openly accused Auguste Coulon of betraying the Walsall men. He was branded a 'Police Spy' and his membership to the club was revoked. It was apparent to them that he was living way above his means.

Back in Walsall the police patiently waited for Westley to return. All his family lived in the town and he had no where else to go. Frustratingly they had to wait until the morning of Tuesday the 12th of January, 1892, when the first train arrived from London. As soon as Westley stepped down from the smoky hissing train, detectives were ready to pounce and surrounded by policemen he had nowhere to go. He appeared to be completely surprised when the officers took him by the arm and 'felt his collar.'

That day, Mr. Taylor travelled to London for an urgent briefing with Sir. A. K. Stephenson, Solicitor to HM Treasury, the heads of New Scotland Yard and the Home Office explosives experts, Colonel Ford and Major Cunliffe. The newspapers reported that, 'As the result of very careful examination it has been established that the bombs found at Walsall would, when filled with high explosive, constitute terrible engines of destruction. It is a curious fact, that, the Walsall bombs are somewhat similar in pattern to those used by the Chicago Anarchists with such deadly effect in 1888. In this connection it may be mentioned that photographs and speeches of the Chicago assassins were found in great quantity in the club at Walsall where Charles and Cails were arrested, but of course the fact does not necessarily imply that the men in custody had anything to do with them. The authorities attach the greatest importance to the arrest of John Westley, as they are confident that it will furnish a missing link in the chain of evidence which the police have been putting together. Great satisfaction has been expressed in London at the skill and energy shown by the Walsall police.' [142]

At half past nine on the morning of Wednesday the 13th of January, 1892, Chief Constable Taylor and Inspector Hamilton visited Ditchfield's house in Green Lane. He was still in bed and his wife shouted up, "Get up, the police have come for you." When the Chief Constable arrested Ditchfield, he said, "I have told you all about it. I have nothing more to say. You can do what you like with me." Ditchfield was taken back to the police station and placed into the cells.

That morning John Westley and William Ditchfield two well known local men, appeared at Walsall Magistrates Court, before B. Beebee and James Lindop. They were jointly charged with Cails and Charles, that between the 1st of November, 1891 and the 7th of January, 1892, they had in their possession or control, explosive substances for an unlawful purpose.

Mr. Richard W. Gillespie instructed by the HM Treasury solicitor appeared to prosecute. He asked the bench to remand both prisoners in custody until Friday, explaining that the case was still in its infancy and they were not ready to proceed at that time.

The Chief Constable said Westley and Ditchfield were both arrested that morning on sworn evidence. He anticipated that by next Friday or some future day, he would be able to prove conclusively that these men had certain explosive substances, for the manufacture of bombs in their possession. Mr. Taylor said the HM Treasury solicitor had instructed Mr. Gillespie to ask for a remand and also asked him to explain that it was undesirable to give any evidence, until the enquiries were finished.

Westley strongly protested at the prospect of being remanded in custody, while Ditchfield said, "I may as well be here as anywhere."

Mr. Gillespie said, "Now that they had the birds, they should have to keep them in a cage."

Westley claimed to be innocent of the malicious and unfounded charges, which bore no reference to him whatsoever.

After consultation, Mr. Beebee said the magistrates could not, "see their way clear to giving bail."

Westley protested saying he was a man of good character with a respectable business and his wife and family needed his support. The magistrates reminded him that it was only until Friday.

A man in the public gallery shouted out, offering a surety of one hundred pound for Westley's bail, but the magistrates said it was not a question of money and ordered the prisoners to be removed to cells.

While the court sat in Walsall, Detective Inspector Melville and Detective Sergeant John Sweeney were out looking for Battolla in London. They observed him walking along Little Titchfield Street,

Soho, with a black bag in his hand. Melville approached Battolla and stopped him in the street saying, "I am an inspector of police and I shall take you into custody for being concerned with Charles, Westley, Cails, and Ditchfield with having implements in their possession at Walsall for the manufacture of bombs."

Battolla replied, "Speak to me in French, I don't understand you." Melville explained to him in French and he replied, "I know nothing about it, except what I have seen in the newspapers." He added, "If I was concerned in it, I should have been out of the country long ago." He was shown a copy of the arrest warrant and then taken to New Scotland Yard, where he gave his details and address of 50, Fitzroy Street. Battolla had in his possession two foreign newspapers, "L' Homme Libre," printed in Brussels and "Il Secolo," in Italian. In his pocket were two door keys that allowed officers access to Battolla's house at 50, Fitzroy Street. At those premises there was a huge amount of Anarchist literature, including La Tribune Libre No.2, with an article on the assassination of police offices, called 'Les Justicieres.' Melville strongly suspected the writing on the bomb sketch found at Charles's lodgings was that of Battolla, so he seized two signed letters as examples. Battolla was conveyed to King Street police station, where he was lodged in the cells.

On Thursday the 14th of January, 1892, Battolla wrote a letter to his wife in Inspector Melville's presence and this letter was also seized as evidence of his handwriting.

That same morning, Joseph Deakin made his second appearance before Marlborough Police Court, having been in custody for a week. He was charged with possession of a cigar box, containing a bottle of white fluid without being able to give a reasonable account for it. Mr. F. J. Maw, a London solicitor appeared to defend Deakin. All eyes and ears were on Detective Inspector Quinn from New Scotland Yard, when he entered the witness box. He said the HM Treasury solicitor had instructed him to offer no further evidence with regard to the London charge, but immediately followed by saying there was a warrant for Deakin's arrest signed by the Walsall Magistrates. Deakin was discharged for the London matter, but his short lived reprieve ended when Chief Inspector Littlechild, head of Special Branch produced the Walsall warrant. It was for an offence of conspiracy, "having in his possession and under his control, an explosive substance, under such circumstances as to give reasonable suspicion that it was not to be used for a lawful purpose." Deakin was taken by the officers to be detained in the cells at New Scotland Yard. It is interesting to note that no proceedings were ever taken in respect of the chloroform and it formed no part of the Walsall case. It's now known that chloroform can be mixed with other substances to become unstable and explode. It can also give off toxic fumes if subjected to fire. Deakin and Battolla were at different London locations, but all six of the Walsall Anarchists suspects were now in custody.

Detective Inspector Melville went with three plain clothed constables to search the Autonomie Club in Windmill Street, believed to be the headquarters of five distinct active Anarchist groups in the United Kingdom. Apart from finding numerous Anarchist leaflets, they uncovered no direct connection to the Walsall case. The Anarchists were well aware the police would be visiting sooner or later.

At around two o'clock that afternoon, Inspectors Melville and Quinn collected Battolla from King Street police station. Quinn instantly recognised Battolla, as the man he saw at Euston Station, just before Deakin arrived in London by train. Battolla was taken to New Scotland Yard to collect Deakin, as both men were going to be transported to Walsall to face the music. Deakin and Battolla sat together in the charge office at New Scotland Yard, without either showing the slightest sign of recognising each other. Both men were conveyed to Euston railway station where they boarded the train for Walsall. Melville and Quinn watched them carefully throughout the journey, but neither showed any sign of acknowledgment and there was no interaction between them at any point between London and Walsall. Melville of course knew that it was a complete charade and they were hiding something. He and Mr. Taylor had observed them together on the 6th of

December, 1891, at Hodgkins coffee house in Bradford Street and later walking together to the Socialist Club.

Around the streets of Walsall, rumour and speculation was rife with all sorts of bizarre stories circulating. Very few facts had been given away by the police during the court hearings and everyone in town wanted to know what was going on with the 'Big London Job.'

The full story was about to break when Battolla and Deakin arrived back in Walsall. The scale of the accusations was going to hit and shock the ordinary people of Walsall, when they realised such a terrible thing was going on under their very noses. The whole affair was so very unusual, that it was causing quite a stir with everyone, from the women in the steam filled laundries to the men in the smokey pubs and beer houses. Boys, girls, men and women in every corner of town waited in suspense, anticipating the next shocking instalment. It was a lot to take in, many were in total disbelief and others were in denial, nobody expected a national bomb plot to happen in Walsall. Why the heck would three respectable Walsall men plot a bombing campaign with a well known Anarchist from Norwich using a false name and two foreign terrorists. The people of Walsall had accepted them into their community, whilst all the time they hid a dark secret to murder!

The next stage was the Committal proceeding at the Guildhall, where the Walsall Magistrates would decide whether there was sufficient evidence to send the case the Assizes at Stafford.

Magistrates Court - Committal Proceedings

In the early hours of Friday morning the 15th of January, 1892, a crowd of spectators began to gather outside the Guildhall, all hoping to gain entry to the courtroom. The courtroom promised real theatre drama for those granted admission to the big event. This was going to be the first time all six Anarchists would be seen together and everybody wanted to witness the event. A broad mix of local people waited to get in, including several ladies, dignitaries and relatives of the accused Walsall men. Once the courtroom was full the doors were closed and police officers prevented anyone further from entering to maintain order and security. It was a rare spectacle at the Guildhall, no one wanted to miss out on the action, the scene was something only witnessed in the most sensational murder trials.

Mr. Alfred Young, appeared to prosecute on behalf of HM Treasury having taken instructions from Mr. R. W. Gillespie. Westley was defended by Mr. G. Rose and Deakin by Mr. Maw of London. Chief Constable Taylor sat in court with Detective Inspector's, Melville and Quinn from New Scotland Yard. Monsieur Vesque Laurent from Lichfield Street, Walsall, was sworn in as official court interpreter for Battolla and Cails.

Everyone in court respectfully stood as the Magistrates entered the room to hear the proceedings. A full team of seven curious magistrates filed into fill the Bench, consisting of the Mayor Alderman William Brownhill, Edward Holden MP, W. Bayliss, J. Newman, W. E. Blythe, J. Lindop and B. Beebee.

The six accused men at the back stood to be jointly charged with having possession of certain explosive substances, without a lawful reason, between the 1st of November, 1891 and the 7th of January, 1892. Cails protested when the charge was read out, but he was silenced by Mr. Loxton the magistrates clerk.

Mr. Young explained that all the charges were brought under the Explosive Substances Act of 1883. Section 4, required anyone in possession of an explosive, to prove it was for a lawful purpose, while

Section 5 made a person liable for assisting offenders. The term 'explosive substance' defined by Section 9 had a broad meaning and included any implement or machine. Mr. Young said that he had been instructed by HM Treasury to apply for a remand in custody for a week, so the numerous outstanding enquiries thrown up from the arrests could be completed by the police. He said the authorities had very good intelligence to suggest these crimes were part of a far broader conspiracy, with ramifications for other English towns. The very serious nature of the case prevented the prosecution from being ready at that time, but Mr. Young suggested the following Thursday would be a suitable day to proceed. He warned them however to expect the case to run for more than one day. Mr. Young reminded the magistrates of 'Jarvis's Act,' which gave them absolute discretion to deal with remand applications, if they thought it was reasonable and advisable.

On behalf of Westley, Mr. Rose complained that the prosecution had kept the defendants in the dark, being extremely vague about the charges. He said Westley could prove his innocence and was anxious to have the matter dealt with quickly.

Mr. Maw protested that Deakin had already been incarcerated for a week on the strength of the most flimsiest of charges, which was absurd in character. He said Deakin was a well known local man, honest, industrious and hard working and there was no chance he would abscond.

Mr. Young apologised for not furnishing full details of the crimes, but said it was not in the public interest to do so. He pointed out that having presented a prima facia case, unlike other offences, it was for the prisoners to show they were acting with a lawful purpose and for them to prove their innocence.

Mr. Rose contested that Westley was from an old Walsall family, born and raised in the town where he lived with his wife and children. He submitted that Westley was a respectable tradesman with his own wholesale brushmaking business and it was absurd to think he would leave town, even if he could. Westley had no convictions and gaol was a severe punishment to inflict on his family who relied on him for financial support. Mr. Rose said several highly respectable gentlemen were prepared to act as substantial sureties in order to guarantee his appearance.

Fred Charles suggested the prosecution were deliberately delaying the case, to enable them to manufacture evidence they didn't yet have and to deny them a proper opportunity to arrange their defence. Ditchfield made no objection to being remanded, but thought it was unfair to their wives and families who relied on them for money. Cails wanted to be dealt with at once, while Battolla said he knew nothing about the charges at all.

Mr. Young reiterated that the magistrates had sole responsibility to decide on the question of bail, but it was customary not to grant it when such serious matters were under consideration. He said he was fully prepared to show the magistrates that Westley was one of the prominent players if necessary, not the innocent man Mr. Rose spoke of.

The magistrates retired and deliberated for three quarters of an hour before returning. They then requested the Chief Constable give them some more evidence. Mr. Young must have thought it was a done deal, as he had left court leaving Mr. Gillespie to stand in for him.

Christopher Taylor entered the witness box to say he arrested Charles and Cails at the Socialist club. At the time of being arrested Charles had been armed with a loaded revolver. He mentioned finding the Anarchist literature, 'The Means of Emancipation,' signed by Cails on the 1st of December, 1891 and other Anarchist papers including, 'L' International.' Charles, he said had the sketch of a bomb with the instructions on how to make it and Cails had a reel of explosive fuse for bomb making. Ditchfield had the bolt for the top of the bomb at his house and he found the mortar, clay and hair, for making bomb moulds in the cellar of the club.

Mr. Rose objected to Mr. Taylor referring to, "a fuse for a bomb" and Cails called out that, "anyone could possess it."

The Mayor who was chairman of the Bench, said they were happy that the Chief Constable's evidence provided them with enough facts to determine that all the prisoners had possession of explosive substances and reasonable suspicion it was without a lawful object. Under those circumstances and due to the gravity of the charges, the magistrates felt compelled to refuse bail. All prisoners were remanded in custody until the following Thursday and were taken to the cells.

That afternoon in the gaol, Deakin appeared unwell and started rubbing his stomach in pain. He refused to see the doctor, but the Chief Constable called one to attend despite his wishes. When the time came to send the prisoners to Stafford gaol, Mr. Taylor did not send Deakin. He was still waiting for the doctor to arrive and thought it was unwise. The doctor eventually came to visit him at about six o'clock that evening. [143]

On that night of the 15th of January, 1892, Inspector Thomas Gore was in charge of Walsall's cell block. At eleven o'clock, Deakin called him over and handed him a handwritten note addressed to Mr. Taylor. The Chief Constable previously gave firm instructions that any incidents should be reported directly to him. When he found out he instructed Inspector Gore to bring Deakin directly to his office. When he arrived, the Chief Constable was sitting with Detective Inspector Melville and Deakin handed him the note. Mr. Taylor asked him if the note was intended for him and Deakin replied, "Yes," followed by "You will excuse me, but I want to tell you all about it. I believe this has been a plant on me, I think Charles is a police spy, what they call abroad an agent provocateur. I feel certain of that as now when I come to remember, he was very particular to know the time I should arrive in London on the occasion I was arrested there."

Mr. Taylor read Deakin's note, where he confirmed the parcel containing the chloroform he took to London on the 6th of January, was given to him by Cails. He said Fred Charles was originally supposed to take it on Christmas Eve, but he did not go. Cails told him to give the parcel to Battolla, who he expected to meet off the eight-thirty evening train at Euston station. Battolla had visited Walsall on the 5th and 6th of December, 1891. Deakin said it was Ditchfield and Charles who made the castings, but he understood Cails intended to use them abroad.

Deakin was also labouring under the false impression that Ditchfield and Charles had already made statements to the police, believing he had overheard Charles talking to an officer.

Mr. Taylor reminded Deakin that any statements he made to the police, could be used against him. If on the other hand, it was intended for his solicitor, it would still be read, but it would be treated as confidential and not used in evidence. Deakin insisted on being supplied with a pen and paper and at about half past midnight, went back to his cell.

At about twenty past five in the morning on Saturday the 16th of January, 1892, Deakin called Inspector Gore and asked if he could speak to the Chief Constable again. Deakin handed him three sheets of handwritten foolscap with writing on both sides. Mr. Taylor went down to the cells and was given the pages Deakin had wrote. The Chief Constable looked into Deakin's cell and asked if the statement was intended for him and he replied, "Yes, Mr. Taylor." The new statement, started, 'Police Station, Walsall, 15th January 1892,' then went on to give following further account. Deakin said that whilst lying in his cell earlier that night, he overheard Ditchfield and Charles making statements or confessions to the police officers. It was this that persuaded him to make his own statement of facts in relation to the charges. Deakin said he had personally known Fred Charles since they met in Paris in July, 1889 and in summer, 1891, he turned up at the Socialist Club from Sheffield, out of work and looking for a job. Many club members already knew Charles by reputation, through the articles he published in the Socialist newspapers. Charles joined Walsall Socialist Club and Westley found him work until he got the job as a clerk at Gameson's. Charles was the first to mention a friend in London named Coulon and it was him who asked them if they could find work for two French comrades. Charles read the letter from Coulon out in the club and they agreed to accommodate one Frenchman, who Charles said could stay with him at his lodgings in Long Street. Charles was supposed to have told Coulon their decision, however on a Saturday afternoon in August 1891, two Frenchmen, Victor Cails and George

Laplace arrived in town. Charles met them at the railway station and they all went to eat at Wright's Dining Rooms, in Park Street. Laplace got lodgings with Charles and Ditchfield found Cails somewhere paid for by the club. Charles later told them that Coulon must have not received his letter about only sending one man to Walsall. Deakin said that he was told that Laplace left Paris to escape conscription and Cails fled from Bordeaux after being involved in some tram strike affair. He said Charles, Laplace and Cails often dined together and Charles always paid. David Young, another club member employed Cails as a trainee chainmaker and Laplace found temporary work with William Ditchfield. Laplace could not find any suitable work as an opera glass maker locally, so he returned to London. Shortly after this Cails wife came to join him on a Sunday from France and they both lived at David Young's house at 54, Green Lane. Cails eventually found chainmaking too hard to do and Young had to let him go. John Westley found Cails work brushmaking, but he couldn't make any money doing that either. On the 4th of January, 1892, the penniless Cails and his wife were given the free use of a room at the club.

Deakin remembered that in late October, 1891 at the club, Cails and Charles had a letter in French from 'Degiani.' Included with it was the sketch of a bomb, the same one seized from Charles by the police. Cails and Charles explained and translated the letter to him, but he understood the bombs were to be used abroad in Russia. Cails, Charles and Westley discussed the matter and decided to get a pattern made for the bombs to be cast. They wrote to Edmond Guillemard's brother, a pattern maker in Brussels for advice, but before he came over to England, they had decided to make the pattern themselves. The brother did come, but ended up paying off all Edmond's debts. One Sunday afternoon, Westley and Charles made a rough wooden pattern together. Ditchfield, said it was too thick, so Westley and Charles hollowed it out even more to make it thinner. Deakin admitted checking the measurements using a pair of callipers with Charles, Westley and Ditchfield. They then needed to find a foundry to cast them, but Charles did not want to use Gameson's foundry as he worked there.

Charles did agree to pay for the bombs to be made and they all agreed to call them 'electric cells.' Ditchfield got the castings and core stocks made, but Charles never turned up to pay him and he ended up having money from the clubs till to buy his family's Sunday meal. The following day Deakin gave Ditchfield a sovereign, but Charles had still not paid him back. The iron patterns were left on a shelf in the club room, but later Cails, Charles and Westley arranged to take them to Bullows foundry in the name of Laplace to get the job done. Laplace had already left town and had nothing whatsoever to do with the matter. Cails wrote to Coulon at Fitzroy Street to tell him the news and he replied to say a man would collect some of the bombs on Saturday. Then there was a problem at Bullows foundry, so Cails wrote to someone at the Autonomie Club in Windmill Street to tell them not to come on Saturday. Despite this on Saturday the 5th of December, 1891, Battolla arrived on the train from London. Deakin said he arranged for him to stay the night at Hodgkin's coffee house, bed and breakfast in Bradford Street. Battolla visited the club on the morning of Sunday the 6th of December, 1891, then left to have dinner with Cails at 54, Green Lane.

After lunch Battolla returned to the club with Cails and Westley, Charles and Ditchfield were there. It was then that Battolla and Cails mentioned examining the bombs at Ditchfield's house the previous day. Battolla said that the bomb was not entirely suitable and demonstrated in detail what was needed, using some sand and mortar. After this meeting everyone knew what was going on including Ditchfield. On that Sunday evening Battolla went to Walsall station accompanied by everyone except for him and Ditchfield and afterwards they reckoned the police had followed them. Deakin said he wanted to make the statement for the sake of his mother and father, because Ditchfield and Charles had betrayed him. Deakin said, he would have never got involved, if he had known the bombs were not for Russia. [144]

The Walsall Bench consisting of the Mayor W. Brownhill, E. T. Holden MP, W. Bayliss, B. Beebee, W. E. Blyth and J. Lindop, presided over a special court on the morning of Thursday the 21st of January, 1892. All six defendants were brought into town from Stafford gaol for the hearing.

Mr. Alfred Young appeared for the prosecution on behalf of HM Treasury, Mr. Maw defended Deakin and Mr. Rose defended Westley. Mr. Cuffe, Assistant Solicitor to HM Treasury was present and Professor Clovis Bévenot, professor of language from Mason College, Birmingham was official interpreter.

Mr. Rose started by condemning outrageous articles of propaganda printed by the press and designed to prejudice the minds of everyone involved in the case. In his opinion the press deliberately printed the content of the Anarchist documents to condemn the accused men even before they had been tried. He also commented that the prosecution had engaged one of the most brilliant advocates on the Oxford circuit, with all the wealth and power of HM Treasury to ensure convictions.

The Mayor assured Mr. Rose on behalf of the whole Bench, that they approached the evidence with open minds and that any articles appearing in the press would have no affect on their impartial judgement whatsoever. On the contrary the Mayor said, he would be only too delighted if the men could clear themselves of all the charges.

Mr. Young expressed his surprise, that Mr. Rose could even suggest the magistrates integrity could be compromised by a few newspaper articles. He personally believed, the Bench would discharge their duties without fear or favour and also pointed out that the documents spoken about were part and parcel of the evidence to come.

Fred Charles appealed to the magistrates on behalf of all the prisoners to be supplied with writing materials, so notes could be made as they went along and this request was allowed.

Mr. Young started by explaining to the magistrates, the particular sections of the Explosive Substances Act of 1883. An offence under Section 4, of making or possessing explosives under suspicious circumstances was punishable by a maximum fourteen years imprisonment. Ordinarily the prosecution had to establish the guilt of a prisoner beyond all reasonable doubt, but under this Act the onus was for the defence to show innocence by proving the prisoner had a lawful purpose. This particular law was created after criminals began to use explosives in connection with political matters and the existing laws proved inadequate. The prosecution, only had to prove the possession of an explosive substance and a reasonable suspicion it was unlawful.

Mr. Young went on to say that anyone who aided and abetted an offender did not have to have possession at all. Section 5 of the Act specifically catered for any person who was responsible for supplying money, providing premises, supplying materials, or in any manner whatsoever, procured, counselled, aided, abetted, or was an accessory to the commission of any crime under the Act. A person guilty under this section was liable to be tried and punished for that felony, as if he had been guilty as a principal.

The term, 'explosive substance' was defined under Section 9 of the Act and included any materials for making any explosive substance, or any apparatus, machine, implement, or materials used, or intended to be used, or adapted for causing, or aiding in causing, any explosion in or with any explosive substance, or any part of any such apparatus, machine, or implement.

Mr. Young said that not withstanding the offences under the Explosive Substances Act of 1883, all the offenders could rightly be charged and convicted with conspiracy to commit an unlawful act.

The case for the prosecution was then opened by Mr. Young. He referred to the importance played by the Walsall Socialist Club, describing it as the meeting place and focal point for all the defendants, who were either members or recent visitors. He acknowledged that every individual person had a right to hold their own strong views, but by the same token there was a line that could never be crossed. The public at large, had an absolute right to be protected from those who secretly planned to commit bloody and outrageous atrocities. In this case, dangerous characters with dark beliefs had conspired together to plan the destruction of human life and property. Mr. Young said there was certainly more than sufficient evidence to demonstrate that the men in the dock were guilty and responsible for perpetrating the crimes. He pointed to the article published in 'L'International' entitled, 'An Anarchist Feast at the Opera,' containing heinous and fiendish ideas. Mr. Young, thought it was abominable and horrendous to contemplate, that any sane Englishman could even consider being associated with such barbaric thoughts or notions. He went on to say that for their own sakes, he very much hoped each defendant had some reasonable account or explanation why they had possession of the explosive substances.

Mr. Young then went through the salient points of suspicion in respect of each prisoner. Charles had a loaded revolver in his pocket when he was arrested, but more importantly he had the sketch and instructions on how to make the bomb and the model of the top bolt in his bag. Charles also wrote the letter to Mr. Bullows using the name of Laplace. Cails had the possession of plenty of inflammatory documents, but he also had the reel of explosive fuse, which could be used to ignite a bomb. Cails lodged at 54, Green Lane, the address given to Mr. Bullows for the fictitious customer. John Westley employed both Cails and Charles at different times in his own workshop making brushes. He also employed the errand boy William Nicholls who took the work to Mr. Bullows foundry and he also accepted the exaggerated quote from Bullows, for the work to be done.

Mr. Young then revealed that Deakin had made a confession to the police about his involvement. He did not however intend to read it out at that time, unless he was ordered to do so. Fred Charles obviously wanted to know what Deakin had been saying and demanded it be read out at once. Mr. Young explained that a confession made by one prisoner incriminating another, would under normal circumstances only be admissible evidence against the maker of the statement. However, in the case of a conspiracy, where criminals acted unlawfully together, it could be used against them all. Mr. Young asked Mr. Loxton the magistrates clerk, to add a charge of conspiracy to the indictment for all the prisoners. A legal argument followed about reading out Deakin's statement and it was agreed by all parties, not to read it out at that point. Mr. Young then spoke about Deakin's dubious and suspicious behaviour in London, when he was caught carrying a concealed bottle of chloroform. Moving on to Battolla, Mr. Young described his visit to the Walsall Socialistic Club from London as highly suspicious, as was his association with the other prisoners.

Chief Constable Taylor was then called to the witness box. He took the oath and commenced by saying he had observed Battolla arrive by train at Walsall on the 5th of December, 1891. Mr. Taylor went through all Battolla's movements for that afternoon and the following day, including his association with the other prisoners at the Socialist Club and finally how he left on the train for London. Mr. Taylor said he went with other officers to Ditchfield's house on the 7th of January, 1892. He found the plaster cast of the bomb, but Ditchfield was not arrested, but went to the police station to help with enquiries. The Chief Constable covered the arrests of Cails, Charles and Piberne at the Socialistic Club and the corresponding search where incriminating items were found. Charles's lodgings at 57, Long Street were subjected to a search and other exhibits were recovered. After this Mr. Taylor went to Bullows foundry and recovered the letter and patterns intended for making the bombs. Mr. Taylor told the court what Charles and Cails had said during their police interviews. Moving to Ditchfield, Mr. Taylor went over the initial account he gave while helping the police with their enquiries and also how he handed over the threaded bolt for the bomb at his house. The chief covered the search of the cellar at the Socialist Club, where he found the parcel of mortar, sand and hair. Deakin he said, provided two written statements on the 15th of January, 1892. In respect of these, Mr. Taylor was questioned about his right to read a prisoners communications, including the ones to his solicitor. Mr. Taylor told Mr. Loxton the magistrates clerk, he had a right and it was his duty under the circumstances.

Rising to his feet, Mr. Rose wanted anything Deakin had to say about Westley excluded from the evidence, but Mr. Young reminded him that unfortunately in a conspiracy case, Deakin's evidence was admissible against all the defendants.

Mr. Loxton the clerk proposed a remand in custody until the following Friday and asked if there were any representations.

Mr. Maw said it seemed perfectly clear that his client Deakin, never had possession of anything of an explosive nature. On those grounds he confidently applied for bail on his behalf.

Mr. Rose said Westley was a well known Walsall man with a business in town and there was scarcely a scrap of evidence against him. He applied for bail saying there was no likelihood of him running away.

Fred Charles made a bail application for himself and his two foreign comrades. He said that being in custody made it too difficult for them to sort out a proper defence and it denied them a fair trial. He complained that a relative who came specifically to assist his defence was turned away. He also claimed all his letters were confiscated and read by the prosecution. It was on those grounds he asked for bail to be granted.

Cails alleged that when he asked for writing materials and access to a solicitor he was told to speak decent English first.

Through Professor Bévenot the interpreter, Battolla made representations about being, 'dragged about like sheep to the slaughter,' from Stafford gaol to Walsall and back. He said he had money in London to secure a solicitor to defend himself, but he had no chance to sort it out on remand.

Mr. Young went through an abundance of evidence connecting them all together and strongly objected to bail being granted. Mr. Taylor disputed their complaints, saying the prisoners had been given every privilege available, while in his custody at Walsall gaol. Mr. Young suggested that the Chief Constable's sworn evidence should undoubtably hold far more weight than the unsupported word of an accused man and he found it personally hard to believe that any man was ill treated by the officials at Stafford gaol.

The Chief Constable confirmed that Charles had been visited by his sister Lucy and her husband. The sister was allowed to see him, but he did have cause to refuse the brother-in-law, because he was Fred Henderson, the well known leader of the Anarchists who spoke two or three languages. In any case, Charles told his sister he would be defending himself. [145]

Ditchfield wanted the court to know, that he gave the police all the evidence against him in the first place. They were happy to let him go then, so it was wrong to keep him in prison now.

Several of them complained about the Chief Constable refusing people admission to the cells for visits, but he said there had to be limits for security reasons. He had a limited number of men to supervise visits and those who insisted on speaking a foreign language were denied, because the conversation could not monitored.

After retiring to consult in private for ten minutes, the magistrates decided to adjourn the case until Friday of the following week. Bail was refused due to the seriousness nature of the offences, but they recommended that the authorities in Walsall and Stafford provided every facility for the men to prepare their defences.

Mr. Taylor said the prisoners had received more privileges than any others since he took charge of the gaol in 1887. They had been treated with the utmost fairness and all their complaints were totally false. All six accused men were formally remanded in custody until the next court appearance and taken down to the cells in the Guildhall. [146]

At eleven o'clock at night after court on Thursday, Police Constable James Power was doing his checks of the cells, when Westley called him over. Westley was scribbling down a note in pencil and wanted to speak to the Chief Constable. Constable Power entered the cell and Westley gave him the note and said, "Never mind, only you give this to the Chief Constable." The letter was given to Police Constable George Ballance in charge of the police station above, who sent it with Police Constable George Robinson to Mr. Taylor's house in Lichfield Street. Westley's note was a request that his order book be returned to his wife. Mr. Taylor wrote back that the order book was being detained to prove his handwriting. When Westley was given the chief's reply, he wrote a second letter admitting that it was his handwriting. Constable Robinson took this back to the Chief Constable just before midnight.

Later that same night, Police Constable Power overheard Deakin and Westley talking to each other from their cells, which both opened on to the same passageway. Deakin was heard to say, "Westley, I will have to die some time." Westley replied, "Never mind, Joe, we shall all die some time, sooner or latter. When I die the people will know what I died for." At this point Police Constable Power cautioned both of them and the talking ceased.

At the end of January, 1892, the editor of a local newspaper received a letter entitled, 'The Anarchist Plot.' It was from someone using the pseudonym 'J.A.P.' This person was a self confessed Socialist, who denied being an Anarchist, but claimed to have heard about a plot to blow up the sewerage farm. He said the charges against the accused men were exaggerated by the police and press and the French newspaper 'The International - No. 7' was not even circulated in England. He called Mr. Taylor callous and cruel for saying, "We just give them as much as will manage to keep them alive" and criticised the prosecutor for the comment, "Now that we have got the birds we will keep then in the cage." 'J.A.P.' scorned the police for accepting praise for their skill, when the accused men made no attempt to escape or to evade arrest. He called Detective Inspector Melville an obvious glory seeker, who was trying to get himself promoted or earn a very good pension. Without naming anyone he said a man had arrived at the Socialist Club, about four months ago, destitute and in rags and was given food, clothes, lodging and work by the charitable members. That same man used his time to worm himself into their confidence and learn all their secrets, so that when the time was right he could betray them and get his fellow comrades arrested. He called their act of trickery unworthy of a lower animal and offered to show the 'despicable animal' what happens to 'spies and traitors.' The identity of 'J.A.P.' is unknown, but he appears to be talking about Fred Charles. [147]

Walsall Magistrates Court recommenced as planned on Friday the 29th of January, 1892. The justices present were, W. Brownhill the Mayor, J. Brewer, B. Beebee. W. E. Blyth, and J. Lindop.

Mr. Kettle appeared to prosecute on behalf of HM Treasury, explaining that Mr. Young was unavoidably detained on the orders of his doctor due to illness, but anticipated that he would be able to resume work on Monday. Professor Clovis Bévenot attended as official interpreter.

Mr. Rose appeared for John Westley and Mr. Maw defended Joseph Deakin. Mr. Rose said that Cails and Battolla did request him to represent them, but he could not accept their instructions. This was most likely due to a conflict of interests, which occurs when potential clients have different accounts of the same incident. Ethically a solicitor can only defend one account.

Before continuing his evidence, the Chief Constable handed the Bench Westley's notes admitting the handwriting was his.

Mr. Maw began to cross-examination Mr. Taylor, who admitted knowing very little about the Socialist Club, other than it was established in 1889. As far as he knew the club was opened quite normally, not in a clandestine way. The Chief Constable said all the defendants were members and regular visitors of the club, with the exception of Battolla. He confirmed that his own suspicions were drawn to the club around the middle of July, 1891, when he became aware of several Frenchmen and other foreigners visiting the premises. He had known Joseph Deakin since he was appointed Chief Constable in 1887, because of his speeches at open-air meetings. He knew Deakin held extreme Socialist views, which he personally found objectionable, but he had never heard him make any direct reference to explosives nor had he been in any trouble with the police previously. Mr. Taylor said that from the 5th of December, 1891, he watched the Socialist Club for a period of about a fortnight until he was taken ill. His understanding was that Assistant Commissioner Robert Anderson, from the Metropolitan Police ordered Deakin's arrest. This resulted from the police enquiries in Walsall on the 5th and 6th of December, 1891 and the communications between Walsall and London that followed. He had a good idea that if any of them travelled to the capital, Detective Inspector Melville would arrest them, but the decision to bring Deakin into the Walsall investigation was only made after his arrest. The Chief Constable was asked what 'explosive substances' substantiated the charges, to which he said, Ditchfield's plaster model and the mining fuse found in Cails portmanteau at the club.

Cails shouted, that the room in the club wasn't his, but Mr. Taylor said he admitted the portmanteau was his, when asked about it at the time.

Mr. Taylor said the other items being relied upon, were the lead bolt from Charles, the core stocks and pattern recovered from Mr. Bullows foundry, the brass bolt given by Ditchfield and the mortar, sand and hair found in the club cellar. He also had grave concerns about Charles motive for having a loaded revolver in his pocket, a strange thing for a clerk to be carrying, but he didn't rely upon it in evidence. Initially, Mr. Taylor thought Ditchfield might have been an innocent agent, unwittingly assisting the others and that was his reasoning for not arresting him straight away. Mr. Taylor was asked about the legitimacy of searching the Socialist Club without a search warrant. He explained that he was the authorised Inspector under the Explosive Act of 1875 and could enter any premises without a warrant under Section 73, if he considered the matter was an emergency and he was looking for explosives. He confirmed that both Charles and Cails were arrested upon his own authority. When asked about the mortar, sand and hair found in the cellar, Mr. Taylor believed it could be used in the moulding process for bombs. Mr. Taylor said that Deakin formed his own impression that Charles was an 'agent provocateur,' based on the fact that he was so interested to know the time his train was arriving in London on the day he was arrested. He said Deakin was quite wrong in his theory, there was no truth that Charles had 'put the job up' to the police. Deakin was certainly not offered any inducement or encouragement to make a statement to the police.

Deakin shouted out, "liar."

Mr. Taylor said that Deakin was cautioned several times and he personally spelt out the consequences of making a statement to the police. The fact was, he purposefully did not take a statement from

Deakin, because of his concerns. Instead Deakin was given a pencil and paper and time to reflect carefully, before he committed anything to paper. Even after Deakin had finished his statement, Mr. Taylor said he only took it from him at his own request. As he read out Deakin's statement to him he kept repeating, "I have done wrong, I have done it, I have done wrong. They will kill me. They will kill me." Mr. Taylor said he never thought Deakin's remarks were wild, hysterical or the result of insanity. That the day before Deakin wrote his statement, he became unwell and complained of stomach pain, but he did not want to see the doctor. One was called anyway, but he did not arrive until six o'clock by which time all the other prisoners had gone to Stafford gaol. That was the sole reason why Deakin stayed behind at Walsall and it was while he was alone in the cells that night, that he requested to make the statement.

The Chief Constable then spoke about the bombs he had made from the castings recovered from Bullows foundry. He said he arranged the manufacture to evidentially demonstrate they could be made. Mr. Maw asked him why he kept referring to them as bombs and Mr. Taylor said he was happy to use the term, after seeing such things during his service in the army.

Mr. Rose asked if the letter recovered from Mr. Bullows foundry was folded up as if to go in an envelope and Mr. Taylor confirmed that it was, but that no envelope had ever been recovered with the letter.

Ditchfield's request to address Mr. Taylor was granted and he complained that Inspector Melville had said, "Ditchfield, you are not telling the truth. You are not telling all you know." Inspector Melville also said, "Do you know who we are?" to which he replied "bum bailies" (Bailiffs) as he expected them, which caused laughter throughout the court. He claimed, Inspector Melville pointed at the plaster cast and said "This is one" and then said, "We want you to tell the truth, where did you get this?" Melville allegedly told him that if he did not tell the truth, he would very likely end his natural life in Pentonville, so "not to spare em."

The Chief Constable said Ditchfield was cautioned in the usual way and warned about the dangers of incriminating himself. He also denied that Melville had said any of the things Ditchfield alleged.

Ditchfield claimed Melville told him not to speak to any of the others at the Socialist Club and to keep away from them.

Mr. Taylor said that when Ditchfield's statement was taken from him, he was stopped several times and told he did not have to incriminate himself.

The Magistrates Clerk advised Cails and Battolla that they could cross-examine the Chief Constable, but it might be better to leave it until they had a solicitor.

In response to Cails, Mr. Taylor said he watched him, Westley, Charles and David Young accompany Battolla to Walsall railway station on the evening of the 6th of December, 1891. He told Battolla, that every statement he had made about him was correct in every detail. Mr. Kettle said he would leave the Chief Constable's re-examination for a future occasion, but confirmed the Attorney-General had authorised the prosecution of all six prisoners.

After half an hour's adjournment for lunch, Colonel Arthur Ford, Inspector of Her Majesty's Explosives and formerly a serving officer with the Royal Artillery, was called by Mr. Kettle. Colonel Ford said the hollow bombs produced in court were made for the police using the pattern and core stocks recovered from Bullows foundry. Mr. Bullows managed to make a mould using clay, mixed with sand, horse hair and charcoal and from it he produced the iron castings or bomb casings. The core stocks were utilised to make the castings hollow. Colonel Ford explained that a lead bolt was required to close the top of the iron castings.

Mr. Rose objected by saying the original moulds used by Bullows should have been produced in court, Mr. Loxton said he would note his objections on the depositions.

Colonel Ford continued by confirming that the brass bolt handed over by Ditchfield was the same calibre as the hole in the top of the casting, but suggested it should be threaded to make it safer to handle.

Ford also said, the holes Ditchfield made in the bottom of the bomb, could be fitted with percussion caps on nipples to explode it.

Mr. Maw complained that the castings produced in court were not made by the prisoners, they were made especially for the police. He asked Colonel Ford to limit his evidence to the things the police actually found. Mr. Loxton, the court clerk pointed out that as an expert, Colonel Ford had already explained that they were made using the originals and it was very important to demonstrate that they could actually be used to create something that could cause an explosion. Mr. Loxton, reminded Mr. Maw that he was welcome to cross-examine Colonel Ford, but he could not object to his evidence.

Colonel Ford went on to say, that the hollow iron castings could be filled with an explosive, secured in place by a bolt fitted in the top. Percussion caps could then be put on nipples where the holes were drilled in the bottom, so that if the bomb was thrown the impact would cause it to explode and shatter into pieces. Colonel Ford compared it to the design of the 'Orsini Bomb' used in the assassination attempt on Napoleon III in 1858, which incidentally was designed and built in Birmingham. Colonel Ford said the reel of explosive fuse was typically used by miners to fire dynamite with a detonator. The fuse could be used with the Walsall bomb, but he thought it was not the best option available if they were meant to be thrown. If however the bomb was intended to be placed somewhere, the fuse would give the bomber time to get away before it went off. He said the mortar, sand and hair found by the Chief Constable in the cellar of the Socialist Club could be used to make a rough mould.

Mr. Maw suggested that all the items produced were altogether rough, but Colonel Ford disagreed by saying the components were in fact, well suited for the purpose alleged by the prosecution. Mr. Maw and Mr. Rose wanted all the items to be examined by an independent expert for the defence, so they reserved their cross-examinations of Colonel Ford.

Mr. Loxton proposed to adjourn the case until the following Wednesday morning.

Mr. Rose appealed for Westley to be released, owing to his business being practically in ruins as a result of his time in gaol. Mr. Maw called for the same on behalf of Deakin and Fred Charles repeated his own application.

Mr. Loxton said the magistrates were performing a serious public duty and had already decided to deny bail to all suspects. He said the delay was in the interests of the prisoners who were still waiting for solicitors to represent them. The case was adjourned until Wednesday morning, but Mr. Loxton told the defence solicitors they were entitled to apply for bail to a judge in chambers if they wanted to. [148]

In Walsall's cells that Friday night after court, Ditchfield attracted the attention of Police Constable James Power, who was in charge of the gaol. Ditchfield said he wanted to make a statement to the police, but was unable to write himself, so he requested Constable Power to write it down for him. The officer carefully and accurately recorded what Ditchfield had to say in his police pocket notebook and then read it over to him. Ditchfield agreed the contents before putting his mark to it.

Ditchfield's statement accused Charles of being the person who asked him to make the pattern. Charles agreed to pay for the work, but when it came to it, he had trouble getting his money. He only got five shillings and the promise of another further thirteen shillings on the following Saturday. Charles, Deakin, and Cails originally told him the pattern was to make French lubricators and that is what he believed. He made a copy for himself, believing it might make him more money than his normal work. When he finally found out the truth, he smashed the plaster model of the core stocks.

Walsall Magistrates recommenced on the morning of Wednesday the 3rd of February, 1892. W. Brownhill the Mayor, J. Brewer, B. Beebee, W. E. Blyth, J. Thorne and J. Lindop were the magistrates on this occasion.

Mr. Young was still too ill to attend, so Mr. Kettle filled in again for the prosecution on behalf of HM Treasury.

Mr. Rose defended Westley, Mr. Maw defended Deakin and Mr. J. N. Cotterell now appeared to represent Cails and Battolla. Ditchfield and Charles remained undefended and Professor Clovis Bévenot served as the official interpreter.

The Mayor announced that the magistrates felt very uncomfortable about the prisoners being constantly remanded from one week to next. He said they would very much prefer the court to sit until all the evidence had been heard.

Battolla started gesticulating with his hands and became verbally excited about something as he spoke loudly in Italian. The interpreter explained that he was very unhappy about the barbaric treatment of his comrade Cails, who had been painfully shackled on the journey between Stafford and Walsall.

When things settled, Colonel Ford was recalled to the witness box to be cross-examination by Mr. Rose. He quizzed Colonel Ford about the mortar and hair found by the police at the Socialist Club. The colonel agreed it was an unusual mixture for making moulds and he had never personally seen it used for casting cores stocks. Colonel Ford said ordinarily explosive fuse wasn't that suspicious a thing to have in a mining district like Walsall.

Ditchfield asked Colonel Ford how two cores could be made from just one stock and said the bolt would not fit the casting when complete.

Colonel Ford believed the lead bolt would fit the casting very well with a little filing around the neck.

The Mayor asked the colonel if the bolt would contract as it cooled, to which Ditchfield shouted, "Hear, hear." Colonel Ford said that it would contract slightly, but not enough to make any real difference.

Mr. Kettle proposed to ask Colonel Ford, if he thought any of the items would give reasonable ground for suspicion and asked permission for him to answer. All the defending solicitors lodged their objection to him answering such a question.

The Mayor however thought the question was the 'pith of the case,' as 'reasonable suspicion' was the determining factor of whether they could be found guilty or not guilty.

Continuing, Colonel Ford stated the sand, mortar and hair could be used to make rough castings. He then started to describe 'Daly's bomb,' named after John Daly, an Irish republican, who was arrested at Birmingham train station on the 11th of April, 1883, for his part in the 1881 to 1885 Fenian dynamite campaign.

Mr. Rose objected, but his objection was overruled.

Colonel Ford said 'Daly's bomb,' was in brass, cylindrical about six inches long and three or four inches in diameter. It exploded on impact and was very similar in many respects to the Walsall bomb.

Fred Charles asked Colonel Ford if he had any personal knowledge of percussion caps being used to explode such bombs, but he hadn't. Colonel Ford told the Bench that he had never heard of an "electrical lubricator" and had no idea if the articles in court could be used for such a purpose.

The next witness called into court was Francis Joseph Bullows, of The Elms, Birmingham Road, a malleable iron founder with a foundry in Long Street. Mr. Bullows explained how he came to receive the parcel at his works and how he deliberately over priced the job, because he didn't particularly want the work. One halfhearted unsuccessful attempt was made to cast the job, but then he paused the work having sent a postcard to the customer. When the postcard came back from the Post Office, marked up 'Dead Letter,' he made no further attempts to make the items, until the Chief Constable asked him to try again. This time the cast was made successfully under his own supervision. He always knew they could make the cast properly, but didn't try too hard initially as he had no interest in the work. It was Mr. Bullows opinion that the top of the casting would be heavier than the bottom, because it was almost impossible to draw up the core.

Ditchfield bellowed out to Bullows remark, "I told you so." The significance was that the Walsall bomb relied on the percussion caps at the bottom striking the ground first and Bullows suggestion contradicted this idea.

Bullows continued by stating that he was never suspicious for an instant that the work could be for a bomb. He agreed the casts could be made thicker and heavier if the core was rubbed at the end, but confirmed when questioned by Mr. Rose, that he had never received any such instructions to alter the core from any of the accused.

A short break in the proceedings followed, after which the young man William Nicholls was called to take the stand. Nicholls said for about twelve weeks on the lead up to Christmas 1891, he worked for Westley. One morning at the workshop, Westley asked him to take a letter and parcel to Bullows foundry in Long Street. Westley instructed him to say it was from someone called Laplace. Nicholls said he knew Cails from working for Mr. Westley making brushes and saw Deakin and Charles during the fortnight before Christmas come to the shop to take Cails for tea.

Sarah Higgins the factory woman who worked at Mr. Bullows foundry in Long Street was the next witness. She lived at 99, Portland Street and said William Nicholls brought the letter and parcel, which she took to Mr. Bullows to price up.

Arthur Gameson from Thomas Gameson and Son, iron founders, of Lower Rushall Street was next in the witness box. He said the company employed Charles as a clerk in their offices and during his employment, he had become very well acquainted with his handwriting. He was confident to say the letter taken to Bullows foundry was in Charles hand.

Police Constable's, Robinson, Ballance and Power all gave evidence in relation to the two letters written by Westley on the 21st of January, 1891. Police Constable Power also spoke about hearing the conversation between Deakin and Westley in the cells on the same day and also recording Ditchfield's statement in his pocketbook on the 29th of January, 1892.

On behalf of Westley, Mr. Rose objected to Ditchfield's statement being read out, saying the evidence was only relevant to Ditchfield and nobody else. Mr. Kettle corrected him by saying the evidence was definitely against Ditchfield, but it was for the magistrates to decide on matters of admission. As the clock approached four o'clock, Mr. Kettle suggested an adjournment until the following day as said he anticipated Mr. Young would return on Tuesday to close the case.

Mr. Maw recommended the court sat until seven o'clock that evening to avoid sitting on Thursday.   Mr. Rose protested against continual adjournments, but Mr. Newman, the magistrates clerk pointed out some of the adjournments were specifically for the prisoners to arrange legal advice. The Mayor decided the court would sit until two o'clock the following day, but after that they would adjourn until Tuesday of the following week. The question of bail was raised again, but the Mayor quickly said that the Bench would not grant bail at that time.

On Thursday the 4rd of February, 1892, the case was resumed before W. Brownhill the Mayor, B. Beebee, W. E. Blyth, and J. Lindop.

Mr. Cotterell started by complaining that on the previous evening, one of his foreign clients had asked for paper and ink, but was only supplied with paper and pencil. His client was very suspicious about the police being able tamper with anything in pencil. The Chief Constable responded by saying that as far as he was concerned, paper and pencil were proper writing materials. Mr. Cotterell demanded to know his reasons, but Mr. Taylor refused to give any further explanation and the Mayor told him that they could not interfere with the Chief Constable's discretion on the matter. The Chief Constable said he was quite willing to take all the responsibility for his decisions, to which Mr Cotterell said it gave the impression the prisoners were being unfairly treated.

The Mayor announced that the treatment of the prisoners would be discussed at a special public inquiry held by the Watch Committee. The Chief Constable instigated the inquiry himself as he wanted to make sure that everything was fair.   The Mayor said each prisoner could attend to air grievances and members of the press would be welcome to come and report on everything.

The case then resumed with the next witness Bernard Ross, who was a brass caster. He talked about how Ditchfield approached him and gave him two halves of a wooded pattern and a wooden model of a bolt he wanted casting. Ditchfield said it was something to do with electric lighting for a man named Purchase, but that turned out to be false. Ross made a plaster cast from the wooden pattern, then asked his brother Thomas Ross, to cast it in metal. Thomas Ross made the lead model and bolt, which he returned to Ditchfield, who eventually paid him sixteen shillings. Ross said the plaster cast recovered from Ditchfield's house by the police was made by him. Later Ditchfield wanted the wooden model enlarging, but he had problems getting his money.

Thomas Ross, his brother was next into the witness box. He produced the pattern, core stocks and bolt from the wooden models, assisted by a man named Brown at the Lambert Works. He gave the finished work back to his brother Bernard expecting to be paid one pound, but received nothing.

Edith, Bernard Ross's wife, said that in November she took the models seen in court to Ditchfield's for her husband. There was also a brass casting similar to the iron one. Ditchfield let her down when he only gave her two shillings, but he did give her another fourteen shillings on the following Saturday. The second time she asked him for five shillings, but he only gave her one shilling and sixpence, so she told him that her husband would be visiting him for the money.

Monsieur Vesque Laurent, a professor of languages at Walsall, said he made translations of the 'An Anarchist Feast at the Opera', a manuscript entitled 'The Means of Emancipation,' signed, 'V. Cailes' and an article called 'Les Justicieres,' about the assassination of police officers (see The Anarchist Literature in Contents). Laurent said he only translated what the police asked him to do and no more. He also said that the manuscript signed 'V. Cailes' was in fact a handwritten copy of an article in 'L' International,' with a few alterations in the translation.

Mr. Cotterell complained that the press had reported that Cails was the author of the work, when in fact he had only copied it from the publication mentioned.

Detective Inspector Quinn from New Scotland Yard was the next witness called. He said he observed Battolla hanging around waiting for someone on the platform at Euston station on the 6th of January, 1892. After Battolla left, he saw Deakin arrive on the next train carrying a suspicious looking parcel under his arm. Deakin was followed and as he approached Tottenham Court Road police station, he stopped and spoke to him. He described how Deakin became evasive and uncooperative, by either failing or refusing to account for the parcel containing the chloroform hidden inside a cigar box. Quinn said he arrested Deakin for the Walsall Bench warrant after he was discharged by Marlborough Street Court. He was present on the train journey between London and Walsall, where Battolla and Deakin displayed no signs of recognition between themselves.

Mr. Maw wanted to know what Quinn knew about the communications between Walsall Police and New Scotland Yard.

Quinn said he knew nothing about any of them, he took his orders directly from Chief Inspector Littlechild in London. Quinn said Deakin was originally arrested under a law that only applied in London, relating to suspected thieves and receivers. When Deakin refused to give a proper account, it gave him reason to suspect the bottle of chloroform was stolen so that was why he arrested him.

Mr. Maw wanted to know if he was ordered by anyone to make the arrest, but the Bench held that question was inadmissible.

The Chief Constable then observed a packet being exchanged between Westley and a man sitting in court and overheard Mr. Rose, tell him to say that it was for him. The Chief Constable asked for the court to immediately impound the packet. Westley said it was a domestic letter for his wife and simply wanted his solicitor to give it to her.

The magistrates asked if the Chief Constable would stop such a letter, to which he replied, "No sir, but I must see what it is first." Protesting in the strongest of terms, the Chief Constable said that it was the first time ever to his knowledge, a prisoner had been allowed to hand something out from the dock.

Mr. Rose expressed his displeasure with the Chief Constable interference. Mr. Newman, the clerk seized the letter and read it to himself, before declaring that it was a communication between a solicitor and client and had nothing whatsoever to do with the case.

The magistrate Mr. Beebee, advised Mr. Rose that the letter should have been handed over to the Chief Constable in the first place. Mr. Rose agreed, but said that he resented the Chief Constable's interference.

The Mayor said the Bench had already discussed the matter of bail at considerable length on several occasions and had come to the conclusion they would refuse it. The Court then adjourned till Tuesday, at quarter past ten. [149]

The court resumed promptly at the Guildhall on Tuesday the 9th of February, 1892. The magistrates present were, Mr. Brownhill the Mayor, B. Beebee, W. E. Blyth, and J. Lindop.

Mr. Alfred Young returned from being sick to prosecute the case, Mr. W. Thompson defended Battolla, Cails, and Ditchfield, Mr. Maw represented Deakin, Mr. Rose appeared for Westley and Mr. Holmes Gore for Charles.

Mr. Thompson called the magistrates attention to the very scandalous behaviour of the daily press, whose reports prejudiced the whole case in the eyes of the public. He objected most strongly to them using phrases like, "a well concocted conspiracy for the manufacture of bombs", "well known conspirators", "notorious Anarchists," and referring to Deakin as, "deeply imbued with the doctrines of the most dangerous class of Anarchists."

The Mayor agreed that the comments were highly improper, but said he had personally been too busy to read the papers. If there were any powers at his discretion, he would use them to punish those responsible for printing such articles.

Frederick Brown, an electrical engineer from Fairy Field, Walsall was the first witness called to the stand that day. He was an associate member of the Institute of Electrical Engineers and ran the Walsall Electrical Company from 57, Bridge Street. His business manufactured electrical machinery and he was well acquainted with all new inventions in relation to electricity. He told the court that he had never heard of an 'electrical lubricator,' but had carefully examined the castings made by Mr. Bullows and concluded they had nothing to do with electrical machinery at all. In fact, in his view the only thing the castings could be used for was bombs, charged with an explosive. He then described various explosive cocktails that could be used in such a device.

Mr. Thompson in cross-examination wanted to know if he was an explosives expert.

Mr. Brown, said he was not an expert, but had studied the subject for many years and had a great deal of knowledge on the subject. He offered to demonstrate how to make a bomb out of a casting if the court wanted him to.

Mr. Thompson challenged him, so Mr. Brown charged one of the castings with gun cotton, pausing to say it would be very unwise to insert a detonator while in the court. Mr. Brown screwed down the top bolt and while doing so commented that a shell made of brass was less dangerous than one made of iron. When Mr. Brown offered to throw the bomb down, the alarmed magistrates advised him that it would be better not to go that far.

Mr. Thompson suggested that he should throw it at the prosecutor, if at anybody at all.

During cross-examination by Mr. Gore, Mr. Brown defined a bomb as a closed chamber containing an explosive, which would shatter upon ignition. Mr. Brown said he had conducted an experiment at his works just outside of town with one of the iron castings. He charged it with less than of quarter of an ounce of gun cotton, then placed it underneath an old wrought iron boiler. He connected a detonator with one hundred yards of wire, then used an electric charge to blow it up. The explosion burst the bomb into numerous fragments which deeply embedded into the ground. The pieces he recovered were exhibited for examination by the court.

Detective Inspector Melville was next to come to the witness box, who as an experienced officer was used to court drama. He described his first visit to Walsall on the 5th of December, 1891 when he went to the railway station with Mr. Taylor. Battolla arrived by train and was followed and observed associating with the other defendants from the Socialist Club. Melville went through the events of the 6th of December and his return trip to London on the same train as Battolla. The next event was at Euston station on the 6th of January, 1892, when Battolla arrived and appeared to be looking for someone. Deakin arrived from Walsall on the next train and was followed away carrying a suspicious parcel. Outside Tottenham Court Road police station he was stopped and arrested, then he urgently returned to Walsall to liaise and update the Chief Constable. Together they went to see Ditchfield at his house and the Chief Constable found the plaster pattern for the bomb. Ditchfield freely admitted the name George Laplace was used. Melville went over the arrests and search of the Walsall Socialist Club and corroborated that Cails admitted the searched bedroom was his.

Cails shouted out, "Thats a lie," but was advised to be quiet by Mr. Thompson, his solicitor.

Finally before lunch, Melville went through the search of Charles lodgings, where the bolt, the bomb sketch and the address book linking him to Battolla were found. He mentioned the Anarchist papers, including, "The Means of Emancipation," and "Fight or Starve," being found, but then they broke off for a lunch break.

When the court returned after the adjournment, they agreed it was impossible to get through all the business before the end of that day. It was agreed when court finished to resume at quarter past ten on Monday.

Detective Inspector Melville then continued by saying he returned to Ditchfield's house with the Chief Constable and the top brass bolt was handed over. He described Battolla's arrest and the search of his premises at 50, Fitzroy Street, London. Melville said that the writing on letters found at Battolla's house was the same hand as that on the sketch of the bomb from Charles lodgings.

Mr. Thompson objected to the assumption, saying there was no proof in what he said.

Melville said Deakin and Battolla sat in a room together at New Scotland Yard trying to give the impression they did not recognise each other. He also brought both men to Walsall by train and all the way back they maintained they were strangers. Melville said he was present with the Chief Constable when Deakin convincingly said Charles was a spy. Mr. Taylor warned him about the consequences of making any statement to the police, but was given writing materials at his own request.

In cross-examination, Mr. Thompson asked Melville what policing experience he had. Melville referred to his part in the 'Gallagher case' of 1883, resulting in four men getting life sentences for planning to blow up the Houses of Parliament. He did meet one of the defendants from that case named Curtin.

Mr. Thompson was eager to probe Melville about his association with Auguste Coulon. Melville admitted being in the company of a well known Anarchist named Coulon who was foreigner, but never at New Scotland Yard. Melville refused to say whether he had paid Coulon money for information, but did say he had paid lots of Anarchists money.

Mr. Thompson asked him outright, "Have you paid him any money?"

Mr. Young intervened, protesting that questions asked merely to obtain the name of an informant could not be put to Inspector Melville.

Mr. Thompson said he had a theory about Coulon being the suspicious element in the case and an agent of the police. Several people in the courtroom started to applaud his suggestion. The Mayor was infuriated and threatened to clear the court and public gallery if it happened again, he told Mr. Thompson that the question should not be answered.

Mr. Thompson said Melville had declined to answer the question, to which Mr. Young interjected saying the Bench had made a ruling that it was not a proper question and he did not need to answer it.

Detective Inspector Melville then described Deakin's arrest in London and the suspicious circumstances. Mr. Thompson asked if there was a search warrant for Ditchfield's house. Melville replied that as a foreigner in Walsall, the address was out of his policing jurisdiction and could not say if Mr. Taylor had a warrant or not, but believed he used general police powers.

Mr. Thompson suggested that the Chief Constable obtained his evidence by unlawful means, because searches without warrant under the Explosive Act of 1875, were only permitted when there was a danger to life.

The case was adjourned until the following Monday at a quarter past ten.

The special public inquiry by the Watch Committee about the treatment of the prisoners was held in the Council Chamber at the Guildhall on the evening of Wednesday the 10th of February, 1892.

The Mayor W. Brownhill, Aldermen Lindop and Roper, Councillors Lester, Beardsley, Noake and Dean, and the Town Clerk, Mr. J. R. Cooper were all present. They assembled to hear any complaints from the six Anarchists about their treatment whilst in the cells at Walsall gaol. The Chief Constable sat in the room throughout the enquiry, together a few members of the press and general public.

Mr. Taylor made representations that each prisoner should be heard individually, largely due to security concerns. The panel discussed his objection and eventually decided the six men should be heard separately.

The first man called in was John Westley who had no specific complaint about any official. Westley asked them to consider his concerns more as suggestions, rather than complaints. The Town Clerk said the whole purpose of the inquiry was to hear any complaints against the Chief Constable. Westley explained that he was quite content to suffer until such time as he could prove himself innocent of the charges.

His first concern was the bed being made of hard wooden boards with only one thin blanket. He suggested a folding mattress and two blankets should be supplied. Westley thought this might ensure prisoners came to court well rested and in a proper state to defend themselves, which he felt sure the gentlemen of the Bench would prefer. Westley complained that his draughty cell was near the yard and caused the symptoms of his neuralgia to return. The Chief Constable said cells were kept at a constant temperature of between 75-80 degrees for comfort. Mr. Taylor thought it was unfair to hold him accountable for the design of the gaol, when five of the ten cells faced towards the yard. Deakin who occupied a cell on the opposite side complained it was too hot and wanted the window left open. Westley said the beds at Stafford had mattresses and proper bedclothes, but the Town Clerk remarked that Stafford was designed to keep prisoners for lengthy periods of time, whereas Walsall was only ever intended as a lock-up for a few days. Westley's next suggestion was that prisoners should be provided with a table and stool to eat their food. The Chief Constable responded by saying meals could be eaten from the benches with them sitting alongside. Westley suggested the black painted cell walls could be whitewashed like at Stafford, as he personally found them very dark and depressing, especially in the dim light. He complained about the inadequate flushing power of the toilet, which often made things very offensive. Mr. Taylor said Walsall's cells were designed to contend with drunken men who made a terrible a mess, unlike Stafford gaol where drink was unavailable. Westley was also unhappy about having to speak to visitors through a barred window and wondered if the door could be left open when a wife or solicitor came, or a reception room could be made available. He also strongly objected to sharing a towel with the cell next door, especially when the old man next to him died. The Chief Constable said there were several roller towels located around the cell block for everyone to use. Westley thought it was unfair that some visitors were disqualified from entering, just because they spoke foreign languages or held particular opinions. Despite all his concerns he admitted the Chief Constable had personally shown him some kindness. The Mayor acknowledged his representations and sent Westley back down to the cells.

William Ditchfield was the next prisoner brought in and his main complaint was about being placed initially in cell No. 5, where he caught a severe cold. The Chief Constable accepted it was the wrong choice of cell for him, but said when he found out he immediately moved him into the charge room to get warm. Dr. Sharp was called to examine him after about an hour and a quarter and later he was placed in the warmest cell in the block nearest the heating system. Ditchfield admitted that Dr. Sharp had been attending him for being unwell even before his arrest. He said when he eventually spoke to Mr. Taylor in his office, he was given some whisky and Mr. Melville gave him a cigar. The Town Clerk asked Ditchfield if he had any complaints about his treatment, to which he replied, "No sir, nothing but kindness." He said, they brought him whatever food he wanted and he was quite satisfied. Ditchfield was then led away.

The next prisoner called in was Joseph Deakin, who said the Chief Constable had given them the impression that friends who brought food could visit them, which was incorrect. The Chief Constable said Deakin was mistaken, what he actually said was food could be brought in at anytime, visits were a different matter altogether. Deakin protested that he and his comrades were paraded up and down from the cells like Punchinelloes (A Punchinello is a short fat humpbacked clown or buffoon in Italian puppet shows). He thought the authorities were treating them in such a way, to give them little chance of getting justice.

Deakin said the Chief Constable's policy on admitting friends was harsh, in response Mr. Taylor said he could only admit relatives, solicitors and business associates and no one else. Deakin accused the Chief Constable of denying him access to the evening newspapers. Mr. Taylor said nobody had ever made any representations to him or been refused newspapers and he walked up and down the cell block repeatedly during the day. It was however standard practice, to cut out any articles relating to a prisoners own case, but they could all read the general news. Deakin accused Mr. Taylor of preventing him from giving Mr. Maw his solicitor, written instructions. The Chief Constable, said that was in consequence of a prisoner attempting to hand out a plan of the Stafford prison grounds the previous day. Interviews with solicitors had never been refused, although it was usual for them to speak through the grating. Deakin said he had no complaints about the bed clothes, which were sufficient, but he did say the walls of the cells were dark and dismal. Mr. Taylor said the walls were painted shoulder height with black varnish, so they could be scrubbed and kept clean.

Fred Charles was the fourth man to attend the inquiry. He complained that the Socialist Club had been searched without a warrant or proper legal authority. The Chief Constable said the premises were searched on his authority and he took all the responsibility for doing so. Charles complained that on the day he was arrested he was given no food to eat. The Chief Constable said he personally asked Charles at seven o'clock if he wanted anything to eat and he replied, "No." He was offered bread and coffee, but would not have any of it. When he first came to Walsall as the new chief, the food allowance was only two loaves, which he thought was insufficient for a strong man and he introduced the additional meal at midday. Now each prisoner had a loaf plus a pint of coffee at breakfast, a loaf with cheese at dinner and a loaf with a pint of tea in the evening. Mr. Taylor said that when he made the throw away comment, "just keeping life in them," it was meant as a joke, due to the fact that some of the prisoners refused his food. As a result of that joviality he received many complaints, including one from the British Medical Journal, who he thought should have more important things to do, than sending him letters. Charles complained that two men came all the way from London to assist in his defence, but neither were allowed to visit. When challenged, Charles admitted that one of the men was his brother-in-law, Fred Henderson who might have been refused because of his previous convictions. The Chief Constable stated that Fred Henderson, had a conviction with three others for rioting and looting shops on the 14th of January, 1887, in Norwich. One of his co-defendants was the notorious Charles Mowbray, known as the 'Anarchist tailor.' Charles claimed he knew nothing about it, which was an obvious lie as he had been present during the riot. The Chief Constable said that people who wanted to visit prisoners for serious offences in Metropolitan prisons had to apply for a magistrates authority and they could be withheld if the police objected in anyway. Solicitors had to apply to the clerk of the court, who could also refuse them permission to visit. Prisoners were allowed to hand notes to their solicitors in court, but any interview in the cells must be in the presence of monitoring officers. Walsall prisoners certainly had better treatment than any others he had ever known and the restrictions he applied were purely in the interests of justice.

The penultimate prisoner was Jean Battolla, who the Town Clerk said he had spoken to on the previous day, where he intimated he had no complaint to make. Speaking entirely through the interpreter, he confirmed that he had no complaints about the food or anything else.

The final defendant called in was Victor Cails, who was assisted by the interpreter as he alternated when answering questions between French and English. He had a pre-prepared written note with his complaints, which was read out. The list included the length of time he spent in custody, between his arrest without warrant and being formally charged. Next was that his companion Marie Piberne was only given dry bread to eat, which she refused to accept. Then Cails complained about his cell being bitterly cold with insufficient blankets to keep warm. He resented being manhandled with excessive force and being handcuffed by both hands when transported between Stafford and Walsall. His last gripe was that he had been deprived of his liberty in the most arbitrary way. The Mayor remarked that the incident regarding the handcuffs had already been answered by the Chief Constable, who conceded it was both unnecessary and contrary to his instructions. It was regrettable he was double handcuffed, but it was simply a case of there being an odd number of prisoners and an over estimation of Cails strength by the police inspector in charge. Cails said, "He is my enemy, but I do not know what the hell they have against me. I am an Anarchist, but I do not want to kill the police. I do not want to kill anybody. It is only the present system I want to kill." Cails did not complain about the food and admitted that the Chief Constable gave them tobacco in the cells against the regulations just to keep them happy.

After the last man was removed from the room, the Town Clerk read a long letter addressed to the Mayor. It was a serious complaint against the conduct of Walsall police by Fred Henderson, Charles's brother-in-law. Henderson said he was greatly distressed after coming all the way from London only to be refused admission. After the Mayor had mentioned fairness in court, Henderson had hoped the Chief Constable would allow him to see Charles to make arrangements for his defence. Mr. Taylor distinctly told him that arrangements had already been made for his defence, but when his wife saw her brother, nothing had been arranged at all. He alleged Mr. Taylor referred to his wife as "this female." In the end he had to return to London without seeing Charles and accused the Chief Constable of deliberate falsehood and being personally responsible for rendering Charles defence impossible. He called the Chief Constable's treatment of an accused man's relatives as nothing short of scandalous. Henderson believed Mr. Taylor's intentions were to secure a conviction by preventing a fair trial, all to get himself promoted and considerably increase his own reputation. Henderson threatened to bring the circumstances before Parliament if necessary by using his connections with the London press.

The Chief Constable in response, said it was regrettable that Mr. Henderson did not personally attend himself to present his tissue of lies. Mr. Taylor said he had been very careful to ensure that every conversation he had with Henderson was in the presence of Inspector Hamilton, who was perfectly ready to tell the inquiry the real truth. Mr. Thompson had a visit with Charles and he genuinely believed it was for the purpose of representing him at court. Mr. Taylor said he personally told Henderson he could not visit Charles, because of his criminal antecedents. Henderson wanted to get written consent from Charles to remove property from his lodgings, so Mr. Taylor allowed his sister to go down and speak with him. Henderson thanked him for granting his wife permission to see her brother. It was Charles himself who told his sister that he had politely declined to allow Mr. Thompson to defend him. The Chief Constable said, he was well aware that Henderson was a reporter for 'The Star,' newspaper in London and that was the reason why he was so careful around him. He knew the class of prisoners he was dealing with, ones that complained about their treatment every time the court sat to listen.

A great deal of discussion followed, which came to the conclusion that the only real complaint against the Chief Constable was his refusal to allow some visitors admission to the cells. The committee concluded that they had no power to interfere in the way the Chief Constable did his duty in his official capacity as Borough Gaoler, because his adopted course of action appeared reasonable to protect the public interest. The inquiry unanimously resolved, "That in the opinion of the committee, after hearing the statements of the six prisoners, no blame attaches to the Chief Constable in respect of their treatment during their confinement in the borough lock-up." [150]

That evening after the inquiry was over, members of the committee visited the cells themselves, to see what the conditions were like. The prisoners engaged in general conversation with the members of the inquiry. Allegedly Cails mentioned his fondness for the 'weed' (tobacco), so compassionately the Mayor sent a policeman out for tobacco, cigars and cigarette papers, which were handed out among the prisoners. The press later reported, 'for nearly an hour the six so-called Anarchists hobnobbed and smoked in an underground cell with the Mayor, the Chief Constable and half a dozen town councillors and aldermen.' [151]

The case at Walsall Magistrates continued on the morning of Monday the 15th of February, 1892. The same legal teams attended to represent their respective clients.

Before any proceedings got underway, the Mayor declared the reports in the press about hobnobbing with the prisoners were a fabrication of the truth. He said members of the Watch Committee paid a bona fide official visit to the gaol after the inquiry had finished, but they did not enter any of cells. A couple of members did leave a cigar or two for the prisoners, but that was strictly on medical grounds and nothing else. Looking directly at the members of the press present in court, the Mayor threatened that he would not hesitate to commence a libel action against any newspaper, that wasn't very careful to report only the truth without any speculation.

Detective Inspector Melville then took the witness stand to be cross-examined by Mr. Thompson. He demanded to know if any action had been taken against the man named Coulon, mentioned in Deakin's statement. Mr. Thompson offered to supply Melville with Coulon's address so they could act on the matter.

Melville asked him what he meant?

Mr. Thompson said, "Will you arrest him?" It was clear that Mr. Thompson thought Coulon was the police informer and was testing Melville for a reaction. Melville was far too sharp, but before he could say anymore, Mr. Loxton the magistrates clerk, told Mr. Thompson it was not an admissible question and that line of questioning was dropped.

Melville said when he first spoke to Ditchfield it was thought he may have been an innocent agent of the others. He did give Ditchfield a cigar in the Chief Constable's office at the same time Mr. Taylor gave him some whisky, but that was only because he appeared unwell and the doctor ordered it on health grounds. Melville said he did not know that Coulon lived at the same address as Battolla.

The Detective Inspector was asked about a man named McCormick convicted at Birmingham the previous week, who told the court that he was helping the police to get evidence against the Anarchists. Melville said he had heard of McCormick and Mr. Thompson asked, "Is that true?"

Mr. Young intervened, strongly objecting to the question which was not answered.

Mr. Rose was next to cross-examine Melville, who said that the anarchist literature found at the Socialist Club was in a room, Cails called his bedroom.

Cails shouted out, "It's a lie."

Unflinchingly, Detective Inspector Melville said the upstairs bedroom was obviously being occupied by a man and woman, but agreed it was not separated in any other way from the rest of the club.

Next, Mr. Maw questioned Melville, who said the first time he ever saw Deakin was on the 5th of December, 1891 when he first visited Walsall. The next time was when Deakin was arrested on the 7th of January, 1892 in London. He said he went to Euston station after receiving information that Deakin would be travelling to London by train. He denied that he ever met with Coulon on the platform. Melville said that Deakin's arrest had previously been discussed with his Assistant Commissioner, Robert Anderson. Mr. Maw wanted to know about what correspondence passed between London and the Chief Constable of Walsall, but Melville said it was not for him to say. Mr. Maw asked Melville, if Mr. Taylor encouraged Deakin to make a statement. Melville said he would have remembered hearing him if it had happened, but it didn't. Melville agreed he told Deakin there were some good things in Socialism and that he sometimes dined at the same restaurant as John Burns. When Deakin's bedroom was searched, he uncovered an assortment of literature, including a number of copies of the Sheffield Anarchist and the Commonweal.

Mr. Thompson proceeded to further examine Melville, asking if he said to Ditchfield "don't spare them, because these men have tried to bring you to ruin," or that he would be sent to Pentonville for the "term of his life natural." Melville denied making either comment, but admitted telling Ditchfield to tell the truth. He also conceded that he referred to a man named John Curtin, who was sent to gaol in 1883 for not telling the truth in a dynamite case he dealt with.

Mr. Young recalled the Chief Constable to give further evidence relating to how he arranged for David Lamont Howie, from Mr. Draycott's studio on The Bridge to photograph all the documents except two. Detective Constable John Ingram said he took the remaining two documents to be photographed and then brought them back to the Chief Constable.

David Lamont Howie the photographer from The Bridge, said he photographed eleven documents relating to the case for the police.

After lunch, Mr. Thompson protested that the photographs taken by David Howie, were enlargements of the originals, especially in respect of the sketch of the bomb.

Mr. Young suggested that the photographs could be clearly marked as 'enlargements,' to suffice.

George Smith Inglis, a handwriting expert from Red Lion Square, Holborn, London was the next witness. Inglis said he closely examined Battolla's letter written in Inspector Melville's presence and the other two seized from his lodgings and in his expert opinion all three letters were in the same handwriting. Furthermore it was the same writing as on the sketch of the bomb found in the possession of Charles. The notes Westley wrote to the Chief Constable were identical writing to the words, "Yes, price will do. Please say when sample 3 doz. will be done," on the return letter to Mr. Bullows at the foundry. He compared a document written by Cails with the manuscript 'The Means of Emancipation' found in Charles bag and found them to be the same handwriting.

In cross-examination, Mr. Thompson asked Inglis about his experience in handwriting expertise. He replied that he had considerable experience in the field of handwriting. Mr. Thompson probed him over a previous controversial court case, but Mr. Inglis refused to answer his questions.

Mr. Young said that concluded the case for prosecution, but Mr. Thompson asked the courts permission to cross-examine the Chief Constable again.

The Chief Constable retook the stand to be quizzed about the authority he used to search Ditchfield's premises and those of the other prisoners. Mr. Taylor said his actions were perfectly lawful and were conducted in a legal manner. In his official capacity as Inspector under the Explosive Act of 1875, he could search any premises where he thought there was a possible danger to life and in these cases he did not consider a warrant was necessary. He did not believe the delay itself would endanger life, but did think life would be endangered if he allowed explosives to be removed from the premises. In the case of Ditchfield's house and workshop, they were not technically searched, as the plaster cast for the bomb was in an open box on show. Mr. Taylor said they originally went to Ditchfield's for information only, he was not under suspicion and they were unaware that he had anything in his possession. For several days, they believed he was an innocent party in the matter and were looking to make him a witness in the case against the others. Ditchfield's extended stay of about eight hours at the police station, resulted from the delay dealing with the arrests and searches of the other prisoners. The truth was Ditchfield could have left at any time, he was not under arrest. Mr. Taylor categorically denied saying to Ditchfield, "They are all rushing up to make statements. I'll give you the first chance." In fact when he did finally speak to Ditchfield he had not spoken to anyone else. Ditchfield gave him the identity of Bernard Ross, when talking about the core stocks. Mr. Thompson asked the Chief Constable if he knew a detective named Kavanagh. Mr. Taylor said he had heard of him, but was unaware if he had ever been a member of the Socialist Club. He knew a man named McCormick very well, as he had been in the police station many times, but he considered him to be a disreputable scoundrel. McCormick came forward to give information about the case and was rewarded with two shillings per day to keep him onside, while the Treasury decided if they were going to use him as a witness. In the end, McCormick was discredited because of his behaviour and was not used in the case.

That concluded the evidence in the case and all the prisoners were formally charged with having possession or control of certain explosive substances, with a reasonable suspicion they were for an unlawful purpose. They were also charged with conspiring together to commit the same offence.

Mr. Thompson thought it pointless to go into an elaborate defence, if the Bench had already made up its mind that a prime facia case had been made out.

Mr. Newman, the clerk indicated that the Bench believed there was a case for a jury at the Assizes. Each prisoner then gave there own reply to the indictments.

Ditchfield said he was not guilty of the charges. Cails said, it made him mad to have things brought against him, when he knew nothing about them. Battolla claimed the prosecution were labouring under a mistake and reserved his defence. Deakin, Charles and Westley also reserved their defence for the Assizes, but none of the prisoners gave any indication of what their defence might be.

The Mayor said the Bench had decided the case would be heard by a jury at the next Stafford Assizes and he formally committed the prisoners for trial.

Bail applications were made by Mr. Thompson for Ditchfield, Mr. Rose for Westley, Mr. Maw for Deakin and Mr. Holmes Gore for Charles.

Mr. Young pointed out that each defendant had a responsibility under the Act to show they had a lawful purpose, yet surprisingly each of them had decided to reserve their defence giving nothing to suggest they were innocent.

Interrupting him, Mr. Gore said by taking advantage of the wording of an Act of Parliament in that way, Mr. Young's approach was quite unfair to the prisoners. Mr. Thompson said that the allegations made by Mr. Young were 'scandalously unfair.'

Mr. Young quickly retorted by saying that anyone in the possession of their seven senses, would give a defence if they had one. In light of the fact that his learned friends felt it alright to verbally attack him, he pointed out that it was their duty to offer a reasonable explanation, rather than allow their clients to be committed for trial.

Mr. Holmes Gore strongly objected to Mr. Young being allowed to disparage the prisoners and questioned his entitlement to even address the court in such a way. Mr. Thompson found the whole procedure indecent on the part of the Crown.

The Mayor said the Bench would be glad to hear from Mr. Young on the question of bail.

Mr. Young said he could only repeat the words he gave before, about the Act of Parliament throwing the onus on the prisoners themselves to prove innocence. If they had any reasonable line of defence, it was in their own interests to give it at the earliest opportunity. He reminded the magistrates that they were happy to refuse bail when few of the facts were known previously and now they had been given so much more incriminating detail.

Mr. Maw rose from his chair to speak, but the Mayor told him they would hear what Mr. Young had to say. As he sat back down he called the court grossly unfair.

Mr. Young warned the magistrates that if they decided to grant bail having heard all the evidence, the responsibility and consequences rested with them and not with him.

With the weight of responsibility on their shoulders, the Bench retired to consult, knowing the prosecution had been sanctioned by the highest authority in the land. The Bench had a duty to be fair, but if the prosecution faltered because of their actions, their heads would almost certainly be on the block. After privately consulting for about twenty minutes, they returned with their decision. The Mayor announced that they would accept bail, in the principle sum of £1,000 with two sureties of £500 (Equivalent to £150,000 in 2023). This was a compromise to demonstrate they were not delivering an unbalanced decision. They offered the prisoners a prospect of bail, but two thousand pound was far beyond the reach of most people. The Magistrates added a safety net in that the police had to approve any surety who came forward with the money. Despite the large sums involved, it was widely known that there were some rich Socialists men in the country, who could easily afford the large amounts. Proving acceptability to the police was more difficult altogether.

Mr. Thompson claimed that the authorities refused to listen and repeatedly ignored complaints made by the prisoners. The Bench had heard enough and directed that the prisoners be taken to the gaol cells.

152

On Friday the 26th of February, 1892, a bail application was made at Walsall Magistrates Court, before the Mayor W. Brownhill, W. E. Blyth and B. Beebee on behalf of Fred Charles.

The two sureties attending were Mr. Robert Sykes Bingham of 8, Wicker, Sheffield, a partner in a provision merchants and Mr. Robert Franklin Muirhead, a lecturer at Mason College, Birmingham. Muirhead had been a member of the Socialist League and was present at 'Bloody Sunday' on the 13th of November 1887.

Mr. Bingham refused to give sworn evidence and said he considered it an insult to be asked, but made an affirmation. He then gave his business details, which were were corroborated by his brother, Mr. J. Bingham. Mr. Muirhead also took the affirmation, stating his personal details and respectability.

The Chief Constable made no objections to either man, commenting that the newspapers had wrongly accused him of deliberately refusing bail and discriminating against people connected to the Socialistic movement. Having considered the application, the Mayor said neither of the Bingham brothers were suitable sureties. They found Mr. Muirhead was satisfactory and agreed to listen again if they could find someone else prepared to put up the £500. It is uncertain if the Chief Constable was aware of Bingham's previous history, but he was a known Anarchist in Sheffield and was indicted for incitement to murder in 1889, although found not guilty. Bingham had also employed Fred Charles and associated with Charles Mowbray and Edward Carpenter. Bingham was a member of Dr. Creaghe's Anarchist Club in Westbar, mentioned earlier. [153]

On Wednesday the 9th of March, 1892 a second bail application was made for Charles at Walsall Magistrates Court. The Bench consisting of B. Beebee, W. E. Blythe, J. Thorpe and J. Lindop examined the two sureties. The Chief Constable confirmed that he had a cheque for £500 in his possession from Mr. Hugh Holmes Gore from Frederick Henderson, of London, which Lloyds Bank confirmed they were prepared to pay. He also had £500 in cash from Edward James Watson, a solicitor living at 11 Berkeley Avenue, Bishopstone. Watson had been involved in the Bristol wave of strikes during 1889-1890. Mr. Taylor said he had no objection to either of the sureties and the Bench made an order for Charles to be released on bail. Henderson said some London newspapers had claimed Walsall Magistrates never intended to accept bail under any circumstances. He wanted it publicly known that there was no substance to those stories. He said the authorities in Walsall had treated him with the utmost courtesy and any delays were entirely down to himself. Mr. Beebee said the magistrates were not answerable for what appeared in the London newspapers. [154]

Stafford Assizes

Stafford Assizes opened at the Shire Hall on Friday the 25th of March, 1892, with the notorious 'hanging judge' Sir Henry Hawkins presiding. The courtroom was crowded reflecting the great interest in a couple of serious cases due to be heard during the sitting.

The dark wooden panelled courtroom was an austere and typically Victorian symbol of authority. Many a person had stood in the dock to be condemned to the hangman's noose. The judge sat centrally at the far end of the room on an elevated platform and beneath a canopy with a Crown signifying his devolved power. The witness box was in the corner, between the judge and the adjacent benches accommodating the jury. The floor of the court in front of the judge contained the seating for the prosecution and defence counsel and the other court officials. The suspects sat at the back and everyone else sat around the periphery which included a gallery to observe the proceedings.

The trial of the 'Walsall Anarchists' was fixed to start on the following Wednesday morning and was expected to last at least until the following Saturday.

The Grand Jury were sworn in to enable Mr. Justice Hawkins to outline the forthcoming proceedings. He discussed the Walsall case and explained the basics about the Explosive Substances Act of 1883. He spoke about the Socialist Club in Goodall Street, where Deakin was secretary and gave a brief resumé of the evidence. He concluded by saying that the defendants could take advantage of giving their defence from the witness box, where it was open to them to tell the jury any lawful reasons for possessing the items. After addressing the Grand Jury for over an hour and a half, he set out the calendar of events and the jury were dismissed. [155]

The trial of the six Walsall Anarchists started properly at the Assizes on Wednesday the 30th of March, 1892. The case naturally attracted a great deal of national and local interest, so admission to the courtroom was strictly limited. A large contingent of police officers under the command of Chief Superintendent Longden from the County Constabulary were deployed to enforce the restrictions. The two front rows of the centre gallery were reserved for ticket holders. Only counsel, others engaged in the case and representatives of the press were admitted to the main body of the Court.

The court started punctually at half past ten, when Mr. Justice Hawkins entered the courtroom and everyone rose to their feet. The prisoners, Fred Charles, Victor Cails, John Westley, William Ditchfield, Joseph Thomas Deakin and Jean Battolla were all brought to stand in the dock at the back. There were two offences on the indictment, firstly, that between the 1st of November, 1891, and the 7th of January, 1892 at the Borough of Walsall, in the County of Staffordshire they were in possession of explosive substances for an unlawful purpose. Secondly, that between the 1st of November, 1891, and the 7th of January, 1892 at the same place, they did unlawfully and wickedly, conspire, combine, federate and agree together to cause by explosive substances, an explosion in the United Kingdom of a nature likely to endanger life, or to cause serious injury to property. Also to make or have in their possession, or under their control, explosive substances, with the intent to endanger life or cause serious injury to property in the United Kingdom.

Prosecuting on behalf of the Crown was the Attorney-General, Sir Richard Webster QC, MP, assisted by Mr. Jelf QC, Mr. Alfred Young and Mr. Sutton. Mr. Willis QC and Mr. Cranstone (instructed by Mr. Hugh Holmes Gore of Bristol), appeared on behalf of Charles. Mr. W. Thompson and Mr. E. F. Lever (instructed by Mr. J. N. Cotterell of Walsall), were counsel for Cails, Battolla and Ditchfield. Mr. J. W. McCarthy (instructed by Mr. F. J. Maw of London), appeared for Deakin. Finally, Mr. Boddam (instructed by Mr. G. Rose of Wednesbury), was for Westley.

The Attorney-General, opened for the prosecution by asking the jury to totally disregard anything they might have read or heard in the newspapers about the case. The innocence or guilt for this most serious felony, should be judged purely on the evidence they saw or heard in the court. He explained that, The Explosive Substances Act of 1883, made it a crime to have 'explosive substances' in your possession where there was reasonable suspicion it was not for a lawful purpose. An 'explosive substance,' as defined by law, was not merely a powder or some other explosive, but parts of a machine or device to cause an explosion. The articles found in the prisoners possession were not actually explosives per se, but they were items intended to be used to create parts of a bomb and therefore came within this definition. The indictment under which the prisoners were charged, allowed them to take the oath and to give an explanation for their possession. The Crown had purposefully selected the charge, to allow the prisoners every opportunity to give an explanation if they had one. He said it was for the jury to decide, how and for what purpose six men of different nationality, with no trade or family ties came together. The Attorney-General asked the jury to focus very narrowly on the facts in making their decision, as to why these men came together in Walsall and acted in concert together. The Attorney-General said the prisoners were open to give any lawful reasons or innocent motives to prove why they came together. The unquestionably the central hub of their activities was Goodall Street Socialist Club, where Thomas Deakin was the secretary. Deakin founded the Socialist Club in 1887 and by 1891 it had forged connections with Anarchist organisations from all around Europe. Deakin was certainly the club delegate who attended the Anarchist Congress in Brussels. It was Deakin who proposed Fred Charles, Victor Cails and another man named Laplace for membership in August 1891 and Westley who seconded them all. All the defendants, with the exception of Battolla were members of the club and when he visited Walsall in December 1891, he went in and out repeatedly with the others. Sir Richard Webster read out the manuscript in Cails handwriting entitled 'Means of Emancipation,' which was found in the possession of Charles. He suggested the document shed some light on what motivated the group of Anarchists and proved that Cails presence in England was for no innocent or harmless motive. He said it was imperative for each of the prisoners in the dock, to give some reasonable explanation, or else the only conclusion to be reached was that they were associating together for an unlawful purpose.

The Attorney-General moved onto the sketch found in the possession of Fred Charles, showing a pear-shaped bomb with three nipples at the base. The drawing came with a set of written instructions, translated as "Substance, cast iron, a screw at this height and very strong; dimensions like a big pear, not larger" and "It is understood you don't trouble about caps, make three holes at the places the same size." These words were in Battolla's handwriting and it would be shown to the jury, that this device could be fitted with percussion caps and thrown to cause an explosion. The jury he said, would have to decide whether or not such an implement could be used for any useful or innocent purpose. The Attorney-General called Ditchfield's motivations into question when he told Bernard Ross the castings were for electro-lighting. Why, if Ditchfield actually believed that story, would he invent an imaginary man named Purchase, a student at the Science and Art Institute who worked at Matthews and Bliss's linen drapers. In reality, Purchase clearly did not exist and there was no practical electrical application connected with any of the articles. Fred Charles wrote the letter sent to Bullows foundry, but signed it in the name of George Laplace, which he knew was false because Laplace was not even in Walsall at the time. Westley's handwriting confirmed the order made to Bullows and he too knew Laplace was not involved. The Attorney-General said the jury needed to question themselves as to why both men used the name of Laplace, if they were conducting a legitimate business. Turning to Battolla, what possible reason did an Italian living in London have to visit Walsall on the 5th of December, 1891. Similarly, why did Deakin really go to London on the 6th of January, 1892? Why did Ditchfield keep the plaster model of a bomb and the brass bolt made by Ross at his house? The Attorney-General said he could not see any obvious or practical reason why Cails needed a reel of mining fuse at the Socialist Club. That is until you read the Anarchist literature, 'An Anarchist Feast at the Opera' when the true reason becomes blatantly clear. The real and sole reason for having the fuse, was that it was intended for making bombs. The Anarchist article describes in awful graphic detail, how two determined men in an extraordinary act of wickedness, could cut gas pipes and plant small bombs, to destroy a whole opera house committing cold blooded murder. To make things worse, these ideas were not just the fantasy or dreams of raving mad men, these things had actually taken place in the real world. After blowing up their victims, the culprits were long gone and far away. The Attorney-General said bombs similar to those in the articles, could be made from the items found in the prisoners possession. The jury were asked to collectively decide, what if any lawful reason or innocent purpose the prisoners came together to make the such castings.

With the opening speech over, the first witness Bernard Ross, a brass caster from 9, Birchills Street was called in. Ross admitted making the castings for Ditchfield, in the belief they were designed by a man named Purchase, who worked at Matthews and Bliss, on The Bridge. Ditchfield informed him they were intended for a new kind of electric light machine.

Robert Young a demonstrator from the Science and Art Institute gave evidence to say that there had never been a student attending the college at Walsall, named either Purchase or Laplace.

Edith Ross, the wife Bernard gave evidence of taking the patterns done by her husband to Ditchfield's house.

Thomas Ross, Bernard's brother, confirmed that he actually did the work of casting, before returning them to his brother.

The next witness was Harry Dudley, who worked at Matthews and Bliss in Walsall. He swore that the company had never employed anyone by the name of Laplace or Purchase at their business.

Westley's errand boy, William Nicholls, of 109, Paddock Lane was next to be called. He recalled one day in November, 1891, when Westley sent him with a heavy parcel to Mr. Bullows foundry in Long Street. When he returned, he was almost immediately sent back to tell Mr. Bullows to get the work done as quickly as possible. Westley told him to say the work was for a Mr. Laplace, of Green Lane. Nicholls told the court Mr. Westley lived next door to the Socialist Club and kept a key for the premises.

Arthur Gameson, from Gameson and Sons iron founders, said that Fred Charles was employed by the firm as a clerk. He examined the letter sent to Bullows foundry signed 'Laplace' and was certain it was Charles handwriting.

Francis Joseph Bullows, said his family owned and run the foundry in Long Street and he remembered receiving the order in question. He spoke about his dealings with it and said that he later made some castings from the pattern and core stocks at the request of Mr. Taylor. These were the ones now produced in court. All the evidence given up until this point was accepted and agreed by the defence teams.

The next witness to be called was the Chief Constable of Walsall Borough Police, Christopher Taylor. Mr. Taylor confirmed that his enquiries revealed nobody by the name of Laplace lived in Green Lane during November, 1891. He said Battolla arrived in Walsall by train from London on the 5th of December, 1891. During his stay, Battolla met with the other defendants and left on the London train the following day at five. Mr. Taylor said on the 7th of January, 1892, he went to Ditchfield's house in company with Inspector Cliffe from Walsall Police and Detective Inspector Melville from New Scotland Yard. It was Ditchfield who told him that the plaster model and a brass casting were taken to his house by Cails and that sometime later Battolla visited to examine the casting. Ditchfield also said he was asked to put three holes in the bottom in a triangular pattern. Ditchfield said he thought they were 'electrical lubricators' and he was getting paid threepence per casting for boring three holes in the bottom. Mr. Taylor said he personally considered the literature 'Means of Emancipation,' 'Fight or Starve' and 'Anarchist Feast at the Opera,' found in Charles bag at Long Street, as undoubtedly revolutionary. When he found the sketch of the bomb and a lead bolt in Charles bag, he refused to say anything about them. That concluded the evidence for that day and the court was adjourned until the following morning.

The case restarted the next morning on Thursday the 31st of March, 1892, with the Chief Constable resuming his position to give evidence. He started by saying how he found the reel of explosive fuse in Cails portmanteau at the Socialist Club. Mr. Taylor said on the sketch of the bomb he found in Charles bag, there was a partly erased drawing of a bolt marked 'five-eighths.' This was an important fact, because the bolt recovered from Charles was actually five-eighths of an inch in length. The drawing was passed around for jury members who examined the document with a magnifying glass to get a better view. The Chief Constable said he had studied the books from the Socialist Club and Battolla's visit was definitely not recorded anywhere.

The prosecution then read out Ditchfield's statement made to Police Constable Power on the 29th of January, 1892. Following that the Anarchist literature, 'The Means of Emancipation,' 'Fight or Starve,' 'Les Justicieres' and "The Anarchists Feast at the Opera", were all read out (see The Anarchist Literature in Contents).

The Chief Constable's evidence turned then to the subject of Deakin's statement made on the 15th of January, 1892. He conceded having a general conversation with Deakin before the statement was made, where he may have mentioned rising up through the ranks to be Chief Constable, but denied saying anything about it being the kind of Socialism he liked.

Mr. McCarthy who represented Deakin suggested that Mr. Taylor's relationship with his client, cast a suspicion over the whole of his second statement. McCarthy likened Mr. Taylor and Inspector Melville to a couple of cats, playing with a miserable mouse.

The Judge said, justice was sometimes defeated by policemen who told an arrested man, "Pray for heaven's sake, say nothing, because if you do it may tell against you." The Judge said his own opinion could be summed up by one of the most eminent of judges, who said to the police, "Keep your eyes open, and your mouth shut." This brought a wave of laughter through the courtroom.

The Judge then allowed the Attorney-General to read out Deakin's second statement. It talked about Fred Charles arriving in Walsall from

Sheffield. It said that Charles received a letter from Coulon asking them to find work for two French comrades, then later Cails and Laplace arrived in Walsall. Deakin admitted making the pattern for the bomb, but said he thought it was for Russia or he would never have had anything to do with it.

The Chief Constable, resumed his evidence saying that on Saturday the 26th of March, 1892, he conducted bomb experiments on land at Sutton Road, assisted by Inspector Hamilton. The top bolt was substituted with a six inch wooden plug. He did not invite any defence solicitors to attend the experiment. The Chief Constable confirmed that he had knew a man named McCormick who first came to Walsall in January, 1892. McCormick made a witness statement to the police on the 9th of January, 1892 and was paid two shillings a day to stop in a common lodging house, while HM Treasury decided whether or not to use his evidence. Later it was discovered that McCormick was a disreputable and unreliable drunk and all links were severed with him. (In November, 1892 the Socialist movement officially declared McCormick a traitor and 'coppers nark' for his continual attempts to infiltrate the organisation with a view of getting money.) [156]

Detective Inspector Charles Cliffe head of Walsall C.I.D., was led through his evidence by the prosecutor Mr. Sutton. Most of what he had to say was to corroborate Mr. Taylor's evidence.

Frederick Brown an electrical engineer from the Walsall Electrical Company was the next person called to give evidence. He said he had never heard of an 'electrical lubricator' and believed the only useful purpose for the casting was as a bomb. Brown who had a lifelong interest in explosives, thought the casting could be charged with a variety of explosives to cause an explosion. He thought the weight was easily sufficient if dropped on one of the percussion caps to cause an explosion and it was certainly potentially dangerous to life.

David Lamont Howie a photographer who worked at Mr. Draycott's Studio on The Bridge, said he photographed the exhibits and several of the other documents for the Chief Constable.

Vesque Laurent, a professor of languages, said he translated, 'An Anarchist Feast at the Opera' and other articles from French into English on behalf of the police and prosecution.

Police Constable Power was the last witness of the day, who gave evidence of receiving the letters from Westley and taking the voluntary statement from Ditchfield, when he wanted to make a clean breast of it. In that statement, Ditchfield said that Charles told him they were 'French lubricators.' Ditchfield admitted making a pattern for himself, believing at the time it might earn him more money than his usual job. Ditchfield told Constable Power he smashed the models when he finally found out they were for bombs.

On the morning of Friday the 1st of April, 1892, the case restarted with the evidence of Police Constable's Ballance, Robinson and Power, being run through in quick succession.

The next witness was Detective Inspector Melville, who outlined Battolla being followed around Walsall on the 5th and 6th of December, 1891. He said he covertly returned on the same train to London with Battolla on the 6th of December. He was present later with Inspector Quinn when Battolla turned up at Euston Station, just before Deakin arrived by train. He witnessed Deakin's arrest in London, but then returned to Walsall to liaise urgently with Chief Constable Taylor. Detective Inspector Melville went through his dealings at Ditchfield's house and the arrests of Cails and Charles at Walsall Socialist Club. Melville said he searched Battolla's house in London and was present when Deakin and Battolla sat at New Scotland Yard, apparently not recognising each other. He said they maintained their charade all the way back on the long railway journey to Walsall. Melville corroborated Mr. Taylor's account about how Deakin's statement was obtained from him. Deakin, he said had convinced himself that Charles was a police spy and that he and Ditchfield had already made statements. Melville denied there was any coercion, threats or inducements given to Deakin encouraging him to make a statement.

Mr. Thompson asked Melville about his relationship with Auguste Coulon. He said he had known about him for a couple of years, but first spoke to him twelve months ago. He believed Coulon was a member of the Autonomie Club in London, but had not seen him within the last few weeks.

Mr. Thompson wanted to know if Melville had ever paid Coulon any money in exchange for information connected with this case. Inspector Melville declined to answer whether he had paid him anything or not. Mr. Thompson insisted on an answer to the question, quoting a dictum from the Master of the Rolls, where the defence of prisoners demanded an answer for the greater public good. Mr. Thompson suggested the whole affair was a concocted plot, invented by Coulon and paid for by the police. He fell short of implying that Coulon was carrying out police orders to entrap the defendants.

The Judge ruled that Detective Inspector Melville should not answer the question, as it was detrimental to the public interest and that line of questioning ended. Barristers seldomly questioned the authority of a Judge.

The next police witness was Detective Inspector Quinn from New Scotland Yard, who corroborated the evidence of Melville regarding the arrest of Deakin. Quinn said he personally knew nothing about Coulon at all and denied following Battolla away from Euston Station on the night Deakin arrived by train.

To continue the courtroom drama, the next witness was Colonel Ford, Inspector of Explosives. He said the castings produced by the police exactly corresponded with the sketch found in Charles's bag at his lodgings. Colonel Ford stated that he was absolutely certain the castings could be used to make a loaded bomb.

George Inglis, the handwriting expert confirmed that the writing on the sketch of the bomb was Battolla's and both Charles and Westley had written on the letter that went to Bullows foundry. The manuscript entitled, 'Means of Emancipation,' and the addresses in the pocketbook were both in the handwriting of Victor Cails.

Mr. Thompson attempted to discredit George Inglis by suggesting that his involvement in the Parnell Commission inquiry, made him both fallible and unreliable.

The Judge pointed out that every witness was fallible and reminded him that nothing in the case that Mr. Thompson mentioned, affected Mr. Inglis's ability as an expert.

The Attorney-General then read out further extracts from the 'Commonweal' publication, giving details of incidents involving bomb explosions in France and Spain. After concluding these readings, the Attorney-General intimated that the case for the prosecution was concluded. This was a convenient time to break and the court rose and adjourned for lunch.

Returning after the recess, Mr. Willis, who spoke for Charles, submitted that there was no case to answer. He said the prosecution had simply failed to provide any evidence to show the possession of anything intended or adapted, to cause an explosion. Furthermore there was no evidence that any of the accused had possession of any machine, or part of a machine, which could cause an explosion. Charles had neither the fuse, the casting, or the brass bolt in his possession, merely a lead bolt, but there was no evidence to say it was ever intended for a bomb. Mr. Willis inferred the Explosive Substances Act of 1883, was only intended to apply to actual explosive substances themselves and no time fuses or acid to detonate bombs was ever found during the whole investigation. He accepted a bomb could explode if thrown, but a shell casing alone could not cause any damage. Mr. Willis submitted that the Explosive Substances Act of 1883, applied to the possession of explosives not empty vessels to put them in. He contended that the only relevant item produced by the prosecution was the reel of explosive fuse, but there was no evidence given to say a fuse would work in these bombs. Mr. Willis said that Mr. Brown had plainly explained that the fuse and the bolt could not be used together. In any case, Mr. Willis contended that the defendants had given up constructive possession long before the police struck.

Mr. Thompson, speaking for Cails, Battolla and Ditchfield said he could only repeat and agree with what his learned friend Mr. Willis had just said. Mr. Boddam said none of the things were in the possession or control of Westley and Mr. McCarthy submitted there was not a scintilla of evidence against Deakin, who never had any of the things in his possession or under his control.

The Attorney-General came to his feet to say, it wasn't necessary to show each and every member of the group had possession, because they all conspired together. He said if Mr. Willis's contention about the Act of Parliament was right, the whole Act of Parliament would be pointless and worse than useless. Sir Richard called Mr. Willis's arguments 'monstrous,' as he was suggesting the possession of a bomb shell would not be an offence. In reality the shell of a bomb was the most dangerous part, because it was designed to kill people or damage property when it exploded. He found Mr. Willis's idea ridiculous, as a situation might arise where, one man could have the shell, another the screw, and so on, and yet none could be convicted.

The Judge asked the Attorney-General, if Mr. Willis was arguing that a man who had a shell he intended to fill with high explosive was committing no crime?

The Attorney-General confirmed that was exactly the argument Mr. Willis was submitting. He also said Mr. Willis was unfortunately mistaken in his understanding of what constituted, 'explosive substances' under Section 9 of the Act, as the real definition was far broader than what he said. Sir Richard also pointed out that Mr. Willis had conveniently forgotten to mention the small point, that Charles had possession of the bomb sketch, with the instructions on how to make it.

The Judge disagreed with the representations made by the members of the defence and told them there was a case to answer and the case must proceed.

Mr. Boddam and Mr. Thompson indicated that they would call Westley and Ditchfield to give evidence in their own defence.

William Ditchfield, was the first to give evidence, describing himself as a hame filer by trade, who could not read handwriting or write himself. Ditchfield admitted he was one of about seventy members of Walsall Socialist Club. He said on the 7th of January, 1892 a number of police officers visited his workshop and at first he thought they were 'bum-baillies.' When he realised it was the police, he thought they had come as supposed friends. Mr. Taylor said "Where's Swain work?" Ditchfield explained, 'Swain' was his step-fathers name, which he used until the age of twenty-one when he discovered his real father's identity. The Chief Constable picked up the plaster cast of the pattern from a box, which had been left there by one of his children who thought it was a doll. Mr. Taylor showed it to Melville, who said, "This is one," and said to him, "Ditchfield, this is a dangerous thing and you'll have to give an account." Ditchfield told them that it was a plaster model for making 'French electric lubricators' belonging to George Laplace. Melville said he knew George Laplace and described him, "A young man very fair complexioned." Ditchfield confirmed he was correct and that Laplace was also a member of the Socialist Club. At this point, Melville stamped his foot and said "Ditchfield, you are not telling the truth." Ditchfield admitted he knew Victor Cails, but denied knowing the Italian who visited with Cails one Saturday in December. Inspector Melville said, "Ditchfield, you are not telling the truth and you will have to go with us," reminding him that he had a large family to consider. Inspector Melville told him that Deakin was already in custody. Ditchfield said he counted at least eleven policemen in his house, as he got his coat. Detective Smith pushed him into a carriage quite forcibly and told him, "I'm going to take charge of my prisoner." At the police station he was banged up in the pen, which the police referred to as the dock. After an hour being guarded by policemen, he began to physically shake from the freezing cold. Inspector Bailey took pity on him and took him into a room where police officers sat writing reports and there was a fire to warm up. At around four o'clock, Mr. Melville walked into the room and he asked him for something to eat. They later brought him some bread and cheese, but nothing to drink.

About six o'clock that evening, Detective Inspector Cliffe led him into the Chief Constable's office, who was sitting in there with

Inspector Melville. Mr. Taylor said he looked ill and handed him a glass of whisky to warm him up. Mr. Melville asked him, "Do you smoke" and he replied, "I would like the chance," and he was given a cigar. The Chief Constable and Melville asked him to go through his story again, so they could write it all down before he went home. His written statement was then taken and he signed it with his mark, this was the one read out in court. After the statement was finished, Melville said, "Now, Ditchfield, there was a man that I knew of the name of Curtin, had you been as big a fool as him and said you did not know these men, he has now ended his life in Pentonville." Shortly afterwards Ditchfield went home. The following Wednesday morning, Ditchfield was in bed when his wife called, "Get up, the police have come for you." He went down to find Mr. Taylor and Inspector Hamilton waiting for him. Mr. Taylor told him, "I have had orders down from London and I must arrest you." Ditchfield said he had been in custody ever since that time. On the 29th of January, Ditchfield made a second voluntary statement taken down by Police Constable Power. That statement was perfectly correct, except that he thought he may have taken the plaster cast from the club in temper after a row with Charles.

Ditchfield explained that he used the phrase, "when I found out what they were for," after the police started following him around and he realised something was wrong. He recalled an incident on the last Monday in November, when Detective Inspector Cliffe called at his house at just after twelve at night, asking if a man named Swinburn lived there. Ditchfield told him, "You know he don't, Cliffe," and went outside to speak to him. It was then he thought he caught sight of Inspector Quinn and Detective officers Smith and Ingram further up the street. At the Socialist Club the following night, Westley, Deakin, Cails, Charles, and several others, were all talking about being 'shadowed.' He was confused, but when they explained to him what 'shadowing' was, he realised he was being 'shadowed.' This was the moment his suspicions were aroused and the 'penny dropped.' He realised something must have been seriously wrong for the police to be following them and he got into a sharpish row with the others. Charles tried to calm him down assuring him they would have nothing more to do with it. Ditchfield told them he, "did not want nothing more to do with Anarchy, if that was a specimen, if that was the way they deceived one another, God deliver him from Anarchy." When he finally left the club that night, he took the plaster cast with him and fully intended to smash it up. Ditchfield said he had been paid his money before that, but he thought he needed to explain about it.

At that point the Judge told the jury, he did not think they would be able to finish before the end of the day, so the Court was adjourned. [157]

Mr. Justice Hawkins continued the case on Saturday the 2nd of April, 1892. All six prisoners and the Crown were represented by the same Counsel as previously.

Ditchfield went back into the box to continue his evidence. He seemed to think the police first came to his house, even before Battolla visited him with Cails. Ditchfield said when they began to talk about 'shadowing,' he could not understand why the police would be following them. He complained to Charles, Deakin and Cails and asked them, "What are they doing it for?" They replied, "There's nothing in it, what have you got to put yourself about for?" Ditchfield said he wished he had never seen Battolla and it was Charles who first asked him to go to Bernard Ross. It was Ross and not him who used the name Purchase and it was also Ross, who showed Charles, Deakin and Cails how to make the wooden pattern. Charles had agreed to pay him, but never turned up as planned and eventually Deakin paid the money he was owed.

The Attorney General asked, "You thought this was quite an innocent matter you were concerned in?"

Ditchfield replied, "If I hadn't, I should not have had anything to do with it."

The Attorney General asked Ditchfield if he knew what an Anarchist was and he said, he did not fully understand the term. Ditchfield said he started to grow suspicious when Charles and Deakin kept changing the name of the thing, from cells, to lubricators and then electric lubricators. Ditchfield admitted being a member of the Socialist Club from the day it was established, but he never fully understood the meaning of the word Socialist either. Ditchfield said the reason he decided to join them was because he listened to the speakers and liked the principles they spoke about.

The Judge asked him if he knew the meaning of the word 'Anarchist.' Ditchfield said he had never troubled himself to find out, but he thought it was something to do with not voting.

John Bailey a barber and jeweller, who lived at 58 and 59, Green Lane, Walsall, gave evidence in support of Ditchfield. Bailey said that in early November, 1891, Ditchfield came into his shop and said he had got a good job for a French electrical company finishing some electrical lubricators. He didn't really know what they were for, but they were pear shaped and he was going to earn threepence each for doing them. A fortnight later, Ditchfield told him a man at the club had failed to pay him for some work he had done. He was very upset because he could not afford to pay for dinner the following day. Bailey had personally known Ditchfield for thirty years and regarded him as a truthful, peaceful and responsible man. Bailey said he was not himself a member of the Walsall Socialist Club.

Mr. Thompson said that concluded his case for the defence of Ditchfield and he did not propose to call either Battolla or Cails to give evidence.

Mr. Willis then called Westley to take the stand, who started by telling the jury he had lived in Walsall all his life and was the son of a local business man. Westley said the first time he ever saw Charles was at the Socialist Club in August, 1891. He admitted to seconding the membership applications of Charles, Cails and Laplace but said he had no previous knowledge of Cails or Laplace at all, although he had heard of Charles from some articles he read. When Charles first arrived in town, he found him work for a short time as a traveller selling his brushes, until he got a better paid job as a clerk at Gameson's. He recalled a time when Charles and Deakin were talking about taking out a patent for a lubricator and they asked him to help them make a wooden pattern. They drew a sketch on a piece of paper and gave him some instructions, but it was not the same sketch produced in court.

The Judge wanted to know if he knew what a lubricator was? Westley replied he did not know. He continued by saying, one day Charles brought a parcel and a letter to his workshop and asked if his boy could run it to Mr. Bullows foundry. Westley said he had no suspicions at the time and Charles told him, "If their price doesn't exceed about twenty-two shillings, you can say that will do." When his boy came back, it was marked up with the price twenty shillings. He did notice that the order was for three dozen castings, signed 'Laplace,' but he recognised it was in Charles handwriting. He wrote back accepting the price on behalf of Charles, but apart from that he had nothing to do with it. Westley said he had never seen or heard of any brass castings, brass bolt, screw or lead bolt and he only helped them in the pure spirit of friendship and took no further part in the business other than that. Westley said he never spoke to Battolla due to the language barrier. He had no idea the wooden pattern he helped them with was for a bomb, or had any connection to explosives until after he was arrested. If he had of known he would have had nothing to do with it.

The Judge asked him about being a Socialist. Westley told, him that he was a Socialist, but one strongly opposed to violence and he personally disapproved in the principal of explosive weapons and the manufacture of firearms. His interest in Socialism was purely from an educational interest from the lectures he attended.

Mr. Willis called Mr. Edward Carpenter, formerly Fellow of Trinity College, Cambridge for the defence. Carpenter was a well known Socialist, who had been a member of both the Social Democratic Federation and the Socialist League. Carpenter was associated with many notorious members of the Socialist and Anarchist fraternity. He was openly homosexual and an early campaigner for gay rights. Carpenter took the affirmation instead of the oath and said he had known Charles since 1890, having first met him at the Sheffield

Socialist Club. He described Charles as a very tender, kindhearted and generous man.

The Attorney-General asked Carpenter if he was an Anarchist?

Carpenter confirmed that he did call himself an Anarchist and had previously contributed articles to the 'Commonweal.' He also admitted that he sympathised with some phases of Anarchism.

Mr. Willis asked him if he agreed with that part of Anarchism, which believed in destruction using bombs? Carpenter replied that he did not consider those views as an integral part of Anarchism.

Robert Mustard, a railway goods agent from Wednesbury and Samuel Statham, a goods agent from Tipton, were both called to give Deakin an excellent character reference for sobriety, honesty and integrity.

Mr. Willis, then addressed the jury on behalf of Fred Charles, calling him a man of undoubted honour, intelligence and standing, who had a good character right up until the unfortunate matter in Walsall. Willis accused the prosecution of using the word 'Anarchist' to frighten people and to prejudice a fair trial. He said the prosecution conducted their case on the principle of terrifying the jury by reading out sensational literature, to compensate for their lack of evidence. Mr. Willis then began talking about the idealism of the Anarchists.

The Judge was unimpressed and reminded Mr. Willis that idealism was not evidence and he was making an inflammatory harangue. Mr. Willis protested at being prevented from giving his thoughtful views and expressing his sympathies, concluding "they are much to be pitied, because by the neglect of political rulers themselves, this organisation has come into existence which, perhaps in its outward movement, if change does not come, may threaten to inflict untold evils on mankind."

Mr. Thompson addressed the jury for Battolla, Cails and Ditchfield. Mr. Boddam followed for Westley and finally Mr. McCarthy spoke for Deakin. Then at this convenient point, the trial was adjourned until Monday.

On the morning of Monday the 4th of April, 1892, the case continued. The Attorney-General stated he very much regretted that the defence sought to accuse him of trying to terrify and alarm the jury. It was the Anarchists themselves who held very objectionable views and unfortunately it was his painful and difficult duty to lay those facts before the jury. It was not necessary to show they all actually possessed the things he spoke about, because if two or more were jointly acting together to commit a felony, they were all guilty. The Attorney-General commended Westley for doing the right thing by going into the box and denying his involvement. Under the circumstances, he believed the jury should reject Deakin's evidence against Westley. It was entirely for the jury to decide if Ditchfield and Westley were innocent, having fallen for the falsehood about the bombs being an 'electric cell.' If the jury should believe anyone, it should be those two who stood in the witness box to tell the truth. Westley gave his account in the witness box and if the jury thought he got mixed up without fully knowing the truth, they should give him the benefit of the doubt. Ditchfield admitted to being a party to making the original casting and putting the worm on the screw, but the jury were entirely at liberty to decide if he had guilty knowledge or not. The Attorney-General said Charles had provided no suggestion as to why he had possession of the sketch of a bomb and his own counsel made no attempt to say it was for an innocent purpose. He then made references to the other prisoners. The Attorney-General asked the jury to try the prisoners by the strictest legal evidence and by that evidence alone and not to return verdicts, purely because the men held violent opinions

Mr. Justice Hawkins then began his summing up, commending the Attorney-General for making it crystal clear in every syllable he spoke that he wanted the case tried in the fairest manner possible. He then advised the Jury on a point of law, that every member of a criminal conspiracy was equally culpable. Cails and Charles were undoubtedly Anarchists, but that in itself did not infer they were bloody minded. Having said that, he thought there was no accidental reason why the Anarchist literature read out in court had come into their possession. If however, the jury could find any innocent explanation for having it, they should consider it. At the end of his speech the Jury were sent out to their room to consider their verdict in private.

Just over an hour passed before they returned to the courtroom with a verdict. The foreman of the Jury stood, as one by one the charges were read out for each prisoner and the foreman gave his heavily anticipated reply. Charles, 'Guilty,' Cails, 'Guilty,' Deakin, 'Guilty,' Battolla, 'Guilty' and the last two Westley and Ditchfield, 'Not Guilty.' The foreman of the jury said they recommended the judge to be merciful in respect of Deakin. The two Walsall men Westley and Ditchfield, who gave an explanation were acquitted and the Judge ordered them to be discharged from custody.

The convicted men were asked if they had anything they wanted to say before sentence was passed. Charles said the translations from the French newspapers, didn't in any way represent Anarchist ideas. He admitted the logical conclusion of Anarchist ideology was to bring down society, but referred to an article written by William Morris in 'The Commonweal.' This says that Socialist revolution, was not a change brought about by riot or violence, but was a change in the basis of society itself. Charles said causing explosions would only turn public opinions against them, defeating the objectives of the Anarchist movement. He always believed the bombs were for Russia and that was the only reason he was willing to lend a hand.

Battolla, through the interpreter, accused Auguste Coulon of being the great intriguer and police spy. He said he was a proud Anarchist, who stood for a humane state of society were men lived in harmony without authority. He wanted to know what punishment the generals of bourgeois society should get for inventing explosive weapons to kill thousands, if they were only guilty of having one shell. The Judge said they did not need or want a general discussion on politics. Battolla said he was glad to be sentenced as an Anarchist, declaring "Long live Anarchy, which is the real future of humanity and the concord of human feelings."

Cails declared himself an Anarchist, but said that was no reason to mistake him for a criminal and Deakin had nothing further to say on the matter at all.

All four defendants were then asked to stand as the Judge delivered his sentence. Mr. Justice Hawkins said the sentences he was about to pass, were not because the men were self confessed Anarchists, as he felt certain many of their persuasion would shudder at the cruelty suggested in those wicked papers. The punishments were based purely on them entering into a very cruel conspiracy to manufacture bombs to cause injury or destruction to human life and damage to property. He believed there was not a shadow of doubt, they were all guilty as charged. Jean Battolla he said sketched the bomb giving instructions on how to make the diabolical weapons. In the eyes of the law it mattered not, whether they were for use in Great Britain, Russia or anywhere else in the world. The crime deserved and demanded an exemplary sentence to suppress such cruel conspiracies being committed again, but he derived no personal gratification by passing sentences upon men, who could have diverted their talents to far more peaceful uses. Under the grave circumstances it was his painful duty to hand out long terms of imprisonment for conspiring to the wholesale destruction of life, the maiming of persons and the widespread destruction of property. He had no alternative, it was his duty and responsibility to pass a sentence, which adequately punished them for their crime.

Charles, Cails and Battolla were each sentenced to ten years penal servitude. In Deakin's case he listened to the jury's recommendation for mercy and dealt with him more leniently by sentencing him to five years penal servitude, saying he thought he was the dupe and the victim of the others standing before him. [158] [159] [160] [161]

Just Rewards?

On the night of Wednesday the 20th of April, 1892, a special meeting of the Watch Committee was held in the Council Chamber at the Guildhall. The Mayor announced that he had received two letters and asked for the Town Clerk to read them out.

The first dated the 16th of April, 1892, was addressed to the Chairman of the Watch Committee and was from Whitehall. It read, "Sir, I am directed by the Secretary of State to acquaint you that the Director of Public Prosecutions has brought specially to his notice the very valuable service rendered by Chief Constable Taylor and the Walsall police in detecting and tracing the proceedings, and obtaining the evidence required for the prosecution of the four persons who were convicted at the last Stafford Assizes of offences under the Explosive Substances Act of 1883. The case appears to Mr. Matthews to have been one of very great public importance and he is satisfied that the credit of bringing the offenders to justice belongs mainly to the Walsall police. I am to ask, therefore, that you will be so good as to convey in some public manner to the Chief Constable and the other members of the force, Mr. Matthews high appreciation of the zeal, energy, and skill which they have shown in dealing with this matter. I am, Sir, your obedient servant, E. Leigh Pemberton."

(Henry Matthews was the Conservative Home Secretary under Lord Salisbury and Edward Leigh Pemberton was the Legal Assistant to the Under-Secretary of the Home Office)

The second letter was from HM Treasury at Whitehall, dated the 16th of April, 1892 and addressed to the Walsall Town Clerk. It read, "Sir, I have the pleasure to inform you that I am authorised by the Lords Commissioners of HM Treasury to pay to Mr. Taylor and the officers acting under his direction in the above case the sum of £50 in recognition of the services rendered by them in furtherance of the ends of justice, and of the zealous and able manner in which they performed their duties. Such sum to be divided between the officers in question such proportions as may be thought fitting by the Watch Committee. I trust that this payment will meet with the approval of the Watch Committee, and in that case I shall be glad to be informed of their wishes as to the manner of its distribution, in order that I may do what is necessary in the matter. In making this communication to you I desire to express my personal sense of the valuable and efficient assistance I received from Mr. Taylor during the course of the inquiry, and to say that, in my judgment, the manner in which he performed his duties which were of a special and difficult character, is worthy of high commendation. I have the honour to be, Sir, your obedient servant, signed H. Cuffe, Assistant Solicitor to HM Treasury." (£50 is equivalent to about £7,600 in 2023)

The Mayor declared that the letters spoke for themselves and he suggested that the £50 should be divided, £40 to Mr. Taylor and £10 to Detective Inspector Cliffe, which was agreed. The Watch Committee unanimously passed a resolution to show their appreciation by saying, "that the Committee express its appreciation of the services rendered by the Chief Constable and the officers of the force, and of the way in which they had discharged their duties."

The Town Clerk said HM Treasury were bearing the principal cost of the prosecution, believed to be between £1,000 to £1,500. The charge to the Borough was £209. 9s. 11d.

The Chief Constable said that neither he nor his officers had any thought of reward at the time, they were simply doing their duty. It was his job to place the facts before a jury, but he was very pleased to accept all the compliments paid to him and his officers. He asked the Town Clerk to include his thanks in the letter of reply to the Home Office. [162]

The verdicts sent a shockwave through the town of Walsall, but Westley and Ditchfield had been cleared and had returned home to their families. To them it was but a mere 'Mare's Nest,' of intrigue!

The Mowbray and Nicoll Trial

After the Walsall Anarchist trial was over, the authorities were keen to put the whole matter to bed. However, certain factions within the Anarchist movement were less prepared to let things lie. From their point of view, the four convicted men had been the victims of rough justice, framed by the police in an establishment plot against them.

On the 9th April, 1892, the 'Commonweal' published an article entitled, 'The Walsall Anarchists - Condemned to Penal Servitude.'

The article read: - "The Walsall Anarchists have been condemned - Charles, Battolla, and Cails to ten years penal servitude, while Deakin has been let off in mercy with five. For what? For a police plot concocted by one of those infamous wretches who make a living by getting up these affairs and selling their victims to the vengeance of the law. Surely we ought not to have to warn Anarchists of the danger of conspiracies, these death traps, these gins set by the police and their spies, in which so many honest and devoted men have perished. Surely those who desire to act can do as John Felton did, when, alone and unaided, he bought the knife which struck down the tyrant. Are there no tyrants now? What of the Jesuitical monster at the Home Office, who murders men for taking a few head of game? What of the hyena who preys upon bodies of hanged men, and whose love of the gallows a few years ago won him the title of 'Hangman' Hawkins? this barbarous brute, who, prating of his humanity, sends our comrades to ten years in the hell of the prisons. What of the spy Melville, who sets his agent on to concoct the plots which he discovers? Are these men fit to live? The Anarchists are criminals, vermin, gallows carrion, well, shower hard names upon us, hunt us down like mad dogs, strangle us like you have done our comrades at Xeres, shoot us down as you did at Fourmies, and then be surprised if your houses are shattered with dynamite, and if people shrink from the companionship of officials of the law as 'dangerous company.' Justice has been done. Has it, gentlemen of the middle classes? 'Justice!' Was it justice that was done in your Courts of

Tuesday, when a cruel wretch belonging to your class bearing the likeness of a woman was let off with one year's imprisonment for torturing her own child to death, while men who loved the suffering people so much that they dared all things for them are condemned to ten years penal servitude? Justice it may be, perhaps, too, it will be just when the oppressed strike back at you without ruth and mercy, only don't whine for pity in these days, for it will be useless. - D. J. Nicoll"

The author of the inflammatory article was David Nicoll, the well known activist and one of the leading voices for the Anarchists release campaign. Nicoll was absolutely convinced that Coulon set them all up under the direction of Detective Inspector Melville. For information, the John Felton in the article was the assassin of George Villiers, 1st Duke of Buckingham at Portsmouth on the 23rd of August 1628. The authorities hung him for the crime, but he was revered by the people who called him a martyr.

On Sunday the 10th of April, 1892, Nicoll made two speeches an hour apart at a Hyde Park rally, regarding the convictions of the Walsall Anarchists. Nicoll was accused of making comments tantamount to inciting the murder of the Home Secretary, Henry Matthews, the trial judge Mr. Justice Hawkins and Detective Inspector William Melville. To protect public officials from acts of violence the authorities were keen to act quickly, before the threatening and inflammatory words gained any more public support.

On Monday the 18th of April, 1892, the police raided and searched the offices of 'The Commonweal,' at 145, City Road. Detective Sergeant John Walsh found the manuscript for the offending article on pink paper. David Nicoll wasn't present at the offices when the police attended, but he was arrested outside 194, Clarence Road, Kentish Town by Inspector William McClinchey on Tuesday 19th of April, 1892. Several articles relating to the Walsall case were recovered from his premises together with copies of the leaflet 'Fight or Starve.'

That same day Detective Sergeant's Patrick McIntyre and John Walsh both from Special Branch went to 44, Probert Street, London. This was the home address of Charles Mowbray, who was believed to be the publisher of the article. Detective Sergeant McIntyre arrested Mowbray, who sobbed in frustration as his wife had just died and lay dead in bed upstairs. After being arrested Mowbray replied, "This is a very bad job, my wife is lying dead, having died this morning." He turned to Chief Inspector Littlechild who was also present and said, "I am not guilty, I have severed my connection with them, I do not believe in violence of any kind." Mowbray said "I disagree with the article in the Commonweal." Various socialist documents were found at his address.

On Wednesday the 20th of April, 1892, Nicoll and Mowbray appeared at Bow Street Magistrates Court charged with Seditious Libel. Nicoll admitted being fully responsible for the article, but Mowbray said he was no longer connected with the 'Commonweal' and had nothing to do with it. Bail was refused and both men were remanded in custody for a week. [163]

Mowbray was granted special permission to attend the funeral of his wife. At about four o'clock on Saturday the 23rd of April, 1892, a group of around two hundred congregated outside the Workpeople's Club, in Berners Street. People carried red banners, one with the words, 'Remember Chicago, there will be a time when our silence will be more powerful than the voices you strangle today' and another had the contentious 'Commonweal' attached. The slow mournful procession proceeded under the watchful eye of Superintendent Arnold, who commanded a large contingent of police officers. The hearse and coffin was followed by the coach containing Charles Mowbray and his children. Behind them was a very orderly, quiet and respectful crowd with a band playing the 'Dead March.' Large numbers of people lined the route along Commercial Road to Manor Park cemetery. Several leading Anarchists spoke of revenge at the graveside, including Madame Louise Michel. [164]

On Wednesday the 27th of April, 1892, Nicoll and Mowbray appeared at Bow Street Court, where they were committed for trial at the Central Criminal Court. Bail was refused for Nicoll, but Mowbray was granted bail with a five hundred pounds surety. Mowbray maintained that he had severed all connections with the 'Commonweal' prior to the article being published. [165]

The case against David Nicoll and Charles Mowbray went ahead at the Central Criminal Court at the Old Bailey on Friday the 6th of May, 1892. A large number of leading Socialists turned up in court wearing distinctive red ties. The Attorney-General, Sir Richard Webster, the same man who prosecuted the Walsall Anarchists at Stafford attended to prosecute the case.

Detective Sergeant John Sweeney said he heard Nicholl speak at Hyde park, where he made references to Jesuit Home Secretary Matthews, Inspector Melville and Coulon. He heard Nicoll say, "two of them must die." He also heard him call Justice Hawkins 'Butcher Hawkins.' Constable Francis Powell corroborated Sergeant Sweeney's account.

Nicoll called a number of witnesses including Fred Henderson, to dispute the words Sweeney allegedly heard at Hyde Park.

The final outcome was that Mowbray was acquitted, but Nicoll was sentenced to eighteen months with hard labour. [166] [167] [168]

Part Three - What Happened, Next ?

This story may leave you wondering what happened next, what came of the people in this story. We already know something about what happened to the Walsall Anarchists from the outcome of the trial at Stafford, but what of Haydn Sanders the man himself, where did he go and did he ever return to his hometown or to the council.

Haydn Sanders

Haydn Sanders did stand as a socialist candidate for a second time in 1892, but this time for the Masbrough Ward, in Rotherham. Sanders lost by eighty-one votes, but said the writing was on the wall and change was coming. He said he would be back, again and again until he succeeded to make the council listen. [169]

The next time we hear of Haydn Sanders, he became embroiled in a strike at Mr. Dobson's, Derwent Foundry. One foundry worker, John Stevenson refused to join his fellow strikers and continued to go into work. One day as he walked to work, a large intimidating crowd followed him, including Haydn Sanders, who he alleged was their ring leader. As a result, Sanders was summonsed to appear before Derby Magistrates on Saturday the 10th June, 1893, for an offence of persistently following Stevenson about under the Conspiracy and Protection of Property Act 1875. Sanders who represented himself, insisted on being tried at the Assizes on indictment, claiming he was only there to prevent a disorder and nothing more. The magistrates had to decide whether there was enough evidence to commit the matter for trial at the High Court and knew a Judge would be very critical if they sent a case without sufficient evidence. Sanders bolshy personality convinced them to dismiss the case, rather than risk a backlash. The decision caused loud cheers from the crowds, both inside and outside the court when the result was announced. [170]

In 1894, Haydn Sanders was advertising in various newspapers offering his services as a lecturer and for organisation work in connection with all trades and labour movements. At this time, he was still the General Secretary of the Stoves Grates Workers Union and lived at 17, Clifton Grove, Rotherham. [171]

On Friday the 8th June, 1894, the Investigation Committee of the National Stove Grate Workers Union met at Masbrough, without any executive members being present. The special meeting was called after the auditor informed the committee that he could not balance the Union books and there was a discrepancy of £25 7s. 6d. The auditor told them that the union accounts over the four years since it began, were so bad, it was almost impossible to show where the shortfall came from. The committee concluded, that Haydn Sanders had conducted their business in such a lax and careless way, he was either grossly negligence, totally incompetent or both. They recommended that he be immediately dismissed as general secretary, with the rest of the executive council. The committee also suggested a change of rules to elect the next general secretary nationally and to properly register the union, which had not been done.

Haydn Sanders and the rest of the executive committee met in private at the Star Inn to discuss matters. Sanders chaired the meeting and they decided to request a direct audience with the auditors to discuss the matter. [172]

The next week the union held a further meeting at Rotherham, where Sanders denied any money was missing, claiming the auditors had overlooked some expenses and a payment made to a barrister during the Warrington strike. Sanders made a speech, telling them they could be proud of the advances they had made in the cause of the Labour movement, but despite trying to butter them up and making excuses, they dispensed with his services forthwith. [173]

On Friday the 15th of February, 1895, Haydn Sanders sued a man named Walter Vickers Russell for two pound at Rotherham County Court. At this time he lived at Percy Street, Rotherham and described himself as the late secretary of the National Union of Stove Grate

Workers. Haydn Sanders prosecuted the case himself before his Honour Judge Ellison. Mr. Gichard, a solicitor defended Mr. Russell. Sanders claim was that at Christmas 1890, Russell borrowed two pounds, which he failed to repay. The Judge asked Sanders, if there was any legal paperwork to support the loan agreement. Sanders said because he trusted the man with a debt of honour there was no paperwork, but he had two witnesses he intended to call to prove the case. The first, Arthur Hodgkinson said he knew them both very well and Russell did borrow two pounds from Sanders to pay for his wedding. The second witness, John Rawson said Russell had actually borrowed four pounds from Sanders, but had since paid him two pounds back. The Judge said that neither of his two witnesses brought anything but hearsay evidence, which was worthless to prove his case. Sanders was undeterred and insisted on being given the opportunity to question Russell himself. Russell went into the witness box and Sanders aggressively accused him of coming to his house in 1890, financially broke and crying for money. Russell denied the accusation, but Sanders was like a terrier and wouldn't let go, becoming more probing and aggressive with every question he asked. The Judge intervened reprimanding Sanders for the terrible way he was treating the witness. Sanders told the judge that Russell was deliberately provoking him by not telling the truth. The Judge disagreed and said Mr. Russell was conducting himself perfectly properly. Sanders sarcastically said that the Judge was so much cooler than him, but then again he ought to be. This brought fits of laughter to the courtroom, which did not impress the Judge at all. In response the Judge criticised Sanders tomfoolery, by saying for a man who called himself a secretary, he knew very little about getting a proper acknowledgement of debt. His Honour Judge Ellison said, if Sanders had bothered to do the right thing, everyone could have been spared the court commotion for a paltry two pounds. He said Sanders had abused Mr. Russell for simply refusing to admit having the money, he called Sanders "one of those witnesses, excited, abusive and ready to say anything to gain his case," while Mr. Russell remained "perfectly calm." The judgement was awarded against Sanders. [174]

Haydn Sanders without any known source of gainful employment, continued to enjoy his sporting pursuits. At the beginning of May, 1895, he caught a huge trout in Derwent Water, one of the largest they had ever seen, weighing in at 5lbs. 12oz. It was two foot long with a girth of thirteen inches and he gifted the fish to the Belper Angling Association. [175]

On Friday the 19th of July, 1895, Haydn Sanders of 20, Percy Street, Rotherham appeared at Rotherham County Court, being sued by John Flavell, the secretary of the Rotherham and District Trades and Labour Council. Flavell claimed that Sanders failed to hand over £12. 2s. 10d., belonging to his members. His Honour Judge Ellison was presiding again and Mr. Gichard represented Flavell. The Judge said, there was a fatal flaw in the case as having carefully read through the rules of Mr. Flavell's organisation, nowhere did they actually define what a member was. In addition the Rotherham and District Trades and Labour Council were unregistered, so not protected by the Trades Union Act of 1871. The previous Act had now been repealed which forced him to dismiss the action against Sanders. [176]

Rotherham County Court had not seen the last of Haydn Sanders, as in March, 1898, he returned again for the none payment of two debts. When Sanders was sacked by the Stove and Grates Workers Union, he unsuccessfully sued the union in the High Court, but he lost and costs of £28 18s. 10d., were awarded against him. In typical Sanders fashion, he rebelled by failing to pay any of the money owed. In June 1897, Rotherham County Court made a judgement of one pound per month against Sanders to recover the debt, but he failed to pay anything from that order. There was a second debt of ten shillings per month from a tradesman who he failed to pay. Sanders told the hearing that he had undertaken no paid work for seven weeks and was "utterly unable to pay." His last paid work on a commission only basis was at the 'Rotherham Express,' newspaper. His honour demanded that Sanders declare his annual income, which he said was about seventy-five pounds. The Judge told him that many people lived comfortably on twenty-five shillings a week. Sarcastically, Sanders remarked, "it was marvellous how they did it," and followed by asking for the amount to be reduced to four shillings per month. The Judge said he believed Sanders had sufficient mental training to understand that this matter could not carry on in this way. Sanders claimed the Union had tried their very best to drive him out of town. The creditors solicitor produced a business card, 'Sanders and Co,' suggesting that he was running a viable business. Sanders said, 'Sanders and Co,' was run by his wife, who was in charge of the 'Rotherham Herald' newspaper as a freelance editor and journalist. Sanders said he lived in a rented house with his wife and four children, but she owned everything including the furniture. The solicitor accused Sanders of hiding behind his wife to escape paying his debts. He pleaded with the court that he was unable to "live in a rough manner like an ordinary workman." The hearing was adjourned for a month. [177]

Slippery as an eel, Haydn Sanders met with the official receiver at Sheffield on the 17th of May, 1898. He filed for the bankruptcy of his business, 'Sanders and Co.,' which traded as advertising contractors, publishers and commission agents. The company had outstanding company debts amounting to £311. 4s. 6d., with assets of only £7. 11s. 6d. He said the business was started in October 1897, but had allegedly made no money at all. He said since being sacked as the secretary of the Stoves and Grates Workers Union in 1894, his only income had been from doing odd lectures and unfortunately he had kept no account books to record his business or financial affairs. A representative from Wilson Brothers printers, said Sanders had placed an order with them six weeks ago, but failed to settle his account, despite him selling the printed work. The printers thought he had only filed for bankruptcy to get out of paying his debts and had obtained the work by false pretences, knowing full well he was not in a position to pay. Sanders denied being dishonest, but the official receiver demanded to see his paperwork. Sanders said there was no paperwork and he had no assets at all, even his watch and chain had gone to a cousin. The Judge demanded the cousins name to verify the facts, but he refused to give it.

Eventually out of frustration the receiver reluctantly wound the business up. [178]

Sanders was back at Sheffield Bankruptcy Court on Thursday the 16th of June, 1898. The Stove Grates Workers Union were still trying to recover their money from Sanders, who had paid nothing despite all their attempts. Mr. W. Gichard appeared for Sanders defence and Mr. A. M. Wilson for the National Union of the Stove Grate Workers. Sanders who resided at 20, Percy Street, Rotherham admitted having unsecured debts of £311 4s. 6d., with assets of only £7. 11s. 6d. Sanders said he severed all contact with the Stove Grates Workers Union four years previously when they sacked him. Apart from odd lectures, the only work he had done was starting the 'Rotherham Herald, Parkgate and Rawmarsh Journal' in October 1897. He told the Receiver he had never kept any account books for his business transactions. This time, he said his wife was not involved in 'Sanders and Company,' which started in February 1898, although she did work for the firm as a journalist. Sanders admitted being insolvent when he started the 'Rotherham Herald,' but earned £77 1s., from advertisements in the four issues he printed. Tillotson's who printed the paper had been paid £32 7s. 6d., but he still owed them £29 14s. 6d. Distribution had cost him £15 and incidentals another £20, so he was down about £20 overall. In addition, he owed Wilson's of Leicester £26 7s. 6d., for printing leaflets. He firmly blamed the pressure the Stoves Grates Workers Union put on him, for preventing him being able to pay Wilson's. He referred to the Union as 'scoundrels,' who robbed him of hundreds of pounds, but the Judge warned him about the words he was using. Mr. Gichard said, Sanders had done his very best to make a living to pay off his debts, but the Union had hounded him ever since he had left their employment. The matter was adjourned for a month. [179]

When the matter came back to court on Thursday 21st of July, 1898, the Stove and Grate Workers Union were not happy with Sanders explanations, but eventually the case was closed and unsettled. No doubt Sanders had made the case 'too difficult to deal with.' [180]

At the time of the census in March, 1901, Sanders lived at 11, Meadow View, Belper, Derbyshire. He described himself as a journalist editor and his wife Louisa was also a journalist. They were both boarding at the address, but none of their children were present. Their son Hampden was at a private school in Derbyshire. [181] [182]

Mr. and Mrs. Haydn Sanders were on a list of society guests who attended a Temperance Garden party at Milford House, Belper in June 1904. The guests were supposedly some of the best known people in the temperance movement. [183]

Soon after arriving at Belper, Haydn Sanders became the Managing Editor of 'The Belper News,' run by The Derbyshire Liberal Press Limited. Haydn Sanders liquidated the company on 20th of August, 1907, when he and his family left Derbyshire to reinvent themselves again, this time in Croydon. [184]

The affairs of the Derbyshire Liberal Press Limited were discussed at Belper County Court in December, 1908. Haydn Sanders was ordered to attend the court, but arrived demanding his travelling expenses by train from Croydon to Belper. Sanders said he owned 1,090 out of a total 2,077 shares at five shillings each when the company was liquidated, but denied anything was dodgy about transferring shares shortly before the company was wound up. They challenged Sanders about one of his books, which appeared to have been tampered with, but Sanders said it was only clerical errors and nothing more. [185]

In 1909 the London Aeroplane and Aerial Navigation Company was created in Croydon by Haydn Sanders and his two sons, Captain Haydn Arnold and Hampden. Captain Haydn Arnold Sanders was the managing director and test pilot of the company, who qualified as a ships captain with the Board of Trade in 1908 and assumed the Captain title. On the 25th of February 1909, Haydn Arnold Sanders applied for several patents all to do with aircraft construction, including one for a bomb releasing and targeting device. In March that year, Haydn Sanders entered into negotiations with the Bridlington authorities to build aeroplanes. They needed to acquire an air strip with a large sixty by forty foot hanger to accommodate a trial plane, being designed and built by Captain Sanders, who he intended to make a series of test flights in July, 1909. [186] [187] [188] [189]

The first aeroplane built by the London Aeroplane and Aerial Navigation Company in 1909 was the Sanders Biplane No. 1. It was built at Kessingland, Suffolk with the assistance of F. L. Rawson and was a single seat biplane, powered by a thirty horse power, four cylinder Brooke engine, with two chain driven 8½ foot long propellers. Captain Haydn Sanders made his first test flight in October 1909, when he flew the Biplane No. 1 across the Benacre Estate, at Benacre Ness, Suffolk.

In February, 1910 Haydn Sanders attended a meeting about creating a Citizenship League at Croydon. He described himself as the former editor of the 'Surrey Daily Argus' and gave a lecture about individuals being responsible for their own actions and the provision of affordable working class housing. At the conclusion of the meeting they resolved to form a Citizens Association for political action and a Citizenship League for the spread of political education in Croydon. [190]

In February, 1910 the Sanders Biplane No. 1 was wrecked in a crash landing, but Captain Sanders was not seriously hurt and he lived to fly another day. In April 1910, the family created the new 'Sanders Aeroplane Co.,' and transferred their aircraft operations to Beccles in Suffolk. The Mayor of Beccles council sanctioned a strip of marshland to be the leased to Captain Sanders, saying he was delighted with the prospect of having an airfield being established in the town. [191]

They built the Sanders Teacher at Beccles, a flight simulation device using standard aeroplane parts to teach pilots balance on the ground. They later used some of the parts to develop their next biplane. [192] [193]

The brothers worked on a new design at their Beccles Common base and later released the Sanders Biplane No. 2. This aeroplane had many modifications, essentially strengthening the overall construction. It had a steel tube and wooden frame, shrouded in a fabric covering and the wings folded. It was powered by a fifty horse power Alvaston engine and test flights began in the spring of 1911.

In March, 1911 the Sanders Biplane was exhibited on stand 75 at the Olympia Aero Show. It was then powered by a 60-80 horse power, E.N.V. eight cylinder engine, fitted with a single nine foot diameter propeller. This aircraft costing £1,000 had a 40 foot wingspan and was 31½ feet long. The wheels were retractable when the machine was in flight. Despite the Sanders Teacher being well publicised in the 'Aircraft,' and 'Scientific American' magazines in 1911, no more was ever heard of it. [194]

Mr. and Mrs. Haydn Sanders sent a wreath to the funeral of William Hodgkins, saddle maker at Ryecroft, Walsall in February 1911. Hodgkins was his brother-in-law, who was married to his sister Priscilla. [195] [196]

On the 2nd of April, 1911, Haydn Sanders, his wife Louise, son Hampden and two daughters Miriam and Gertrude all lived at 23, Blenheim Park Road, Croydon. Haydn was described as the manager of a rubber company and his son, Hampden was an aeronautical engineer. His eldest son, Haydn Arnold Saunders was an aircraft maker and resided with his family at 45, Station Road, Beccles, Suffolk. [197] [198]

In July 1911, the partnership known as the Sanders Aeroplane Company, between Haydn Sanders, Hampden Sanders, Haydn Arnold Sanders and J. Hirst was dissolved and by 1913 had gone out of business. [199]

Haydn Sanders, described himself as a fifty-two year old manager of a rubber company, when he joined the Lewisham Lodge (2579) of the Freemasons on the 9th of November, 1912. Mr. and Mrs. Haydn Sanders were on the guest list of the Lewisham Freemasons annual Ladies Night at the Liverpool Street hotel in April, 1914. Sanders remained a member of that lodge until he resigned in August 1919. [200] [201]

On Thursday the 26th of February 1914, Haydn Sanders and his son Captain Haydn Sanders were at Newcastle Assizes, suing Mr. George Robson from the Combination Metallic Packaging Company for £150 worth of damages to an aircraft in 1912. Mr. Robson from the North East Aero Club had approached Haydn Sanders senior about his son's services at their flying club. Some agreement was reached and Captain Sanders, arrived at Gosforth Park on the 6th of April, 1912 and Robson built a hanger at Chevington. The Sanders airplane sustained £150 worth of damage in a flying accident and they were seeking compensation. Before the case was fully heard at court, Robson agreed to settle and pay the £150 to close the matter. [202]

During the First World War, Haydn Arnold Sanders initially served with the Royal Navy where he was mentioned in despatches at least twice and then with the Royal Air Force. In 1914 Hampton Sanders joined the 4th Battalion "The Queens" as a private, but was later granted a commission in the Indian Army, where he rose to the the rank of Captain and was awarded the Military Cross. [203] [204]

In 1921 Haydn Sanders lived with his wife Louisa and son Hampton at Pine View, Ockham Road, West Horsley. Haydn was a sixty-one year old journalist and his son was described as a retired Indian Army captain. The family employed a sixteen year old girl as a live in servant. [205]

On the 11th of July, 1924, a man who described himself as a Socialist from Chalfont St. Peter, wrote into a local newspaper. Sanders wrote a response on the 21st of July, 1924, describing the Socialist "characteristic of the party writers and street corner leaders, a diatribe filled with envy and hate and a zealous attachment to ideals not only utterly impractical but calculated to bring disaster to the very class, the proletariate who he champions." Haydn Sanders political views had certainly shifted, this sounded very similar to how he was described when he served on Walsall Council. Sanders went further, promoting the Unionist Party, saying their ideas were based on centuries of hard work and not just words. Sanders called Socialism a highly contagious disease, capable of bringing ultimate disaster to the country and said the idea that society was run by profiteers out to fleece the public was untrue. This was a monumental shift from his views as a young man, he even branded the bulk of Socialists as the anti-Christ, while the Unionists practiced the Fatherhood of God and were loyal to the King. Sanders claimed that real British people, who wanted to prosper were being forced to leave for the United States, because the Socialists had ruined working ethics and reduced overall production. Sanders was now living at Elmwood, Stoke Park, near Slough. [206]

The same Socialist from Chalfont St. Peter replied to his letter, and criticised Sanders, who wrote back again, this time to put down the Socialist cause and criticise the Trades Unions for falling under the Socialists spell. [207]

The South Buckinghamshire Conservatives and Unionist Association held a garden party in August, 1924 at the Manor House, Little Marlow. Haydn Sanders gave a speech on the evils and menace of Socialism and Communism and expressed his regret that Trades Unions had been lured towards Socialism. [208]

On the 10th of May, 1930 the South Buckinghamshire Conservative and Unionist Association met at Slough. The Conservative peer William Grenfell, who was Lord Desborough presided at the meeting. Haydn Sanders of Stoke Poges was elected onto the General Purpose Committee of the Conservative and Unionist Association, completing his total transition from Red to Blue. Councillor Brownhill had made a prophesy at a Walsall Council meeting in September 1889, that 'Mr. Sanders was becoming a true Conservative.' How right he seems to have been. [209]

In 1932 a statement printed in the Walsall Observer claimed that Mr. Dean was the first labour councillor in Walsall. Joseph Deakin wrote to the newspaper to point out that Haydn Sanders became the first labour councillor in England in November 1888. Deakin still lived at his old family home of 238, Stafford Street,. [210]

Haydn Sanders of Elmwood, Stoke Poges died on the 4th of April, 1937 at a Lowestoft nursing home, leaving an estate valued at £115. His daughter Gertrude Ivy Clark was the sole executor of his will. Gertrude married Alfred Clark a New Yorker, who made a fortune in early gramophone and movie recording. She died a millionaire at the Connaught Hotel in London in 1976 aged 85 years. [211] [212] [213] [214] [215]

Sanders nephew Vivian Stranders, the son of his sister Miriam also served in the military during the First World War. He got to the rank of

Captain in the RAF, after initially serving in the Royal Field Artillery. In 1926 he was caught spying for the Germans and imprisoned for two years. After release he settled in Germany and served with the SS during World War Two engaging in Nazi propaganda under the code name 'Mediator.' He died in 1959, having lived the rest of his life in West Germany.

Surprisingly, very little has ever been written about Sanders, so I hope in some small way this has managed to put some colour to his monochrome memory. Despite his success in 1888, I had to dig fairly deep into the archives to discover some of the missing chapters relying heavily on historic documents. As to what kind of man Haydn Sanders really was, I leave it up to the reader to make their own judgement. Only a small side street, Haydn Sanders Square, at the end of Brace Street, where he used to live memorialises the name of a man who otherwise slipped into Walsall obscurity. He rarely features in local history and does not make the list of the most famous sons and daughters of the town, but maybe some wanted to forget him all together!

The Walsall Anarchist Case

What became of the characters involved in the Walsall Bomb Plot of 1892, after the dust had settled? In the aftermath of turmoil the traumatised town slowly began to return to business as usual. Most people probably just wanted to move on, but the Labour movement had suffered a sever blow to its credibility. Nationally the Anarchists were making noises about a miscarriage of justice, with accusations of conspiracy and subterfuge on the part of the police. Some left wing groups still talk about these theories even now, as the Walsall Anarchists earned a place in their history's calendar of events.

One of the leading voices of the day, campaigning for the Anarchists release was David Nicoll. After he was released from prison for publishing the inflammatory articles, he pushed for a judicial review into the Walsall case. Nicoll wrote a pamphlet called, 'The Walsall Anarchists, Trapped by the Police, or the Truth about the Walsall Plot,' and sold it for one penny to raise funds for the appeal.

To drum up support, Nicoll who was the editor of the 'Anarchist,' publication planned a mass meeting in Walsall on Sunday the 25th of March, 1894. He had large posters printed to advertise the meeting, believing that the people of Walsall remained sympathetic to the fate of the convicted men. Nicoll and George Cores from the Leicester Trades Council were the two prominent Anarchists speakers due to attend. The poster claimed the four men, Charles, Deakin, Cails and Battolla were imprisoned as the victims of a sham dynamite plot instigated by a spy of the Russian and English police.

The first meeting at the end of Park Street, was scheduled for eleven o'clock that morning. They expected thousands of 'working men' to attend at the allotted time, but when Cores climbed onto the folding stool to speak only about twenty or so had turned up. The Chief Constable and a couple of his detectives watched as he began to speak. The crowd grew to about two hundred and Cores explained that the police were only allowing the meeting, providing they stuck to the rules of no disorder or incitement to violence. Cores said Anarchists never advocated trouble, unless they were denied their common rights of meeting in public. Some of the advertised speakers were unfortunately unable to attend due to poverty preventing them from travelling.

It appears that Nicoll and Cores totally misjudged the strength of support in Walsall for the Anarchists, as the reception was cool to say the least. When Cores announced the Anarchists had been entrapped, someone shouted, "They deserved twice as much." Cores said one of the men was his associate and the same voice shouted, "Then you ought to be with him." Several of the crowd started to laugh and jeer at Cores. Next to speak was David Nicoll, who said all of the men, were industrious, sober, orderly men, whose employers gave them good character references. Nicoll claimed that Scotland Yard were employed to find Anarchists, but when they could not find any, they created them instead. He said, Coulon 'the traitor' was rewarded with hundreds, while Inspector Melville got thousands of pounds.

A second meeting was advertised for eight o'clock at the bottom of Bradford Street. This gathering was attended by numerous men, who were less than hospitable to the visiting Anarchists. Threats were exchanged and a free for all started, with the Anarchists retreating hastily back towards the railway station. Things turned ugly at the station, when one of the Anarchists pulled out a knife and stabbed a man named Hawkins in the hand. This was the catalyst for a riot and the knifeman had to flee for his life across the rail tracks, pursued by several angry men. He managed to get away, but dropped the weapon on his as he ran. The Walsall men gave some of the Anarchists a severe beating, including Cores who was struck across the head and sent flying across the rails. Strangely there is no mention of the police attempting to break the fight up, prior to the Anarchists leaving town. It is known that the Chief Constable had talks with the Home Office and HM Treasury before the meeting took place, so it may have been part of the strategy. [216] [217]

At five past eleven on Sunday the 4th of November, 1894, a bomb was placed outside on the doorstep of 2, Tilney Street, Mayfair. The device shattered every window in the street and caused severe damage to the house and adjoining properties. Fortunately none of the occupants of the house were seriously injured, but it is strongly believed that the bomb was intended for the house door. The occupant next door was sitting in his house by the fire and would have almost certainly been killed or seriously injured by the blast. His name was Sir Henry Hawkins, the Walsall Anarchist trial judge. Within a short time after the blast, Chief Inspector Melville and Inspector Quinn were quickly on the scene of the dastardly devastation. [218] [219]

The Walsall Bombers campaign for clemency was finally decided on the 1st of July, 1896 when the Home Office at Whitehall issued a statement regarding the mens convictions. The communication on behalf of the Secretary for State said, "he is unable to discover any sufficient ground to justify him, consistently with his public duty, in advising Her Majesty to interfere in this case." [220]

Any hope of an early release was gone and the three remaining Walsall Anarchists still in prison had to serve out the remaining years of their sentence. We will now take a look at what happened to the four convicted men, before moving on to discuss the other characters.

Joseph Thomas Deakin was sentenced to five years imprisonment for his part in the Anarchist plot, half of the ten years given to the others, because the jury recommended him for mercy. The judge, listened to their request and remarked that he also believed Deakin was the, 'dupe and the victim of the others standing before him.' The Judge's comments suggest that Deakin was a man, who in the presence of stronger personalities was to some extent swept along. Rather than the leading light, he must have given the court the impression that he was a much weaker character, naive or easily led. In the presence of Charles, Cails and Battolla this is easy to see. Deakin however, was certainly not stupid and was widely known for his strong Socialist views. No doubt the main reason why Deakin went to prison was because he ran the Walsall Socialist Club, which provided a safe haven for extreme Anarchists. Whether the others actually exploited and took advantage of him may never be known. Deakin was released from prison in January, 1896 and he returned to his home town of Walsall, where he continued with his life. [221]

The experience of prison must have weighed heavy on Deakin's mind, as he never sought to take a prominent role in politics again. He did however retain his strong Socialist views and interest in politics keeping strong connections with the labour movement.

At the time of the 1901 census, Deakin was forty-two years old and employed as a commercial clerk. He lived with his elderly parents and two sisters at the family home of 238, Stafford Street. [222]

By the 1911 census, Deakin was a fifty-two year old wood turners clerk, still living at 238, Stafford Street. Both of his parents had passed away, but three of his adult sisters, Lucy Ann, Eliza and Ellen all lived with him. All his siblings, except for his brother Charles were unmarried and childless. His two older sisters ran a fancy ladies outfitters shop. [223]

Joseph Deakin lived a relatively long life, dying in Walsall aged seventy-nine on the 7th of September, 1937. This was just a few months after his friend, Haydn Sanders died in Lowestoft. Whether they ever kept in touch is unknown, but it seems unlikely due to Sanders drastic change in his political beliefs. Deakin's funeral was at Ryecroft Cemetery on the 10th of September, 1937. The burial was attended by his brother Charles and other family members, but also the Mayor of Walsall, A. J. Stanley, Aldermen Millerchip, Thickett and Hucker and Councillor Whiston.

An obituary appeared in the local newspaper confirming that he was not forgotten by the Walsall Socialists, it simply read "Joseph Thomas Deakin, last of the old Socialist guard. He nailed his colours to the mast and steadfastly kept the faith." It was sent in by Comrades Johnson, Farnol, Giles and Cooper.

Apart from his involvement in the Anarchist Plot, he lived a relatively quiet life and never married. In the eyes of many, he was forever viewed with suspicion, tainted as the 'Anarchist.' Despite this he was well regarded and respected by the Socialist and Labour groups.

They saw Deakin as a clever knowledgable man and valued his opinion. To the very end Deakin maintained to his closest friends, that he was framed for the Anarchist Plot. [224] [225]

Fred Charles was visited in prison at Portland by Councillor Roberts from Walsall on Whit Monday, 1896. Charles told him he had trained as a carpenter, wood turner and mechanic and earned all the good conduct points for an early release. They discussed the impending decision on the sentences, but Charles never expected a day off his term. Charles told him that Cails was also at Portland, working in the quarry and Battolla was at Dartmoor shoemaking. [226]

Charles was visited in late 1896 by his friend Edward Carpenter, who gave him the sad news that William Morris had died on the 3rd of October. The news of his friend's death, allegedly brought tears to his eyes. Charles struck up a 'pen pal' relationship at prison with Charlotte Skerritt, an independently wealthy teacher and fellow Anarchist from Oxford.

In 1899, after seven and a half years of his ten year sentence, Charles was released and Skerritt met him at the prison gates. Her money took him on a grand tour of Europe, to help him recover from the years of incarceration. When they returned to England in the spring of 1900, they married at Norwich and set up their first home in his birth town. [227]

Later the couple moved to the Summertown district of Oxford, where Charlotte previously lived. In March 1909, Dennis Hird the principal of Ruskin College, Oxford was sacked for his socialist teachings. A new college was set up, where until the middle of 1911, Fred Charles did occasional lectures on political history.

At the time of the 1911 census, Fred and Charlotte lived at Bedford Lodge, South Parade, Oxford. He was described as 'living on his own private means,' which basically meant they still had money in the bank to live off. [228]

The couple invested money in a couple of failed market gardening ventures, first at Marston, just outside Oxford and then at Kidlington. In the 1920s they both retired to the Whiteway Colony of Socialists, where they worked as volunteers. In her book, Nellie Shaw described him, 'the picturesque sturdy figure, with sun-tanned face and white hair and moustache, clothed in a rough tweed knickerbocker suit, who with the inevitable heavy walking-stick, trudged about in our midst. He really looked just like a retired military officer, though a more peacefully disposed man never existed.'

Fred Charles always was and stayed throughout his life a full supporter of the Communist Soviet way. His wife Charlotte, died and was buried at St. Andrew's, Miserden in August 1925. [229] [230] [231]

Fred Charles died at the Whiteway Colony on the 17th of November, 1934 and was buried three days later in the same grave as his wife. [232] [233]

Victor Cails and Jean Battolla were the last of the Walsall Anarchists to be released from prison. Cails left Portland prison in December, 1899, but found it very difficult to get work as a foreigner without any references. He believed his written references were seized by Walsall Police when he was arrested at the Socialist Club in 1892. In desperation he wrote to Walsall Police asking for any paperwork to be returned and on the 8th of March, 1900, Chief Inspector Gore wrote back, to say that everything had gone to Stafford Assizes and nothing was retained to Walsall. [234]

Cails visited New Scotland Yard hoping to speak with William Melville about his paperwork. He waited over two hours for Melville to turn up, only to be told that the case was dealt with at Walsall and their Chief Constable had all the documents. [235]

In April 1900, Walsall's Town Clerk wrote to Cails saying that he had found some English translations from the original trial papers, including two certificates from former employers. [236]

When Cails and Battolla were released they sought out old friends in the East End of London for help, both were supposedly broken men in a pitiful physical condition. David Nicoll arranged a musical charity event at the Imperial Rooms, Mile End on the 28th of April, 1900 and sold tickets at sixpence each to raise funds. [237]

In September 1900, Cails made an official complaint against the Metropolitan Police, because he was convinced they were still 'shadowing' him. After making his complaint he believed they stopped. [238]

Cails maintained his friendship with other prominent Socialists, including Louise Michel and Dr. Creaghe and eventually found some work as a mariner.

In November 1905, Cails gave evidence at the libel hearing in London of the retired Scotland Yard detective, Inspector John Sweeney. John Sweeney was one of the officers present when Battolla was arrested in 1892 and he gave evidence at the Mowbray and Nicoll trial. Sweeney was being sued by a successful Italian antiques dealer named Luigi Parmeggiani, because he had openly accused him of being a notorious 'Anarchist' and a receiver of stolen goods. The truth was Parmeggiani had been an Anarchist, but had since come good as a successful businessman and turned his back on his old comrade friends. When he decided to sue Sweeney it backfired, as several of his old Anarchist friends were ready to bring him down for betrayal.

Victor Cails told the court that he was an Anarchist, who had been sentenced to ten years imprisonment for manufacturing bombs at Walsall in 1892. Cails confirmed Parmeggiani was an Anarchist and a frequent visitor to the Autonomie Club in its heyday. After Cails was released from prison, Parmeggiani made it clear it was bad for business and told his old Anarchist friends to keep away from him. Parmeggiani lost the case and Sweeney was awarded costs. [239]

In March 1926, the French anarchist newspaper L'En Dehors (The Outside), reported his death, "Victor Cails, who was built with lime and sand.., had courageously set to work and had exhausted himself there." [240]

Jean Joseph Battolla was released from Dartmoor on the 16th of September, 1899, around the same time as Cails. Both struggled on the outside of prison and relied on the help of old friends.

On Wednesday the 7th of January, 1903, Jean Battolla appeared before Bow Street Police Court having been summoned for failing to maintain his wife. Battolla was described as a boarding house keeper, living at 99, Gower Street, London and his wife Josephine Eugenie, was staying at 30, Goodge Street, Tottenham Court Road. Battolla's wife was represented by a solicitor Mr. Harry Wilson, who said they were married at Marseilles in 1883. He said that Battolla was released from prison in 1899, after being convicted of manufacturing bombs at Walsall in 1892. Wilson said it was at Battolla's request that his wife visited him and she stayed at one of the several boarding houses opened with the proceeds of a fund collected for him on his release. After a few days, Battolla demanded she leave as his housekeeper was unhappy. The housekeeper ended up assaulting Mrs. Battolla and was bound over to keep the peace by the magistrates. Mr. Wilson said that Battolla had an income of around £20 per week from three boarding houses he ran in partnership with a woman named Bennett who lived with him. The Magistrate commented that he never heard a worse case and ordered Battolla to pay £2 per week maintenance and two guineas costs. [241]

Sometime later Battolla returned to his native Italy. He sailed from Genoa, Italy on the 19th of April, 1910, aboard the SS Oceania landing at New York on the 2nd of May with a new family. He was forty-eight years old and his 'wife' Caterina was twenty-five. They had two children, a son Dante, who was five and a daughter Algeriade who was four. [242]

On the 31st of October, 1911, Battolla swore an oath of allegiance to become a citizen of the United States. In doing so he had to clearly declare that he was not an Anarchist, a prerequisite of citizenship and he signed to secure his stay. [243]

On the 1st of June, 1915, Battolla lived with his twelve year old son, Dante at 223, Sullivan Street, New York. He was employed as a boot maker, so he evidently kept to his old trade in order to make money in the new country. [244]

In 1920 he lived alone in 49th Street, New York, where he still worked as a shoe maker. From that time onwards, both him and any of his known family disappear into obscurity and I have found no further records or references about them. 245

William Ditchfield stayed in Walsall after being acquitted at the trial. The 1901 census at the end of March, shows his family resided at 97, Hatherton Street, Skating Rink Yard and comprised of three daughters, his son-in-law and three grandchildren. Unfortunately his wife, Ellen had been admitted to the lunatic asylum at Burntwood in 1900 and she died there in 1902. 246 247 248 249

In 1904, Ditchfield aged fifty-six married a widow Matilda Adams at Dudley and they had a daughter named Rose together that year. 250 251

At the time of the 1911 census, Ditchfield lived at 145, Portland Street with his wife Matilda, his two youngest daughters, Lucy and Rose and his step-daughter, Alice Adams. Ditchfield was a sixty-three year old spring bar maker with his own business. 252

In 1912 the Ditchfield's became the proprietors of a fried Fish and Chip shop at 1, Portland Street. They were still in business at the same address in 1916, during World War One. 253 254

William Ditchfield died on the 16th of January, 1928, aged 79 years, leaving an estate valued at £1,647 8s. 1d. At the time of his death he still resided in Portland Street. His wife and daughter Rose, put a verse in the local newspaper, 'He bore his pain, he bore it well, what he suffered none can tell.' 255 256 257

John Westley returned to his wife and family in Walsall after his acquittal. He was active in the Anarchist campaign for the release of the others and took part in the anniversary demonstration conference at Walsall on Easter Sunday, on the 2nd of April 1893. 258

In 1895, Detective Sergeant McIntyre (see below) published his memoirs in Reynolds's Newspaper after resigning from the Metropolitan Police. Westley wrote a letter in response to his article, suggested that Coulon was the reason why Battolla and Melville came to Walsall and why Deakin and Battolla were to meet at Euston. John

Westley thought the bombs were always destined to be captured by the police. [259]

In 1901 Westley was a forty year old commercial traveller, dealing in brushes and lived at 33, Ford Street with his wife and five daughters. By 1911 the family had moved to Rose Villa, 32, Hillary Street, Pleck, where he worked as a brush salesman. [260] [261]

John Westley died at Walsall aged fifty-three years on the 20th of January, 1916. [262] [263]

Edmond Joseph Guillemard was first mentioned by Deakin when he spoke to the police in the cells at Walsall. Deakin said Guillemard's brother in Brussels was a pattern maker and they asked him for help. Ultimately the brother had no involvement, but did end up paying off Edmond's debts, suggesting he was in some sort of financial difficulty at the time.

Mysteriously, Guillemard is almost conspicuous by his absence in the proceedings as he was both a member of the Socialist Club and a Frenchman, with the language skills to understand what was going on. Some suspicion must fall on Guillemard as there is no evidence to suggest that he was ever questioned by the police at any time. This is strange, because of his closeness to the others and adding to the intrigue, is the fact that after the trial, although his family were well settled with strong family ties in the town, he up sticks and left without any apparent reason. [264] [265]

In 1901, the whole family seem to have reinvented themselves at 2, Pond Street, Lincoln, where peculiarly they dropped the name Guillemard in favour of his wife's maiden name of Acton. Edmond also gave his birthplace as Cardiff, maybe to explain away his French accent? [266]

At the time of the 1911 census, the fifty-five year old Edmund Acton, now born in Caerphilly was employed as a brass moulder living at 11, Norfolk Street, Lincoln. [267]

On the 20th of October, 1917, at the age of sixty-one, Guillemard was convicted at Lincoln under the name of Acton for receiving stolen metal. He pleaded not guilty, but was sentenced to twelve months imprisonment with hard labour. [268]

Guillemard died on the 11th of February, 1924 at Lincoln and was buried at Newport Cemetery three days later. His wife died on the 1st of April, 1926. Both their deaths and burials were registered under the correct legal name of Guillemard. [269] [270] [271]

His actions after the trial bare all the hallmarks of a man running away from something. It also stinks of him having received some money from an uncertain source to facilitate it. His later conviction for receiving stolen goods, casts a doubt over his integrity, was he the man who helped convict his fellow comrades, was he a dishonest character or police informant? After changing his identity, there is no evidence to say he ever returned to Walsall. Whatever his reasons, it must certainly be considered very suspicious.

Auguste Coulon, under the control of Detective Inspector William Melville is the prime suspect for being the police informant on the job. Melville always refused to answer certain questions about him, either at the Magistrates Court or the Assizes, but to be fair this was standard practice under those circumstances. He was certainly suspected by David Nicoll, who named him when he wrote 'The Walsall Anarchists - Trapped by the Police' in 1892. In that document, David Nicoll credits Coulon with very little intellect and suggests that most of his ideas came directly from Melville himself. Nicoll's dislike of the police and the authorities was well known, so his views are far from impartial and he did have convictions himself. It must be said, that even if Coulon was a police informant, it is a leap of faith to say he engineered the whole plot. The payment of an informant does not in itself imply that they were an 'agent provocateur,' a term given to someone who acts in a certain way, to make a crime happen. In simple terms a police informant is simply someone who tells the police about something they have found out about, in the normal course of their day.

Coulon was undeniably well placed to supply information about the Anarchist groups with his strong links to the Autonomie Club.

Either way there is little doubt that, Charles, Cails and Battolla were extremist Anarchists, well capable of thinking up the plot all by themselves, without any assistance from Coulon.

Coulon was thrown out of the Autonomie Club after the arrests were made and he was openly accused of being a police spy and traitor. For a time he vanished from his address at Fitzroy Square, as some Anarchists went looking for him. Allegedly they went to his address, but were quickly surrounded by police officers who warned them about their conduct. The Anarchists took this as proof he was under police protection. David Nicoll, was convinced the police were paying for a safe house above a tobacconist shop in Brixton, while Coulon lived the life of Reilly.

In 1894, Coulon asked for an announcement to be published in the 'Liberty' newspaper. Instead of the announcement they put a message to him saying, 'We have thrown your announcement into the waste paper basket. In future limit your communications to Scotland Yard.' At that time he lived at 85, Sistova Road, Balham. [272]

In 1901, Coulon was described as a fifty-five year old house decorator, living with his wife and two children at 97, Cathles Road, Streatham, London. On the 1911 census, he was a sixty-five year old paperhanger living with his wife at 61, Bedford Road, Clapham. It was clear that any money he did get from the police was long gone. [273][274]

Auguste Coulon, died aged seventy-eight on the 22nd of October, 1923 and was buried at Wandsworth cemetery. [275] [276]

Charles Wilfred Mowbray never stopped his political activities after his acquittal at the trial with David Nicoll in 1892. In May 1893, Mowbray and Louise Michel gathered a crowd of about five hundred Anarchist's at Hyde Park. A handbill was circulated entitled 'What Anarchist's Want' and contained the words, "Force and violence keep you in chains while your master robs you. Force can only be repelled by force. By force alone you will at last be able to break the chains of your slavery." [277]

By the end of 1893, Mowbray was making threats of violence at Tower Hill with John Williams, warning the authorities to feed the poor before they rise up against them. He issued a veiled threat to property in London, by saying anything could happen under the cover of a few days of fog. [278]

In summer 1893, Mowbray and other Anarchists were excluded from the Second International of the Socialist Zurich Congress. Mowbray wrote an article, 'Trades Unionism and the Unemployed,' where he called for unity between the employed and unemployed, an overtime ban, an eight hour day and the abolition of piecework.

The Socialist League finally disappeared in 1894, around the same time that Mowbray married his second wife Charlotte Smith.

Mowbray travelled to the United States to preach the word, but his Anarchist agitation got him expelled from the country. He returned via Liverpool on the 25th of February, 1900, on board the SS Etruria. [279]

At the time of the 1901 census, he lived with his wife Charlotte and their children at 31 Eve Road, West Ham. [280]

He became involved in the unemployed movement which evolved after the 'Triangle Camp' fiasco in West Ham. His wife Charlotte died in 1906 and he married for a third time in 1909, to Eliza Hunt. [281]

In 1906, together with some other Socialists, he accepted a job of Tariff Reform lecturer. He toured the country for the National Union of Conservative Associations, denouncing most of the causes he had once staunchly advocated.

In December, 1910, while his family were back at home at Chestnut Grove, Forest Gate, he was on tour in Bridlington, Yorkshire supporting the Conservative Major Mark Sykes. On Friday the 9th of December, 1910, his dead body was found in the hotel bed where he was staying. By some strange twist of fate, Major Sykes opponent was Sir Luke White, the Coroner for the district, in which capacity he oversaw Mowbray's inquest. The final outcome was that he died from heart failure at the age of fifty-four. [282]

His obituary described him as the once, "sinewy, athletic, black-haired, determined man, with the blazing eyes of a fanatic and tempestuous eloquence that stirred many open-air meeting." He was buried in West Ham cemetery, but his grave has been subsequently been built over. [283] [284]

William Melville's long career was filled with adventure. On the 4th of April, 1894, he was boarding a train with his wife at Victoria Station, when his attention was drawn to a man on the platform who he thought he knew. The man was in fact the notorious French Anarchist, Théodule Meunier wanted for a bomb attack at the café Very in Paris on the 25th of April, 1892, where several people were killed. Meunier had been on the run for almost two years, but as Melville got closer he recognised him. There was a desperate attempt to escape, as Melville tried to arrest him and the two men fell on the station platform locked in a violent struggle. Melville's strength prevailed and he managed to overpower Meunier and detain him. Mrs. Melville casually walked over and handed both men their silk hats, which had fallen off in the commotion. At Bow Street Magistrates Court, Meunier looked directly at Melville and yelled, "To fall into your hands, Melville!", " You, the only man I feared, and whose description was engraved on my mind." Meunier was extradited to France where he was sentenced to life imprisonment. He was killed trying to escape from Cayenne penal colony in 1907. [285]

On the 19th of April, 1894, William Melville was promoted to Chief Inspector and took charge of the department at New Scotland Yard.

Melville's detective reputation was well established when he and his family visited his home town of Kerry for a holiday in September 1896. A local newspaper ran the story, "Chief Inspector Melville of Scotland Yard... is a native of Sneem in this county and has been there on holidays lately. He acted as one of the judges at the sports recently held in Sneem, and only left there for London on Monday week. Mr. Melville was a promising athlete before he went to London many years ago and was considered one of the best hurlers in South Dunkerron at the time. He takes a great interest in athletic sports and is a prominent supporter of the Gaelic Athletic Society." [286]

In 1896, Melville met and recruited the spy, Shlomo Rosenblum, who later assumed the name Sidney George Reilly. This man, has been the subject of books and television programmes and is generally believed to be the first 20th century super spy. Ian Flemming supposedly modelled his character James Bond on the exploits of Reilly, created in real life by Melville. It is also believed that Melville was the inspiration for 'M' the head of the Secret Service in the movies.

On the 2nd of January, 1900, Melville, became Superintendent at New Scotland Yard's, Special Branch, when John Littlechild his predecessor retired. In June 1900, Melville allegedly met the stage entertainer and magician, Harry Houdini, who went to New Scotland Yard to showcase his abilities as an escapologist. Houdini demonstrated how easy it was to release himself from police issue handcuffs and Melville befriended him and reputedly learnt lock picking.

At the time of the 1901 census, Melville lived at 16, Lydon Road, Clapham, with his wife and three children. [287]

He retired as superintendent from the Metropolitan Police with his last working day being on the 30th of November, 1903. In reality Melville had not retired at all, he was head hunted for a special secret role at the War Office, who set up a Directorate of Military Operations in 1903. Melville worked covertly on secret missions under the pseudonym of William Morgan from an office at 25, Victoria Street, adjacent to New Scotland Yard.

In 1909, the Government Committee on Intelligence, established a new Secret Service Bureau, with a Home Section under the command of Sir Vernon Kell and a Foreign Section under Sir Mansfield Cumming. Melville was second-in-command at Vernon Kell's department, which although acting in Home matters, remained subordinate to the War Office. By 1910, Kell's department, the Security Service (MI5) separated from Cummings, Secret Intelligence Service (MI6).

At the time of the 1911 census, Melville was described as a sixty-year old police pensioner, living at 24, Orlando Road, Clapham with his wife, daughter Kate and son James Benjamin. [288]

Melville's department at the Security Service bore fruit in 1912, when they uncovered Gustav Steinhauer's network of German secret agents. When war broke out in 1914, the entire network of twenty-one German spies were rounded up in one go, crippling the Kaiser's operation in Britain.

The Secret Service rapidly expanded during World War One, and this included the addition of a 'Spy School' to train new recruits, enhancing the nations intelligence capabilities. Melville frequently lectured at the new facility, but the war ultimately proved exhausting for him. Melville's health deteriorated drastically and he was forced to retire from the service on the 31st of December, 1917. King George V awarded Melville an MBE in the New Year Honours of 1918, in acknowledgement of all his hard work. [289]

Unfortunately, Melville was gravely ill and following an unsuccessful operation at Bolingbroke Hospital, Wandsworth, he died of kidney failure on the 1st of February, 1918. He was buried at St. Mary's Roman Catholic Cemetery, Kensal Green, London. [290] [291]

Probate was completed at London on the 20th of April, 1918, with Melville's estate worth £11,170 7s. 10d. (£920,400 approximate value 2023) [292] [293]

When Melville died, he was the most internationally decorated detective officer the Metropolitan Police had ever known. His talents had led him to end his career at the very top of the Secret Service. During his service Melville amassed a large collection of jewels and gifts, which were left to his children. These included gifts presented by Queen Victoria, King Edward VII, King George V, the German Emperor, the King of Spain, the Czarevitch, Princess Beatrice and several others. He left his manuscripts and memoirs to his son James Benjamin, on the understanding that if they were ever published, the proceeds would be divided between his three children. A lot of his work was of course covered by the Official Secrets Act at that time. [294] [295]

In 2016 his medals were auctioned at Lockdales of Ipswich. They included his, MVO, Royal Victorian Medal (No. 41), MBE, Coronation Police Medal 1902, Neck Badge of the Commander of the Order of Isabel la Catolica (Spain), Officer of the Legion of Honour (France), Order of St. Sava 1883 (Serbia), Order of Saint Sylvester 1905 (Vatican). Included was his police whistle, four original testimonials issued by the Mayor of the City of Westminster and a type written Branch Memoranda giving a full account of his career from 1903 to 1917. The valuers estimation was given at between £1,000 - £1,200, but the hammer went down at £4,400.

Both Melville's sons served in the British army during World War One. James Benjamin Melville was a barrister and strangely defended many Anarchists, including Yourka Dubof and Jacob Peters in 1911. They were suspects in the Sidney Street siege or Battle of Stepney, a gunfight in the East End between the police and a gang of Latvian revolutionaries. Three policemen were killed and two others injured and the army had to be called in to bring the siege to an end. At court, James Melville managed to get both men acquitted, which badly embarrassed the then Home Secretary, Winston Churchill.

James Benjamin Melville was appointed to the King's Counsel (KC) on 29th of March, 1927. At the time he was the youngest person to have held the title and remained so for a number of years.

The name Melville briefly returned to Walsall in 1927 when James Benjamin Melville KC, son of the detective became the prospective parliamentary Labour candidate for Walsall. On Saturday the 27th of March, 1927 Melville spoke at the annual re-union of the Walsall Labour Party in the Town Hall. Who knows if Joseph Deakin was present in the same room, or if he got to meet the son of the man who convicted him?

James Melville became HM Solicitor-General on the 12th of June, 1929 and was knighted two days later at St. James's Palace by the Prince of Wales. When it came to the 1929 General Election, Sir James Melville did not stand for Walsall, but he did become the Labour MP for Gateshead, where he served until his death on the 1st of May, 1931. He died aged forty-six, his life being cut short by the effects of injuries he sustained during World War One. He left an estate valued at almost two million pound by todays (2023) prices. [296] [297] [298] [299] [300]

Sir Patrick Quinn was an Irishman by birth, born in County Mayo in 1855. In 1903 he succeeded William Melville as Superintendent in charge of the Special Branch. He amassed numerous honours during his police career. These included being an Officer of the Legion of Honour and an officer the L'Instruction Publique (France), a Knight of the Order of the Dannebrog (Denmark), of the Order of Vasa (Sweden), of the Order of St. Olav (Norway), of the Order of St. Stanislas (Russia), of the Order of the Redeemer (Greece), of the Order of the Crown (Italy) and of the Order of Villa Viçosa (Portugal), a member of the first class of the Order of Military Merit (Spain) and of the fifth class of the Royal Victorian Order MVO. He was awarded the King's Police Medal KPM.

He retired from the police in 1919 and was knighted at Buckingham Palace on the 18th of March, 1919, being the first police detective to be awarded the honour. He died at his home 28, Montserrat Road, in Putney on the 9th of June, 1936.

Hugh Holmes Gore, who was the solicitor, representing Fred Charles at Walsall Magistrates, mysteriously went missing and vanished in 1898. It is generally believed he engineered his own disappearance, when he was about to be exposed as an homosexual. Was he trying to avoid scandal, no one knows, he never turned up again!

William Nicholls, the young lad who took the parcel to Bullows foundry for Westley, never married and died at Walsall in 1907, aged just 28 years. [301]

Sarah Higgins the woman at Bullows foundry, went on to be the manageress at Henry Moseley & Sons in Bath Street in 1911. At that time she was still a fifty-one year old single lady. It was reasonably unusual for a woman to hold such a high position at the time, especially as she was from Irish descent. I can't find any confirmed records for a marriage or subsequent death for her. [302]

Frederick Brown, the electrical engineer cum explosive man, originally started in Walsall as a photographer in partnership with Mr. Draycott on The Bridge. Later he became the manager of the Wednesbury and Wolverhampton district of the National Telephone Company. He resigned from the company on the 31st of December, 1884 and created the Walsall Electrical Company. When the company was 'limited' in 1892, he became the managing director. He was appointed as the Walsall Corporation electrical engineer and in that capacity he went on a fact finding mission to the United States looking at trams. He was instrumental in the design and introduction of the trolley system of electrically powered trams on his return to Walsall. Apart from his connection to the Chamber of Commerce, he took no real part in public life. He died at his home Brynllyn, Rosemary Hill Road, Streetly on the 8th of August, 1913 aged sixty-five. [303]

Fred Henderson, who was Fred Charles controversial brother-in-law, served his whole life in politics on Norwich Council, becoming an Alderman and later Lord Mayor 1939-1940. In 1947, Henderson was granted the freedom of the City of Norwich, where sixty years earlier in 1887, he had been imprisoned in Norwich Castle gaol. He died on the 18th of July, 1957 aged 90 years. [304]

David John Nicoll, scraped his way through later life, suffering from mental health issues and poverty. He could be found at times selling pamphlets on street corners for a few pennies. At the age of fifty-nine he was admitted to St. Pancras Hospital, where he died on the 2nd of March, 1919. He was buried in an unmarked grave at St. Pancras and Islington cemetery.

Patrick McIntyre, was one of the Detective Sergeants who worked with Melville and arrested Charles Mowbray. He was born in Northern Ireland and joined the Metropolitan Police in 1878 at the age of eighteen. In 1883 he became one of the original officers on the Special Irish Branch working under Melville. McIntyre was later busted down from Detective Sergeant to uniformed constable, by Assistant Commissioner Robert Anderson. McIntyre said the official reason was for falsifying a report after returning from leave. The real reason was his association with a widow Mrs. White, an Anarchist, who he first met after she visited David Nicoll at Newgate Prison. McIntyre claimed his relationship with her was purely professional, but he still resigned from the police. In 1895, McIntyre released a series of stories in the columns of Reynolds's Newspaper about his life in the police. These stories cover several of the jobs he worked on, but he hardly mentions Melville. In his column, he said that many agent provocateurs were known to frequent the Autonomie Club, so the wise refugees such as Prince Kropotkin never went there. He also said an agent provocateur manufactures more 'danger' to make money when 'danger' diminishes. Auguste Coulon wrote to the paper stating that McIntyre was a liar, selling his story for money and that some of what he said was "twaddle." Coulon did admit however, that he offered his services to Scotland Yard and they accepted them. In reply to Coulon's letter, McIntyre said, Coulon was an informant, but he was not the only one in employed by Scotland Yard at the Autonomie Club. [305] [306] [307] [308] [309]

The Bombs - In 2005 John D. Harper wrote a detailed article about the Walsall Bombs, which was published in Historical Metallurgy Journal. John was well qualified to write on the subject, being an expert in his field and the great nephew of Frank Bullows at the Walsall foundry in Long Street. In his personal possession, he had two of the three known surviving examples of the Walsall Bomb, the other being held by Walsall Museum. The bombs themselves were basically a primitive design for a hand grenade, although the British Army had no comparative weapons of this description in 1892. Harper's article concludes, 'Despite the unanswered questions, the physical evidence and trial reports leave no doubt that the principal conspirators, whether or not victims of a police trap, were guilty of trying to make bombs for terrorist purposes. They were not however very competent. The design of the bombs, and of the patterns and casting method used to make them, is technically inept, showing ignorance of foundry methods and elementary ballistics. More competent terrorists would have recruited someone with technical experience and briefed the pattern-makers more carefully.'

I think his opinion fairly represents the evidence produced at court. Interestingly Alfred Bullows foundry in Long Street did go on to make hand grenades, The Mills No. 36 for the British military during World War Two. In the 1960's Bullows became a subsidiary of Binks an American firm making spray equipment. Binks Bullows was at Bullows Road in Brownhills until its final closure.

This book probably raises more questions than it answers, please feel free to fill in the gaps, I hope you enjoyed the history!

You probably think I forgot about Christopher Taylor, the illustrious Chief Constable. His story will be told in full in my next book!

The Shadow of Yesterday
Follows the Light of Today
Into Every Tomorrow!
PR©

The End

The Anarchist Literature - Used at the Trial

Means of Emancipation.

Firstly, in order to arrive at a complete emancipation of humanity, brutal force is indispensable, whatever may say all Theoreticians (the Devil take them). In fact, it is absolutely necessary to act with violence against all that is bad. Otherwise, we shall always be slaves and starving. If we look in the most distant history, from tribe to tribe we see everywhere that violence is and always will be the mother of conquest.

Property in any form is nothing but the result of theft and assassination. Consequently, the more a man has assassinated and robbed, the more he has become rich and powerful. That is why we Anarchists always affirm that property is a theft. This method of individual property, being consequently the true cause of human misfortune, ought to be destroyed entirely, because it has produced a whole arsenal of infamous laws; it has created skilful robbers, able to defend so far all that they have robbed, and who enjoy, boldly and peacefully, the fruit of their crimes.

Then, if it is necessary to put down all political, military, and religious authority, as well as all those law manufacturers, it is absolutely necessary to burn the churches, palaces, convent, soldier barracks,, prefactures, mayors houses, lawyers and barristers' offices, fortresses, prisons, and to destroy entirely all that has lived till now, without contributing to it.

We must then, at any cost, take possession of the land, machines, all working instruments, railroads, telephones, and all that gold and science have placed till now in the hands only of the rich, who use them to make us produce the gold. We must also pull down our huts, for so long witnesses of our sufferings and we must inhabit those beautiful palaces we have built. After that only, we shall be able to proclaim loudly the era of justice and humanity. As it is necessary to place all the national riches at the disposal of those who work, we shall contrive also that

the blood which will flow in the streets be not ours, but that of the infamous rich who have starved us. Henceforth, that is our first and veritable work, without minding the band of politicians and Orators of the Congress. As to the tactics which consist the establish Communism, and to set rules for the future without having first put down the barbarous system of the rich, we do not hesitate to declare them entirely

wrong. In fact, in all the revolutionary periods, ambitious men have always made use of known programmes in order to satisfy their greed of power, and having reached it, they have only put by the grand day of social conquest which is to consecrate at last the entire liberty of the workers. That is why, after so many regulations, the slaves still remain and increase constantly the number of those who are starving. On the other has, how do we know that

amidst the future revolution, we shall not find among obscure men, some resolute spirits, fall of audacity and possessing ideas greater and more advanced than ours. Consequently, if, as in the past we were seeking by established precedent to create a narrow circle for future, we should be compelled to slaughter all those who should attempt to infringe the limits of the programme decided on; and certainly in the effervescence of the struggle for or against the said programme, many superior, intelligent, men would be the victims of poplar ignorance, or of the hatred of opponents. That would certainly happen if one or the other of the parties, Socialists or Collectivists, who both have chiefs, should obtain the supremacy against the Anarchists, who will have no chiefs, nor programmes for the future. Then the real misfortune of the next revolution would be to see these men becoming the masters of the battlefield of the social contest. Well, no more organisation, no dictators; and rather than to lose a precious time in
serving as a ladder to those rascal deceivers, let us occupy ourselves with chemistry, and let us manufacture promptly bombs, dynamite, and other explosive matters, much more efficacious than gun and barricades, to bring the destruction of the actual state of things, and, above all, to spare the precious blond of our comrades. Courage, companions! Long live Anarchy!
Signed, V. Cails., Walsall 1st September 1891. [310]

The International - No. 7 - An Anarchist Feast at the Opera

Who is the starving wretch, an Anarchist or slave, that has not shuddered with rage in thinking of the luxurious enjoyments that the rich come to seek (by means of a little gold) in a box at the opera, on the evening of a first representation? In fact, on that day, the sweaters, financiers, middlemen, magistrates, diplomatists, and moralists, all the cream of the rich and rulers of the people, have gathered together, certain of not being elbowed by low people, in order to enjoy in comfort and without trouble, a fresh spectacle, or the intoxicating music, the singing and the feminine forms (more or less tainted by disease), and to incite their senses and to awaken the passions never satiated of that race of bandits, who on the morrow are unanimously ready to draw the sweat and blood of the workers in order to recover at once the handful of gold spent on the previous evening. Well, comrades, we for whom the opera has never had any charms, because it has not been established to admit us at the auditory of the magnificent soirees, where the munificence of art contends with the brightness of diamonds and lights, can we not likewise enjoy in our turn the delightful spectacle of seeing on a fine day, or rather on a fine evening, this splendid building all in flames in the middle of a brilliant feast, and as a veritable apotheosis carried towards heaven?

Would not a single one among us feel his heart beat with an immense joy in hearing the shrivelling of the grease of the rich and the howling's of that mass of flesh swarming in the midst of that immense vessel all in a blaze? In fact, what delight, in our town, to see, even at a distance, such a red conflagration, a thousand times more beautiful to our eyes than the dazzling of the purest diamond, to hear howling's, the cries of pain and rage of the wolves, their females and young ones in midst of the furnace a thousand times more vibrating and more pleasant to our ears than the songs of half-a-dozen prostitutes above an orchestra? As to our sense of smelling, what delight of smell that flesh burning alive an odour a thousand times more pleasant to our organs than the most delicious perfumes with which that race of men and women impregnate themselves in order to conceal the rottenness which runs out of their bodies. Ah! how happy are the cannibals to be able, when chance favours them, not only to smell the flesh of their enemies boiling, but also to eat it. "The corpse of an enemy smells nice," said a despot.

Then, comrades, admitting that all tastes are natural, and ours, though different they may be, have need to be appeased in their turn. We will content ourselves by indicating the means which we think proper to satisfy them. For the present we will continue the series by saying what we think suitable concerning a gala reception at the opera. In fact, nothing more easy. A single man may act, but two are better, in order to succeed properly in the operation without any danger to them. Thus, two comrades, each provided with a strong knife, having a saw blade, and each man carrying a small bomb of very small dimensions, loaded with chlorate of potash, and having in the middle a small glass tube containing a tablespoonful of sulphuric acid. This small tube is placed erect and buried half its length in the chlorate, must be closed at top by a strong cork, and at bottom by a round piece of cork four millimetres thick (if you wish the bomb to burst at the end of two hours), because the acid requires about half an hour to pierce each millimetre through the thickness of the round piece of cork. If you wish the bomb to burst at the end of three hours the round piece of cork must be six millimetres thick, and so on, half an hour for every millimetre thickness. Moreover, comrades may try beforehand with a small pinch of chlorate (the explosion in the open air does not make much noise), and cover their faces and hands for fear of the broken pieces. These little preparatory experiments will serve them to appreciate the quality of the acid and cork used, as well as the exact time which the acid requires to pierce each millimetre of cork of the same piece. As we have said, the bombs do not require to be voluminous a simple small glass mustard pot, having the shape of a small cask lengthened, is quite sufficient for

the quantity of matter, of which here is the description: - Let us suppose that the vase contains 500 grammes of matter. You will then put first, three-fifths, viz., 300 grammes chlorate of potash ; 2nd, two-fifth, viz., 100 grammes sulphur, 3rd, one-fifth, viz., 100 grammes sugar, maintaining always these proportions according to the size of the vase. Afterwards each of these matters must be ground very fine separately, then mixed gently and thoroughly (although the operation offers not the least danger). The efficacy of the operation depends on the fine grinding and perfect mixture. After that charge the bomb, as it has been said, in a manner that the round piece of cork, four or six millimetres, be fully mixed in the matter above mentioned. These matters cost but little. The chlorate of potash is sold nearly in powder and crystallised. It must be quite dry. The sulphur is sold in small sticks of two or three centimetres diameter. The sugar must be of good quality, and quite dry. All these matters are easily crushed, afterwards the mixing is easy. The greater expense is for the two comrades, on account of the payment of their seats, which must be hired beforehand, on gala days especially. Their seats must be at the top of the theatre. Thus, the two comrades having their tickets in their pockets, go home and load their bombs only at the moment of setting out for the theatre, having calculated for the time of explosion at the end of three hours, supposing that time to be suitable. Afterwards let us suppose they have required half an hour to reach their seats in the theatre, the bombs will have then only two hours and a half to sleep. As soon as arrived the men will keep as close as possible to the walls or pillars along which the gas pipes are fixed. Then, when no one is noticing them, they begin by bursting slightly those pipes with their saw blades. It is easily done, because the lead can be cut through without any noise. When two, or three, or four of these pipes are slightly open, the men place their bombs on the ground by the side of the pipes, concealing them as much as possible from the sight of the public. They may go away quietly at the end of the first act ; the rest of the operation will be completed without them. Then they have time to go home, and even go to bed, so as to prove an alibi at the time of the explosion. Now, this is how the rest of the operation will conclude. At first, the gas escaping will ascend and accumulate under the vault of the theatre during the two hours required for the explosion of the bombs. At that time there will be a quantity sufficient to set fire everywhere and burst the roof and walls of the theatre, and the debris falling back will have the effect of grapeshot on the jolly spectators. Afterwards the fire, fed by the wood, the stuffs, and the grease, will terminate the operation suitably. As we have said at the beginning, the work is easy for two companions who live in a town where there is a large theatre suitable to receive the higher class of the inhabitants. For that it requires only hatred in the heart and to be pitiless. After all, what do we care for feelings of humanity, even with regard to the women and children of that race of robbers and real criminals? Do not their young become wolves likewise? Are their females less eager for prey than the males? On another part the workers or starving people may be tranquil, because none of them are to be seen at those feasts of gold and diamonds which too often are given in honour of any travelling monarch at the expense of the poor people. Therefore, it is pious work to profit by those frequent occasions; to crown worthily those revels which the bandits throw as a defiance at our misery and sufferings. For an Anarchist gala of that kind the little money necessary must be easier to find than for a platonic propaganda. It is saying, comrades, that certain enjoyments are still permitted to us, waiting for the grand day when the social equilibrium will be brutally established.

La Tribune Libre No.2 - 'Les Justicieres'

The monstrous errors embedded in the brains through long centuries of heredity will disappear only with the iniquitous laws which rule us; but sometimes a group of free men, sometimes a fact, make a large breach in the old edifice. The man who crushes the head of a viper or kills a mad dog has never heard other men accuse him, and never at the time when caverns existed no one among the human tribes happened to take part with the tiger or bear against those who contended for the shelter. Among men, called civilised, he who kills the mad criminal is reputed a criminal, and unfortunate men feed their children with bread red by human carnage, the killers of monster's become the executioners. Thus, Padlewsky has delivered the earth from the policeman

Seliverstoff, the assassin of 15,000 brave men by means of Siberia or the scaffold. Advice or warning to the criminal potentates of empire or republics, who mow the people as one mows the grass in the meadows. A warning to the wolves of capital and power; to all human beasts; to all them who kill by thousands in their slaughterhouses so much as the blood soaks the earth. "Blood causes vengeance to flourish as water causes the gras to bloom," said the bard of Gael. The human beasts hunting has begun, we can hear the hallali sounding through the world, when will the general scouring begin? Ah! you believe, you tyrants of Russia, France, and others, that it may last for ever, that there are no more destroyers of monsters, and that the judges wigs, the decorations, tinsel, ornaments, and fine clothes of all these potentates hinder from seeing the assassins faces. More and more frequent are the executions of policemen, traitors and tyrants of the peoples. A warning to the friends of Seliverstoff! We are no manufacturers of idols, but long live the tigers killers! Long live the revolution! Whose turn is it now? Which despot will perform so much that the act of justice would become necessary, and who will give the example of courage? For, know it well, you all, who comment only the perfect propaganda, it requires, more courage to kill than to be killed. Such is the effect of the Anarchist doctrines, they show at the same man enslaved by all the fatalities of actual society, and the necessity for destroying the institution. instead of destroying the individual. They prove also the implacable necessity not to fight, like the savages, with zagays against howitzers. In the house of combat, clemency becomes treason, we must be merciless if we do not wish always to recommence, it would be stupid and cruel. Although we are convinced that it is the duties entrusted from cursed society to its privileged ones, that make monsters of them, however, we recognise the necessity of removing these beings one removes obstacles. Now is the to time to tear every weakness from our hearts. Everyone of us ought to say If it is necessary, I will kill or shall be killed, in order that the scaffolds, the Siberians, the Tonkins may lack bodies and the milestones which crush the masses leave off grinding. The assassin of Nihilists who has been justly punished is not like the only policeman who has ended as a Czar. Katorewski who was executed by a stab was, an agent of police. Mesenzeff, who was found near a gate at Petersburg with a dagger in his back, was the chief of the secret police. The Chief of Police of Azkangel was stabbed in him own house. Sonderkine, a policeman, who searching for the executioners of Alexander II., was knocked down and killed like a dog on the banks of the Keva. There are traitors also. One of them was killed by woman named Kaluka, another was stabbed in his own house. There are some of all kinds, governors, generals, officers of gendarmerie, Maykins, Kaloff, &c, and the Russian women are as firm as the men to strike the tyrant or the traitor. Verowo which and others. Let the death of the policeman, Seliverstoff pas like a zephyr, on the faces of those who will follow. Bravo, Russians You kill the great wolves of the north. Elsewhere Duval, Pini, and all those who are led by their convictions to snatch from the talons of the capital, a particle of what has been robbed by the eternal expedition to throw it as a propaganda under the nose of the monster; everywhere those who understand that society as it is is theft and organised murder will hesitate no longer. Who has ever seen anyone scrupulous in order to escape from the cutthroat where he is struggling against the slaughterers? The whole earth but a slaughter house, where they bleed the weak and knock down the people.

Long Live the Executioners

Fight or Starve - Fellow Slaves

As the slaves of Rome were known by their scars and chains, we, the Modern Slaves, are known by our rags and pinched faces. We, of the Intentional Secret Society, appeal to you, our fellow slaves, to bear this miserable life no longer. At the present we hear horrible tales of misery and deaths from starvation, and this in the richest city and country in the world. It is a crying disgrace to us as workers that such a cowardly disposition should, exist among us, that we should hesitate.

To Take Back the Wealth - Already created by the labour of our class. He is a Coward only worthy of being a slave who will allow wife, child, or self to die in the midst of plenty. Our masters, by law, offer as the brutal alternate of the workhouse prison or casual ward, the conditions of life and labour in each being such to make it preferable to Steal—Steal. nay, Taking back part of our own! Feasting in there luxurious homes on sumptuous fair, clothed and housed as hot-house plants, what do our masters care about our misery and woe so long as we are content to starve without murmur?

Is it possible that we are so Cowardly that we will die rather than fight? Nay! a thousand times nay, Better die fighting thous starving! It is true our masters have organised Forces on their side, but we have no need to fear their Force with the Weapons which we could soon bring to hand, and such Weapons as would speedily render it utterly impossible for Police or Soldiery to act up to the brutal orders of their "commanders!" Every Worker living in a slum, or working in a Factory, knows.

The Power of Fire! - A dozen Fires in one night would render the services of fire engines useless, and if Police and Soldiers are engaged in putting out fires they cannot be engaged in firing on us!
This action on our part may be called by the rich thieves, who newer did a useful day's work in their lives, and don't mean to do, a

Destruction of Property - And some unenlightened workman will re-echo the rich thieves sentiment! But, we ask, who has the more right to Burn and Use Property—the Idlers or the Producers ? What use is the Property to us if we are to look at it and Starve? Quiet reasoning is of no avail with the Propertied Class. It is only by Striking Terror into their craven hearts by an Attack on Property that we may expect to better our lo!

There are many ways doing this, such as Non Payment of rent, Individual or Collective Thieving, or any other method which might suggest itself to you. This apathy inactivity meet not continue. Have done for ever with Charity at the hands of rich thieves, and refuse to enter their brutal Oakum Shods and Doss houses.

Revenge Revenge for the deaths of those who are daily murdered by the brutal system! For every one done to death of our class let a life of a rich robber be taken. Let no hypocritical cant on their part, solitude for the moral and spiritual welfare of the poor deceive you! They only want to humbug you into putting up with the daily miseries you endure. How do you like to read that whilst you are Slowly Starving, the wretches who live upon year Sweat and Tears are engaged in all kinds of pleasures? Have you not the courage to at least disturb their peace or will you Silently Perish in the midst of the Wealth created by yourselves? If you are not strong enough to meet them openly and wrest from them the means of life, you have at least the capacity to
Destroy their Wealth, and disturb the quiet enjoyment of their Unearned Luxuries! Sea to it, at all events, have Revenge! Revenge! [311]

About the Author

Paul Reeves was born in Walsall Wood, Staffordshire in the early 1960's, but his family has a strong affiliation with Walsall for more than two hundred years.

'Walsall Borough Police and the Hotbed of Anarchy' comes following the success of his first book 'Remember Me - The Life of A Walsall Lad' released on Amazon in June 2021.

It tells the story of his relative Henry Reeves, who had an amazingly adventurous life for a nineteenth century Walsall lad. Henry served in Walsall Borough Police during the Victorian era and by strange coincidence, Paul retired after thirty years from West Midlands Police in 2016, completing his service at Green Lane, shortly before the police stations demise. He unknowingly walked in the footsteps of Henry, without ever suspecting there had been another policeman in the family, let alone in Walsall. Most of Paul's police service was as a detective, where he wrote hundreds of lengthy Crown Court files for serious offences.

Dedication

This book is dedicated to my wife Paula, who must have sometimes wondered what the hell I was doing. She deserves a medal. - Paul R.

Acknowledgments

I was overwhelmed by the diverse range of people, who left kind comments or sent words of praise after the release of my first book in 2021. They were mostly from people who I had never met, but their simple, yet sincere reviews, were undoubtably the encouragement for me to write again, so a big thanks to everyone. The one thing I did learn from writing my first book, was there is a great interest in the local history of Walsall, so this book is for you!

Writing historical accounts is no simple task, this book alone has taken almost two years of research to obtain the material necessary. Independently publishing a book is not an easy process either, but selling and promoting is even harder.

I would like to thank the many social media pages, both local and police related, who have given me their permission to advertise my books. Most of all, the hundreds of followers who purchased my book.

Particular thanks goes to Phil Buckley (Karma Times admin), for his encouragement, reviews, photographs and general words of wisdom, but most of all for his help in promoting my work and that of other local people. Thanks also to the West Midlands Police Museum, at Steelhouse Lane Lock-up for stocking my book on their shelves.

Finally, a huge thank you to my team of proofreaders, Paula and Jenny, who spent hours to iron out some of the dyslexic spelling mistakes and basic errors I made along the way. If any mistakes have made it through, it's probably because of my constant edits due to OCD.

In writing this book, I'm fully prepared to stand corrected if any sources used prove to be factually incorrect, or if additional material was inadvertently overlooked or undiscovered. By relying on historic sources, there is always the possibility it may be wrong, or in the case of newspapers articles, tainted or biased by the political or personal views of the authors. I always welcome being informed if any mistakes are identified!

Further Reading

Research for this book has been completed using many internet based resources, which would be too exhaustive to list, but include the following: - Ancestry.co.uk, The British Newspaper Archive, Find My Past, Wikipedia.

Some of the articles and books I have read or referred to, but in no particular order: -

- Dictionary of Labour Biography: Volume XIV, edited by Keith Gildart, David Howell, Palgrave Macmillan - 2018
- Kites, Birds and Stuff: Aircraft of Great Britain Makers and Manufactures, Volume 3 - P. D. Stemp 2013
- Knights Across the Atlantic - Steven Parfitt - 2016
- The Slow Burning Fuse - The Lost History of the British Anarchists - John Quail - 1978 - theanarchistlibrary.org
- Articles Christopher Draper - radicalhistorynetwork.blogspot.com - 2017
- Romantic to Revolutionary - William Morris by E. P. Thompson - 1955
- Whiteway - A Colony on the Cotswolds - Nellie Shaw - 1935 - C.W. Daniel Company
- The Walsall Anarchists - Trapped by the Police - David Nicoll - 1892
- The Life of William Morris - J. W. Mackail - 1901
- The Walsall Anarchist Trial 1892 - West Midlands Police Museum
- The Walsall Bombs - John D Harper - Historical Metallurgy Vol. 39 No. 1 2005
- William Melville – Spymaster. An Exhibition at Kerry County Museum 2007 - Helen O'Carroll
- M: MI5's First Spymaster - Andrew Cook - 2006
- Confessions of an Anarchist - W.C. Hart - Wyman and Sons, Ltd. - 1906

Signposts to the Past - Source Records

[1] England & Wales, Civil Registration Birth Index: Charles Wilfred Mowbray born Bishops Auckland Q3/1856 (Volume 10a, Page 12)
[2] 1871 England Census: Class: RG10; Piece: 5089; Folio: 85; Page: 8; GSU roll: 847387
[3] 1881 England Census: Class: RG11; Piece: 5002; Folio: 7; Page: 8; GSU roll: 1342204
[4] The Globe - Monday 21 September 1885 - Page 5
[5] Eastern Evening News - Monday 28 September 1885 - Page 3
[6] Eastern Evening News - 18 February 1886 - Page 3
[7] Eastern Evening News - 24 February 1886 - Page 2
[8] Eastern Evening News - 4 March 1886 - Page 3
[9] Eastern Evening News - 7 April 1886 - Page 4
[10] Eastern Evening News - 8 April 1886 - Page 3
[11] Norfolk News - 17 April 1886 - Page 12
[12] Illustrated Police News - Saturday 5 June 1886 - Page 4
[13] London Evening Standard - Tuesday 15 June 1886 - Page 4
[14] Lynn Advertiser - Saturday 22 January 1887 - Page 3
[15] The Salisbury Times - Saturday 22 January 1887 - Page 7
[16] England & Wales, Criminal Registers, 1791-1892: Class: HO 27; Piece: 207; Page: 280
[17] Lowestoft Journal - Saturday 22 October 1887 - Page 2
[18] Commonweal - Saturday 12 November 1887 - Page 361
[19] Illustrated London News - Saturday 17 December 1887 - Page 6
[20] London Evening Standard - 19 December 1887 - Page 3
[21] England & Wales, Civil Registration Birth Index: Haydn Sanders born Walsall Q1/1860 (Volume 6b, Page 582)
[22] 1861 England Census; Class: RG 9; Piece: 2012; Folio: 22; Page: 38; GSU roll: 542902
[23] 1871 England Census; Class: RG10; Piece: 2965; Folio: 49; Page: 8; GSU roll: 836429
[24] 1881 England Census; Class: RG11; Piece: 2828; Folio: 13; Page: 19; GSU roll: 1341677
[25] England & Wales, Civil Registration Marriage Index: Haydn Sanders married Louisa Arnold at Birmingham Q3/1882 (Volume 6d, Page 301)
[26] Justice - Saturday 21 November 1885 - Page 5
[27] Commonweal - Saturday 19 February 1887 - Page 59
[28] Commonweal - Saturday 7 February 1887 - Page 152
[29] Walsall Observer - Saturday 16 April 1887 - Page 3
[30] Commonweal - Saturday 10 December 1887 - Page 399
[31] Commonweal - Saturday 25 February 1888 - Page 64
[32] Commonweal - Saturday 4 February 1888 - Page 40
[33] Walsall Observer - Saturday 19 May 1888 - Page 3

[34] Walsall Observer - Saturday 14 July 1888 - Page 3
[35] Justice - 11 August 1888 - Page 6
[36] Walsall Observer - Saturday 13 October 1888 - Page 3
[37] Walsall Observer - Saturday 13 October 1888 - Page 5
[38] Walsall Advertiser - Tuesday 16 October 1888 - Page 2
[39] Walsall Observer - Saturday 20 October 1888 - Page 8
[40] Walsall Observer - Saturday 20 October 1888 - Page 7
[41] Birmingham Daily Post - Tuesday 30 October 1888 - Page 6
[42] Walsall Observer - Saturday 27 October 1888 - Page 5
[43] Walsall Observer - Saturday 27 October 1888 - Page 8
[44] Walsall Observer - Saturday 3 November 1888 - Page 5
[45] Walsall Advertiser - Tuesday 16 October 1888 - Page 2
[46] Walsall Observer - Saturday 10 November 1888 - Page 5
[47] Walsall Observer - Saturday 10 November 1888 - Page 6
[48] Walsall Observer - Saturday 10 November 1888 - Page 7
[49] Walsall Observer - Saturday 24 November 1888 - Page 6
[50] Walsall Observer - Saturday 15 December 1888 - Page 7
[51] Walsall Observer - Saturday 5 January 1889 - Page 6
[52] Walsall Observer - Saturday 19 January 1889 - Page 3
[53] Walsall Observer - Saturday 16 February 1889 - Page 3
[54] Walsall Observer - Saturday 16 March 1889 - Page 3
[55] Walsall Advertiser - Tuesday 19 March 1889 - Page 2
[56] Walsall Observer - Saturday 13 April 1889 - Page 3
[57] Birmingham Daily Post - Monday 8 April 1889 - Page 8
[58] Walsall Advertiser - Saturday 13 April 1889 - Page 2
[59] Walsall Observer - Saturday 11 May 1889 - Page 2
[60] Walsall Observer - Saturday 15 June 1889 - Page 3
[61] Walsall Observer - Saturday 22 June 1889 - Page 7
[62] Walsall Observer - Saturday 22 June 1889 - Page 5
[63] Walsall Observer - Saturday 13 July 1889 - Page 3
[64] Walsall Observer - Saturday 27 July 1889 - Page 5
[65] Walsall Observer - Saturday 17 August 1889 - Page 2
[66] Walsall Observer - Saturday 28 December 1889 - Page 3
[67] Walsall Observer - Saturday 31 August 1889 - Page 8
[68] Walsall Observer - Saturday 31 August 1889 - Page 5
[69] Walsall Observer - Saturday 14 September 1889 - Page 3
[70] Walsall Observer - Saturday 12 October 1889 - Page 5
[71] Walsall Observer - 26 October 1889 - Page 5
[72] Walsall Observer - Saturday 2 November 1889 - Page 5
[73] Walsall Observer - Saturday 16 November 1889 - Page 7
[74] Walsall Observer - Saturday 23 November 1889 - Page 5
[75] Commonweal - Saturday 30 November 1889 - Page 383
[76] Walsall Observer - Saturday 14 December 1889 - Page 3
[77] Walsall Observer - Saturday 4 January 1890 - Page 5

[78] Walsall Observer - Saturday 4 January 1890 - Page 6
[79] Walsall Observer - Saturday 18 January 1890 - Page 3
[80] Walsall Observer - Saturday 26 April 1890 - Page 3
[81] Walsall Observer - Saturday 24 May 1890 - Page 6
[82] Walsall Observer - Saturday 31 May 1890 - Page 5
[83] Walsall Observer - Saturday 14 June 1890 - Page 3
[84] Walsall Observer - Saturday 13 December 1890 - Page 3
[85] Richmond and Ripon Chronicle - Saturday 18 April 1891 - Page 5
[86] 1891 England Census; Class: RG12; Piece: 3846; Folio: 109; Page: 1; GSU roll: 6098956
[87] Walsall Observer - Saturday 24 October 1891 - Page 5
[88] Commonweal - 19 January 1889 - Page 24
[89] Commonweal - 23 February 1889 - Page 61
[90] Commonweal - 29 March 1890 - Page 99
[91] Freedom (London) - Wednesday 1 April 1891 - Page 6
[92] Shields Daily News - Tuesday 24 March 1891 - Page 4
[93] Sheffield Evening Telegraph - Wednesday 12 August 1891 - Page 3
[94] Census Returns of England and Wales, 1891; Class: RG12; Piece: 2253; Folio: 48; Page: 8; GSU roll: 6097363
[95] England & Wales, Civil Registration Birth Index: Joseph Thomas Deakin born West Bromwich Q3/1858 (Volume 6b, Page 63)
[96] 1871 England Census; Class: RG10; Piece: 2989; Folio: 19; Page: 32; GSU roll: 838870
[97] 1881 England Census: Class: RG11; Piece: 2784; Folio: 99; Page: 14; GSU roll: 1341667
[98] England & Wales, Civil Registration Birth Index: John Samuel Westley born Walsall Q1/1861 (Volume 6b, Page 575)
[99] 1861 England Census: Class: RG 9; Piece: 2013; Folio: 65; Page: 29; GSU roll: 542903
[100] 1871 England Census; Class: RG10; Piece: 2961; Folio: 38; Page: 26; GSU roll: 836427
[101] England & Wales, Civil Registration Marriage Index, 1837-1915: John Westley married Ellen Larkkom at Walsall Q4/1884 (Volume 6b, Page 1052)
[102] England, Select Marriages, 1538-1973: FHL Film Number: 1526195, Reference ID: 2:3HWDPFV
[103] England & Wales, Civil Registration Death Index, 1837-1915: Horace John Westley died aged 2 at Walsall Q1/1889 (Volume 6b, Page 456)
[104] Census Returns of England and Wales, 1891; Class: RG12; Piece: 2249; Folio: 48; Page: 20; GSU roll: 6097359
[105] England, Births and Christenings, 1538-1975: FHL Film Number: 1526196, Reference ID: item 12 p 343
[106] 1871 England Census; Class: RG10; Piece: 2963; Folio: 5; Page: 5; GSU roll: 836428
[107] Select Marriages, 1538-1973: FHL Film Number: 1526195, Reference ID: 2:3HWC7HQ.

[108] Staffordshire, England, Church of England Marriages and Banns, 1754-1900: Anglican, Page number: 87.
[109] England & Wales, Civil Registration Marriage Index, 1837-1915: William Ditchfield married Helen Edwards at Walsall Q2/1871 (Volume 6b, Page 830)
[110] 1881 England Census: Class: RG11; Piece: 2824; Folio: 91; Page: 19; GSU roll: 1341676
[111] Census Returns of England and Wales, 1891; Class: RG12; Piece: 2252; Folio: 57; Page: 18; GSU roll: 6097362
[112] England & Wales, Civil Registration Birth Index: Frederic Christopher Slaughter born Norwich Q2/1864 (Volume 4b, Page 103).
[113] England & Wales, Civil Registration Death Index, 1837-1915 - Christopher SLAUGHTER died aged 73 at Norwich Q1/1868 (Volume 4b, Page 79)
[114] England & Wales, Civil Registration Marriage Index, 1837-1915: Christopher SLAUGHTER married Lucy Emily BOWMAN at Norwich Q4/1861 (Volume 4b, Page 403)
[115] 1881 England Census: Class: RG11; Piece: 1953; Folio: 10; Page: 18; GSU roll: 1341470
[116] 1871 England Census; Class: RG10; Piece: 1808; Folio: 49; Page: 13; GSU roll: 838803
[117] 1891 England Census: Class: RG12; Piece: 206; Folio: 141; Page: 25; GSU roll: 6095316
[118] Archives de l'Etat civil de Marseille 1700-1922. Série 31 : Mariages femmes 1810-1915. Paris, France: ARFIDO S.A., 2010.
[119] Church of England Marriages and Banns, 1754-1900
[120] England & Wales, Civil Registration Marriage Index, 1837-1915 : Edmond Josephe Guillemard married Rhoda Elizabeth Acton at Walsall Q1/1873 (Volume 6b, Page 703)
[121] Census Returns of England and Wales, 1881: Class: RG11; Piece: 2826; Folio: 59; Page: 14; GSU roll: 1341677
[122] Census Returns of England and Wales, 1891; Class: RG12; Piece: 2252; Folio: 54; Page: 11; GSU roll: 6097362
[123] Birmingham Daily Post - Saturday 9 January 1892 - Page 5
[124] Census Returns of England and Wales, 1891; Class: RG12; Piece: 2251; Folio: 53; Page: 37; GSU roll: 6097361
[125] Ireland, Civil Registration Marriages Index, 1845-1958 - Volume: 2, Page number: 523, FHL Film Number: 101254
[126] Commonweal - Saturday 11 September 1886 - Page 192
[127] 1888 Dublin Post Office Directory - Page 370
[128] 1889 Thom's Official Directory - Page 1888
[129] Commonweal - Saturday 19 April 1890 - Page 127
[130] Census Returns of England and Wales, 1891; Class: RG12; Piece: 120; Folio: 79; Page: 15; GSU roll: 6095230
[131] Metropolitan Police Pension Registers, 1852-1932: MEPO 21
[132] England & Wales, Civil Registration Marriage Index, 1837-1915: William Melville married Catherine Rielly at St. Saviour Q1/1879 (Volume 1d, Page 199)

[133] 1881 England Census: Class: RG11; Piece: 547; Folio: 68; Page: 20; GSU roll: 1341124
[134] England & Wales, Civil Registration Death Index, 1837-1915: Kate Melville died aged 33 years at Lambeth Q1/1889 (Volume 1d, Page 363)
[135] Census Returns of England and Wales, 1891; Class: RG12; Piece: 407; Folio: 88; Page: 10; GSU roll: 6095517
[136] England & Wales, Civil Registration Marriage Index, 1837-1915: William Melville married Amelia Foy at the Isle of Wight Q3/1891 (Volume 2b, Page 1083)
[137] Commonweal - Saturday 28 November 1891 - Page 156
[138] Sheffield Anarchist - 4 October 1891 - Page 3
[139] Commonweal - Saturday 28 November 1891 - Page 156
[140] Walsall Observer and South Staffordshire Chronicle - Saturday 9 January 1892 - Page 5
[141] Pall Mall Gazette - Monday 11 January 1892 - Page 5
[142] Walsall Observer - Saturday 16 January 1892 - Page 5
[143] Walsall Observer - Saturday 16 January 1892 - Page 5
[144] Walsall Observer - Saturday 23 January 1892 - Page 7
[145] England & Wales, Civil Registration Marriage Index, 1837-1915: James Frederick Henderson married Lucy Bowman Slaughter at Holborn Q2/1892 (Volume 1b, Page 1300)
[146] Walsall Observer - Saturday 23 January 1892 - Page 7
[147] Walsall Observer - Saturday 23 January 1892 - Page 7
[148] Walsall Observer - Saturday 30 January 1892 - Page 5
[149] Walsall Observer - Saturday 6 February 1892 - Page 3
[150] Walsall Observer - Saturday 13 February 1892 - Page 7
[151] Walsall Observer - Saturday 13 February 1892 - Page 5
[152] Walsall Observer - Saturday 20 February 1892 - Page 3
[153] Walsall Observer - Saturday 27 February 1892 - Page 5
[154] Walsall Observer - Saturday 12 March 1892 - Page 7
[155] Walsall Observer - Saturday 26 March 1892 - Page 5
[156] Justice - Saturday 5 November 1892 - Page 1
[157] Walsall Observer - Saturday 2 April 1892 - Page 7 & 8
[158] Walsall Observer - Saturday 9 April 1892 - Page 7
[159] Birmingham Daily Post - Tuesday 5 April 1892 - Page 8
[160] England & Wales, Criminal Registers, 1791-1892: Class: HO 27; Piece: 223; Page: 60
[161] UK, Calendar of Prisoners, 1868-1929: Reference: HO 140/140
[162] Walsall Observer - Saturday 23 April 1892 - Page 6
[163] The Newcastle Daily Chronicle - Thursday 21 April 1892 - Page 8
[164] Sheffield Independent - Monday 25 April 1892 - Page 5
[165] The Gloucester Journal - Saturday 30 April 1892 - Page 3
[166] Royal Cornwall Gazette - Thursday 12 May 1892 - Page 2
[167] Old Bailey Proceedings Online (www.oldbaileyonline.org, version 8.0, 27 January 2023), May 1892, trial of DAVID JOHN NICOLL (32) CHARLES WILFRED MOWBRAY (35) (t18920502-493).

[168] Home Office: Calendar of Prisoners, 1868-1929 Reference: HO 140/138 & Central Criminal Court - After Trial Calendars of Prisoners; Reference: 38 CRIM 9
[169] Sheffield Independent - Monday 2 November 1892 - Page 6
[170] Manchester Times - Friday 16 June 1893 - Page 7
[171] Clarion - Saturday 17 November 1894 - Page 4
[172] Derby Mercury - Wednesday 13 June 1894 - Page 8
[173] Derby Mercury - Wednesday 20 June 1894 - Page 7
[174] Yorkshire Factory Times - Friday 22 February 1895 - Page 8
[175] Sheffield Independent - Monday 6 May 1895 - Page 5
[176] The Evening Telegraph and Star - Friday 19 July 1895 - Page 3
[177] Sheffield Independent - Monday 21 March 1898 - Page 3
[178] Sheffield Daily Telegraph - Wednesday 18 May 1898 - Page 7
[179] Sheffield Daily Telegraph - Wednesday 17 June 1898 - Page 9
[180] Sheffield Independent - Friday 22 July 1898 - Page 6
[181] 1901 England Census Class: RG13; Piece: 3228; Folio: 53; Page: 24
[182] 1901 England Census Class: RG13; Piece: 4347; Folio: 105; Page: 5
[183] Belper News - Friday 24 June 1904 - Page 8
[184] Derbyshire Times - Wednesday 11 September 1907 - Page 2
[185] Belper News - Friday 04 December 1908 - Page 4
[186] Masters and Mates Certificates, 1850-1927, Certificate Number: 004.476 - National Maritime Museum.
[187] Hull Daily Mail - Tuesday 16 March 1909 - Page 6
[188] The Yarmouth Independent - Saturday 20 March 1909 - Page 5
[189] International Patents, 1890-2020: Publication Date: 24 Feb 1910, Publication Number: GB190919874A.
[190] Croydon Advertiser and East Surrey Reporter - Saturday 05 February 1910 - Page 7
[191] Norfolk News - Saturday 23 April 1910 - Page 5
[192] The Aero, 14 December 1910, pages 474 & 475. Dorothy M. Haward
[193] British Patent 12,195 of 1910; Improvements in Flying Machines. Application Date: 18 May 1910. Inventors: Hampden Sanders, Haydn Arnold Sanders.
[194] Field - Saturday 25 March 1911 - Page 30
[195] Walsall Observer - Saturday 11 February 1911 - Page 6
[196] England & Wales, Civil Registration Marriage Index, 1837-1915: William HODGKINS married Priscilla SANDERS at Walsall Q3/1878 (Volume 6b, Page 822)
[197] Census Returns of England and Wales, 1911 - Registration District Number: 39, Sub-registration District: South Croydon, ED, institution, or vessel: 40, Piece: 3321.
[198] Census Returns of England and Wales, 1911 - Registration District Number: 217, Sub-registration District: Beccles, ED, institution, or vessel: 03, Piece: 11009.
[199] Suffolk and Essex Free Press - Wednesday 24 July 1912 - Page 7
[200] Freemasonry Membership Registers; Description: Membership Registers: London I 2206-2535 to London J 2545-2738; Reel Number: 36
[201] West Kent Argus and Borough of Lewisham News - Friday 10 April 1914 - Page 5
[202] Newcastle Journal - Friday 27 February 1914 - Page 3
[203] Naval Medal and Award Rolls, 1793-1972 : Class: ADM 171; Piece: 63

[204] UK, British Army World War I Service Records, 1914-1920 : First World War WO363 - Haydn Sanders
[205] 1921 Census of England & Wales
[206] Uxbridge & W. Drayton Gazette - Friday 1 August 1924 - Page 8
[207] Uxbridge & W. Drayton Gazette - Friday 22 August 1924 - Page 9
[208] Bucks Herald - Saturday 02 August 1924 - Page 2
[209] Uxbridge & W. Drayton Gazette - Friday 16 May 1930 - Page 6
[210] Walsall Observer - Saturday 05 November 1932 - Page 4
[211] Calendar of the Grants of Probate and Letters of Administration made in the Probate Registries of the High Court of Justice in England. London, England © Crown copyright.
[212] Uxbridge & W. Drayton Gazette - Friday 9 April 1937 - Page 4
[213] England & Wales, Civil Registration Marriage Index, 1837-1915: Alfred CLARK married Gertrude I SANDERS at St. George Hanover Square Q3/1921 (Volume 1a, Page 1298)
[214] England & Wales, Civil Registration Death Index: Gertrude I CLARK born 19 December 1890 died aged 85 years at Westminster Q2/1976 (Volume 15, Page 1854)
[215] Principal Probate Registry. Calendar of the Grants of Probate and Letters of Administration made in the Probate Registries of the High Court of Justice in England. London, England © Crown copyright.
[216] Walsall Advertiser - Saturday 31 March 1894 - Page 2
[217] Walsall Observer - Saturday 31 March 1894 - Page 2
[218] Leeds Times - Saturday 10 November 1894 - Page 7
[219] Sheffield Evening Telegraph - Monday 5 November 1894 - Page 3
[220] Reynolds's Newspaper - Sunday 19 July 1896 - Page 1
[221] Walsall Observer - Saturday 11 January 1896 - Page 2
[222] 1901 England Census: Class: RG13; Piece: 2701; Folio: 71; Page: 24
[223] Census Returns of England and Wales 1911: Registration District Number: 370, Sub-registration District: Walsall, ED, institution, or vessel: 07, Piece: 17164.
[224] England & Wales, Civil Registration Death Index, 1916-2007: Joseph T Deakin died aged 79 years at Walsall Q3/1937 (Volume 6b, Page 563)
[225] Walsall Observer - Saturday 11 September 1937 - Page 9
[226] Reynolds's Newspaper - Sunday 14 June 1896 - Page 5
[227] England & Wales, Civil Registration Marriage Index, 1837-1915: Frederic Christopher Charles married Charlotte Elizabeth Skerritt at St. Faith's, Norfolk Q2/1900 (Volume 4b, Page 185)
[228] Census Returns of England and Wales, 1911: Registration District Number: 152: Sub-registration District: St Clement, ED, institution, or vessel: 20, Piece: 8131
[229] Daily Herald - Friday 28 August 1925 - Page 4
[230] Gloucestershire Church of England Parish Registers; Reference Number: P219 in 1/11
[231] England & Wales, Civil Registration Death Index: Charlotte E Charles died Stroud Q3/1925 (Volume 6a, Page 335)

[232] England & Wales, Civil Registration Death Index, 1916-2007: Frederick C Charles died aged 70 years at Cheltenham Q4/1934 (Volume 6a, Page 487)
[233] Gloucestershire, England, Church of England Burials, 1813-1988: Reference Number: P219 in 1/11
[234] Reynolds's Newspaper - Sunday 18 March 1900 - Page 1
[235] Justice - Saturday 07 April 1900 - Page 3
[236] Reynolds's Newspaper - Sunday 08 April 1900 - Page 1
[237] Reynolds's Newspaper - Sunday 13 May 1900 - Page 1
[238] Reynolds's Newspaper - Sunday 16 September 1900 - Page 1
[239] Weekly Irish Times - Saturday 4 November 1905 - Page 14
[240] L'En Dehors - 15 March 1926
[241] Sheffield Daily Telegraph - Thursday 08 January 1903 - Page 8
[242] New York, U.S., Arriving Passenger and Crew Lists: Microfilm Serial: T715, 1897-1957; Line: 24; Page Number: 20
[243] Index to Petitions For Naturalizations Filed in Federal, State, and Local Courts in New York City, 1792-1906; NAI Number: 5700802; Record Group Title: Records of District Courts of the United States, 1685-2009; Record Group Number: Rg 21
[244] New York; State Population Census Schedules, 1915; Election District: 18; Assembly District: 01; City: New York; County: New York; Page: 07
[245] 1920 United States Federal Census: Manhattan Assembly District 5, New York, New York; Roll: T625_1193; Page: 3B; Enumeration District: 420
[246] 1901 England Census: Class: RG13; Piece: 2700; Folio: 8; Page: 8
[247] England & Wales, Civil Registration Death Index, 1837-1915: Ellen Ditchfield died aged 49 years at Walsall Q3/1902 (Volume 6b, Page 248).
[248] UK, Lunacy Patients Admission Registers, 1846-1912: Class: MH 94; Piece: 36
[249] 1901 England Census: Class: RG13; Piece: 2655; Folio: 158; Page: 26
[250] England & Wales, Civil Registration Marriage Index, 1837-1915 : William Ditchfield married Matilda Adams at Dudley Q2/1904 (Volume 6c, Page 191)
[251] England & Wales, Civil Registration Death Index: Rose DITCHFIELD was born Wolverhampton Q3/1904 (Volume 6b, Page 594). Mothers name BOUCHER.
[252] Census Returns of England and Wales, 1911: Registration District Number: 370, Sub-registration District: Aldridge, ED, institution, or vessel: 11, Piece: 17198.
[253] 1912 Kelly's Staffordshire Directory - 1 Portland Street, Walsall - Fried Fish Dealer - Page 794
[254] 1916 Kelly's Staffordshire Directory - 1 Portland Street, Walsall - Fried Fish Shop - Page 469
[255] England & Wales, Civil Registration Death Index, 1916-2007: William Ditchfield died aged 81 years at Walsall Q1/1928 (Volume 6b, Page 745)
[256] National Probate Calendar (Index of Wills and Administrations), 1858-1995
[257] Walsall Observer - Saturday 28 January 1928 - Page 16
[258] Freedom Vol. VI No. 72 - December 1892 - Page 83
[259] Reynolds's Newspaper - Sunday 5 May 1895 - Page 3
[260] 1901 England Census: Class: RG13; Piece: 2703; Folio: 61; Page: 52
[261] Census Returns of England and Wales, 1911: Registration District Number: 370, Sub-registration District: Walsall, ED, institution, or vessel: 28, Piece: 17185.

[262] England & Wales, Civil Registration Death Index, 1916-2007: John Samuel Westley died aged 53 years Q1/1916 (Volume 6b, Page 846)
[263] Walsall Observer - Saturday 22 January 1916 - Page 12
[264] Birmingham Daily Post - Saturday 9 January 1892 - Page 5
[265] Reynolds' News - 24 January 1892 - Page 3
[266] Census Returns of England and Wales, 1901 - Class: RG13; Piece: 3062; Folio: 7; Page: 5
[267] Census Returns of England and Wales, 1911 - Registration District Number: 418, Sub-registration District: Lincoln, Home, ED, institution, or vessel: 22, Piece: 19741
[268] Home Office Calendar of Prisoners; Reference: HO 140/337
[269] England & Wales, Civil Registration Death Index, 1916-2007: Edmund J Guillemard died aged 67 at Lincoln Q1/1924 (Volume 7a, Page 687)
[270] UK, Burial and Cremation Index, 1576-2014
[271] England & Wales, Civil Registration Death Index, 1916-2007: Rhoda E Guillemard died aged 70 years at Lincoln Q2/1926 (Volume 7a, page 501)
[272] Liberty - Sunday 1 April 1894 - Page 4
[273] Census Returns of England and Wales, 1911: Registration District Number: 25, Sub-registration District: Stockwell, ED, institution, or vessel: 34, Piece: 2040
[274] 1901 England Census: Class: RG13; Piece: 474; Folio: 152; Page: 44
[275] England & Wales, Civil Registration Death Index, 1916-2007: Augustus COULON died aged 78 years at Wandsworth Q4/1923 (Volume 1d, Page 669)
[276] London Metropolitan Archives; London, England; London Church of England Parish Registers; Reference Number: Wabg/132/02
[277] Globe - Tuesday 2 May 1893 - Page 5
[278] Derby Daily Telegraph - Friday 29 December 1893 - Page 2
[279] Board of Trade: Commercial and Statistical Department and successors: Inwards Passenger Lists.; Class: BT26; Piece: 155; Item: 57
[280] 1901 England Census: Class: RG13; Piece: 1570; Folio: 132; Page: 35
[281] England & Wales, Civil Registration Marriage Index, 1837-1915: Charles Wilfred Mowbray married Eliza Hunt at West Ham Q4/1909 (Volume 4a, page 225)
[282] England & Wales, Civil Registration Death Index, 1837-1915: Charles W Mowbray died aged 57 years at Bridlington Q4/1910 (Volume 9d, Page 235)
[283] Shoreditch Observer - Saturday 17 December 1910 - Page 3
[284] Web: UK, Burial and Cremation Index, 1576-2014
[285] Kerry Evening Post - Saturday 6 October 1894 - Page 4
[286] Kerry Evening Post - Wednesday 23 September 1896 - Page 3
[287] Census Returns of England and Wales, 1901: Class: RG13; Piece: 461; Folio: 42; Page: 25
[288] Census Returns of England and Wales, 1911: Registration District Number: 26, Sub-registration District: Clapham. ED, institution, or vessel: 01, Piece: 2251.
[289] The London Gazette - 4 January 1918 - Page 401
[290] England & Wales, Civil Registration Death Index, 1916-2007: William Melville died aged 66 years at Wandsworth Q1/1918 (Volume 1d, Page 664)
[291] www.findagrave.com: Find a Grave Memorial ID: 114032862

[292] England & Wales, National Probate Calendar (Index of Wills and Administrations), 1858-1995
[293] Web: Ireland, Calendar of Wills and Administrations, 1858-1920
[294] Forest Hill & Sydenham Examiner - Friday 26 April 1918 - Page 3
[295] The Globe - Wednesday 24 April 1918 - Page 5
[296] Walsall Observer - Saturday 16 April 1927 - Page 8
[297] Walsall Observer - Saturday 2 April 1927 - Page 6
[298] The London Gazette 14 June 1929 - Issue 33506 - Page 3940
[299] The London Gazette 14 June 1929 - Issue 33507 - Page 4028
[300] England & Wales, National Probate Calendar (Index of Wills and Administrations), 1858-1995
[301] England & Wales, Civil Registration Death Index, 1837-1915 - William Nicholls died aged 28 years at Walsall
[302] Census Returns of England and Wales, 1911: Registration District Number: 370, Sub-registration District: Walsall, ED, institution, or vessel: 19, Piece: 17176
[303] England & Wales, Civil Registration Death Index, 1916-2007: Frederick BROWN aged 65 years died at Lichfield Q3/1913 (Volume 6b, Page 510)
[304] England & Wales, Civil Registration Death Index, 1916-2007: James F Henderson died aged 90 years at Norwich Q3/1957 (Volume 4b, Page 476)
[305] Reynolds's Newspaper - Sunday 3 March 1895 - Page 5
[306] Reynolds's Newspaper - Sunday 7 April 1895 - Page 6
[307] Reynolds's Newspaper - Sunday 21 April 1895 - Page 4
[308] Reynolds's Newspaper - Sunday 28 April 1895 - Page 4
[309] Reynolds's Newspaper - Sunday 19 May 1895 - Page 5
[310] Walsall Observer and South Staffordshire Chronicle - Saturday 16 January 1892 - Page 5
[311] Walsall Observer and South Staffordshire Chronicle - Saturday 9 January 1892 - Page 5

Printed in Great Britain
by Amazon